BABY GAMES

The Joyful Guide to Child's Play from Birth to Three Years

ELAINE MARTIN

With Contributions By

Katharine Smithrim
Thoma Ewen
Judy Taylor

Running Press
Philadelphia, Pennsylvania

Canadian representatives:
Stoddart Publishing Co., Ltd.,
34 Lesmill Road, Toronto, Ontario
M3B 2T6.

International representatives: Worldwide Media
Services, Inc., 115 East Twenty-third Street, New
York, NY 10010.

9 8 7 6 5 4 3 2 1

Digit on the right indicates the number of this
printing.

Library of Congress Cataloging-in-Publication
Data number 87-43258

ISBN 0-89471-617-4

Cover Design: Toby Schmidt
Text Design: Brant Cowie/Artplus Limited
Ilustrations: Janet Wilson
Cover Photo: (c) Elyse Lewin/The Image Bank Canada

This book may be ordered by mail from the
publisher. Please include $1.50 for postage.
But try your bookstore first!
Running Press Book Publishers
125 South Twenty-second Street
Philadelphia, Pennsylvania 19103

Contents

A Note to Parents

Dear Parent,

You have been blessed with a child who brings her own individuality to your budding relationship. No matter what your childcare manuals tell you about raising a baby, I don't know of a baby yet who has "read the book." She has not read the charts and tables about what an "average" baby does at an "average" time. She really doesn't care what the chart says about what is "normal." Bright children may be six months ahead of "the book," and yet even a genius occasionally wants to step back to the familiar for comfort.

Your baby will do what she wants to do when, and if, she is ready to do it. She has her own individual personality. She is like no other human being who has ever lived. She comes with her own disposition, her own activity level, her own emotional intensity, her own moods.

She will progress up her own developmental ladder at her own pace. She will want to establish her own patterns for eating, sleeping, loving, and playing. She will have her own special needs that need to be met that are different from those of any other baby, even her identical twin. She may be shy and retiring, or adventurous and outgoing. All of this individuality is reflected in her play preferences. For instance, some babies do not want soft lullabies and cuddling, but do want to be bounced. Other babies don't want to be bounced, but do want soft singing and cuddling. Some babies want both cuddling and bouncing.

To make maximum use of this book, use the entire book and make it your own. Don't limit yourself to our timetable and our categories. If you enjoy certain games, use them forever. Some games will come and go, and come back again as your child grows. The age groupings of the games in this book are OUR way of organizing the wealth of play materials available for quick and easy use. As with any book about babies, this book is written according to "average" developmental levels at an "average" time. There are no such real categories. YOUR BABY IS NOT AVERAGE.

We have selected three-month age breakdowns until eighteen months because certain physical changes occur rapidly, and are somewhat chronologically related to age. For instance, three-month-olds don't usually crawl around the room quickly, and nine-month-olds don't usually speak in complete sentences. There are physical stages that all babies pass through in some sort of usual sequence. For instance, a baby usually crawls before pulling herself up to cruise around the room holding onto furniture; then she walks; then she runs.

At about 18 months your baby's developmental pattern changes. She starts to realize she is an individual person. She recognizes that she is a social being. She starts to become creative and intellectual, rather than primarily physical, in her approach to the world. The changes she is experiencing in her development are more personal, and not as age-related. Therefore, we have changed to six-month age intervals for our game periods after 18 months of age.

The games in this book are based on the experience of a great number of children at the level we have suggested for the game. We have organized the games according to what has worked for us. Our children, the children in the nursery schools where we have participated, and the children in Katharine's classes, all have unique personalities. Thus, we have culled a wide range of games that have appealed to a wide variety of children. Because your baby is unique, she will NOT like EVERY game we have presented. She may be ahead or behind our arbitrary groupings according to age. There are times when she will be completely absorbed in certain activities and totally uninterested in others suggested for her age group. There are games that she may not WANT to play this week, but next week may want to play for hours. There are many games, such as "Hokey Pokey," that we have introduced as circle games for the social development of older toddlers, but that could be categorized just as arbitrarily as a "dance around" game for a newborn. We have presented most of our lullabies in the early sections of the book, while many three-year-olds still enjoy cuddling and singing softly with you.

Many of the games played and songs sung will be favorites for years to come. Some will grow in use over time, while others may never please your individual child. Your baby is unique in her play choices. Use this book as a play resource to find her own, and your own, favorite games and rhythms of play.

We seek games that children love totally. Please send us your favorite games, songs, rhymes, and play activities that your child enjoys over and over. We are looking especially for traditional games from other cultures. If your game is in another language, an English translation would be useful. We invite your comments so that future editions can be even more fun. Our address is: BABY GAMES, Stoddart Publishing Co. Limited, 34 Lesmill Road, Don Mills, Ontario, Canada M3B 2T6.

HAPPY PLAYING!!!

Elaine Martin
WITH: Katharine Smithrim
Thoma Ewen
Judy Taylor

Source Material

Many of the songs and rhymes in Baby Games are traditional folk material. Some authors are known, and we have so indicated. Some items are so ancient as to have origins concealed in the mists of antiquity. Many are still evolving in the nearest playground.

We have tried to indicate the specific locality or country of origin, or the first publication when it is possible—for instance England, Newfoundland, United States, Tanzania, Wales. When specific origin of material is not known, we indicate where it appears widely, in a general area, such as Great Britain, North America. Some of the material is familiar around the world, some of it is very local.

Children's rhymes and songs are from the oral tradition. Every effort has been made to ensure that we have not infringed on any copyright in the songs and rhymes we have learned in playgrounds and nursery schools. If we did inadvertently quote material not in the public domain, please accept our apologies. When you see "Traditional, adapted," Katharine Smithrim did the adaptation.

A Note on His and Her

Babies come in both genders. In order not to show preference for either gender, the use of the male and female pronouns will alternate with each chapter.

Prologue
Baby Games and the Adult

Childhood is an extended holiday; a holiday which enables a person to grow, to experience new aspects of life without the day-to-day pressures and tedium of adult responsibilities. Childhood is the most fascinating time of life. It is the spontaneous creation of a new person, and that person changes and grows daily. Your child wants to copy, copy, copy and learn, learn, learn to gain familiarity with everything in his life. He loves an audience, he laughs at jokes, and joins in the fun when others are laughing. He is a comedian. He can make YOU laugh and enjoy all your playful fun.

Your baby's childhood is enriched and enlivened by the magic of rhymes, songs, and play. And because it is so much fun, your child wants you to join him and enjoy his world. Enter his world and leave your sensible adult cares behind!

Your caring presence and a good sense of silliness are what is required of you in your baby's world. You don't have to be a professional actor or athlete to exhibit the versatility and strength to keep your baby amused. A little fun and attention can go a long way with a baby. And even if your voice sounds like a wild goose honking his way south, don't worry; you will never have a more appreciative audience than your baby.

Here are the rules of this play guide. We insist that they be followed, or the bogeyman will GET you!

PARTNERS: You are never to criticize your partner's ability to play with your child under any circumstances, EVER. You must support your partner, no matter how silly a game looks or sounds. Your most constructive criticism is your own participation. If you can't stand the sound, or the mess, simply leave the room and KEEP QUIET. Comments about fat bottoms in the air, or singing in eight-part harmony with nobody else present ARE SIMPLY NOT ALLOWED. If you are not participating in the play, DO NOT INTERFERE.

SAFETY: Be sensitive to the safety needs of your baby in the specific types of play being performed. No heavy roughhousing for tiny infants; babyproof and toddlerproof environments for all children at all times. Never allow play with paints, scissors, bubbles, glue or anything else potentially harmful (or frightening) without adult supervision. Check outdoor areas for animal feces and toxic plants. Check indoor areas for toxic materials, toxic plants, litter boxes, and detergents. Follow your pediatrician's suggestions for childproofing and NEVER leave your child unsupervised.

SUITABILITY: Recognize that your child is a unique individual who is the best judge of the games he wants to play. Some days he may feel adventurous, and other days he may feel fragile, so accept his choices. Feel free to initiate a new activity, but if he isn't interested, leave it for now and try it again later.

ENVIRONMENT: Spend the time necessary to organize your home to make daily life as easy as possible. MOVE the breakables. Put up the stair gates, reorganize your living space so you can spend as much time as possible with your baby. Figure out how you are going to store his toys so he can find certain ones when he wants to play with them. Make sure that your child CAN do what he is READY to do in an environment that is as safe as possible for him, and as simple as possible for you.

THE FUN of CHILDHOOD
for the ADULT

Being with your child and getting in touch with your own happy childhood memories brings back your personal sense of joy. When you have a baby, your own creative training begins. Because of your child, you are now finding new powers and performing amazing feats: you are an entertainer, an audience, an inventor, a creator, and a teacher. Yet the teaching you do is unique. With your baby you are working with a clean slate. You are not dealing with someone who has been taught before. You appreciate the perspective of the beginning thinker—who has much more clarity than ANY adult. You don't see adult biases, and you don't see cultural blindfolds in your baby's thought processes.

Your child can teach you many things that you may have forgotten. Your child can show you:

- how to learn
- the rhythms of life and learning
- how to meet emotional needs
- the joy of being alive
- creativity
- carefreeness
- the capacity to laugh
- the magic of life
- interest in the world
- how to meet new people

Through play we recreate ourselves. We return to just being truly human.

GAMES FOR GROWNUPS

Bonding

The most important task you and your baby have is falling in love with each other. This is the ongoing process experts call "bonding." Bonding is essential for your baby's development. This mutual love forms the core of a working relationship between you and your child.

This love allows your baby to develop trust in you to care for him. Also, you know and understand your baby and what works with him from your OWN experiences and intuition. You develop essential confidence and trust in your own abilities.

Bonding is very much a "hands-on" experience. Your baby needs to love you. Through touching, talking, stroking, cuddling, singing, playing, holding, and gazing into each other's eyes, you bond quickly and easily. This bond enables you and your baby to establish your own rhythms and to become attuned to each other's needs. You will know how fast he likes to rock, how he likes to be tickled and stroked, which songs and games he likes best, and which games he finds boring or dislikes.

Silly Game for Grown-ups

This is a game that must be done at LEAST every month just so you can keep up with your baby.

What can your baby do now? What does the world look like at your child's level of development? You don't know? It's time to find out! Pretend you are your baby at his current level of development. Explore his world from his perspective, see what he sees, touch what he touches, smell what he smells, taste what he tastes, and hear what he hears. As your baby matures, add to your own repertoire. Roll, crawl, creep, climb, or toddle according to your child's abilities.

Lie on the floor and investigate the world as he sees it—gaze up under the tables, pull yourself up, practice cruising and taking those first tentative, toddling, wobbling steps, and then fall down on your bottom. What does the inside of his crib look like? The ceiling over his head? Is his world manageable? Interesting? Stimulating? Safe? Can it be made better?

After playing this game, you KNOW what this age can do, and what is reasonable for your baby to do. You also know what you must do to babyproof.

Move Your Life Down

The safest place for your baby is a babyproofed floor. I suggest you use the floor FOR EVERYTHING—changing, dressing, eating, and playing. The floor is the space your baby inhabits. Join in the fun and sit or stretch out on the floor. You immediately RELAX. The change from sitting in uncomfortable chairs and dealing with uncomfortable furniture is refreshing. The floor also puts you into a play frame of mind. Your baby will never fall off the floor.

About the Content of Traditional Nursery Material

A common criticism of traditional nursery fare is that it is violent. Much of it is violent, aggressive, and full of surprises. While recognizing human gentleness, there is also an acknowledgment of the all-too-real capacity for human evil.

Nursery rhymes work because they are magic. They diffuse the real stress of establishing this new relationship between caregiver and baby. The rhymes, songs, and stories of the nursery have survived for generations because they allow the resolution of underlying conflicts in our lives in an appropriate way. We'd all like to boil up baby in a pot one day, or have someone, maybe even Bonaparte, take baby away for a while to give us perhaps a 15-minute nap. By saying a rhyme or singing a song, and allowing the fantasy to evolve

and then dissipate, the need, the very real need, to do so in the real life disappears!

Songs like "Baby, Baby, Naughty Baby," and rhymes like "Davy, Davy Dumpling" are wonderful because they permit your baby to be naughty, but they also enable you to threaten all sorts of consequences if the awful activity continues. The parent gets to believe, at least in fantasy, in ogres who will deal with unmanageable situations. The parent-child relationship is not threatened, while the behavior is noted and censured. In fact, this type of song and rhyme reinforces the parental care for and protection of the baby from the bogeyman, for both baby and parent. Songs, rhymes, and stories of this nature allow all of us to use our own wiles and cleverness to deal with the supremely awful in our world, and to triumph over adversity.

Try these games when you get exasperated (as we all do). You and your baby may both end up in giggles on the floor at 3:00 a.m., and at least you will feel better after using this "magic." Try it and see....

Baby, Baby, Naughty Baby

(A good lullaby for a colicky baby, as you gallop around the room together. Ham up your performance.)

(Tune: "Reuben and Rachel" "I Am Slowly Going Crazy" or "Mabel, Mabel, If You're Able")

Baby, baby, Naughty baby
Hush you squalling thing, I say.
Peace this moment, peace, or maybe
Bonaparte* will pass this way.
    (Strut and salute.)

Baby, baby, he's a giant,
    (Pretend to be a giant.)
Tall and black as Rouen steeple,
    (Form a steeple with arms high in the air.)
And he breakfasts, dines, rely on't,
    (Growl and belch.)
Every day on naughty people.
    (Shake finger at baby and at yourself.)

Baby, baby, if he hears you,
(Cup one ear.)
As he gallops past the house,
(Gallop around.)
Limb from limb at once he'll tear you,
(Pretend to rip a pillow apart.)
Just as pussy tears a mouse.
(Pounce and bounce around.)

And he'll beat you, beat you, beat you,
(Beat up the pillows.)
And he'll beat you all to pap,
(Pretend to eat slowly with a spoon.)
And he'll eat you, eat you, eat you,
(Pretend growl and pretend to "eat" towards
Every morsel, snap, snap, snap.
baby's tummy. Snap fingers.)

** Substitute your favorite villain. The original may
have been Oliver Cromwell.*

(Traditional, England)

Davy, Davy, Dumpling

____, ____, Dumpling
(Use your baby's name.)
Boil him in the pot.
(Tickle him all over.)
Sugar him and
(Tap him lightly.)
Butter him and
(Stroke him lightly.)
Eat him while he's hot.
(Pretend to gobble him up—go "Grrrr!"
towards his belly button and give him a hug.)

(Traditional, Great Britain)

If you are still unconvinced about the content of nursery rhymes, read *The Uses of Enchantment* by Bruno Bettelheim. Of course, you are free to adapt any traditional material to meet your own needs and values.

Using Nursery Rhymes

Nursery rhymes can be used in a variety of circumstances. You can use them for tickle games at bath or change times. You can use them as poetry for your wide-awake and playful baby. You can croon them to your sleepy baby, or sing them as you gallop around the living room together. You can say the rhymes to start a conversation when you have nothing to say. You can use them to add color and fun to your baby's feeding experiences.

Nursery rhymes are the basic "tool" in the "toolbox" you can use to entertain your baby, any time and any place. Adapt any traditional rhyme to your own needs. If you notice a place where you can insert your child's name, nickname, or initials, do so. Change the rhyme to fit the gender of your child, for instance "Georgie, Porgie" can be changed to "Lucy, Goosie." If you feel a certain rhyme is sexist, such as "Little Miss Muffett," have Miss Muffett frighten the spider away rather than vice versa. Try to use your baby's name in almost every rhyme you use, for instance:

Baa, Baa, Black Sheep

Baa, baa, black sheep,
Have you any wool?
Yes, sir, yes, sir, three bags full:
One for my master, and one for my dame,
And one for little Jessica
Who lives down the lane.

(Traditional, England)

If you aren't sure what to do next, and your baby wants to be entertained, use your rhymes to initiate your own play. These rhymes will be your basic tools, to be adapted and developed to suit your own daily circumstances for years to come.

Let Your Words Flow

Poetry and music are your baby's connection to the oral traditions of our literary legacy. Don't hold back—let your words flow!

During your baby's first two years, he is learning the groundwork of his verbal language. Give him the rhythm, the patterns, the sounds, the music, and the tune of his language. Let the words cascade from your mouth, let him hear and enjoy! The gift of fluency is precious, and lifelong.

Learning Rhymes and Songs

It is easy to learn the words of any song or rhyme. Simply start with two lines at a time, repeat them four or five times, and then add the next two lines. Say the words aloud to your baby during the day, using the rhyming words to help you remember. Later on, when your baby starts to talk, he is able to use the rhymes he's learned as a tool when learning to speak in complete sentences. Nursery rhymes and songs are word toys; they are fantastic training for your baby's memory.

Songs and rhymes are a wonderful way to play with your baby. The more rhymes you know, the more material you have at your fingertips for use in the car, on your long walks, and as jokes that you share with your baby. Whenever you or your baby gets bored or tense, say some rhymes or sing some songs, wherever you are. The more you use your songs, rhymes, and games, the more fun you will have with your baby throughout his childhood. He will derive a great deal of comfort and joy from his favorite rhymes and lullabies.

Singing

When you make music with your baby, you are a participant, not a solo performer. Your voice is your baby's most important musical instrument because it is YOU singing with HIM. The finesse of the rendition just isn't important. Relax, and concentrate on singing enthusiastically. Don't worry about your vocal talents; the ability to sing improves through usage. Start with simple, familiar songs, and add to your repertoire daily.

The more songs you learn, the more you will be able to entertain your baby. I can testify that singing off-key to a cranky baby on an overcrowded bus, while stuck in traffic, can turn into a sing-along party. Songs are magic!

Buy or borrow some good children's records, learn the melodies, and add your own words, or a familiar rhyme, as lyrics. For instance, "Head and Shoulders, Knees and Toes" can be sung to the tune of either "London Bridge is Falling Down" or "There Is a Tavern in the Town." When you can't think of an existing tune to fit your baby's favorite rhyme, make one up. Composing music is easier than you think. Try it!

Photographs, Photo Albums, and Videotape

Invest in a good camera, film, and whatever else you want and need in order to take pictures of your baby. You will never regret capturing those priceless moments. Gabriel's grandmother, "Bubba," has been confiscating just about all of the photographs of Gaby, and mounting them in large and weighty albums. Gaby adores them.

Creating your own pictorial heirloom is a magical process. Your baby finds it fascinating to go through his history in pictures. As your baby gets older, he will begin to recognize himself, his parents, his grandparents, his friends, and it all becomes meaningful and special to him. Don't throw away the pictures that "don't make it." Keep them separate, to be cut up for your baby's personal books later on.

A Day in the Life of Baby When He Was This Old

Photograph everything your child does in a day. Do this for special days, such as your child's Birth Day. Do this also for some of those not-so-special days, as a record of what happens when your baby is five months old, eight months old, toddling, walking, running.... You will be amazed at how soon you forget what happens at all the various stages of your child's development.

Separate the pictures for any one day and make a book for your child that describes his activities. Add the words for what he saw, what he did, and where he went. This will make a pictorial record your child will cherish.

A Diary for Your Child

My most priceless baby present was from my friend, Jenny's "Aunt Susan." It was a five-year diary with four lines for each day. It takes only a minute or so a day to jot down what happened—and as a record, it's priceless!

Peer Friends

Babies need friends their own age. It is never too early to introduce your newborn to "playmates." Newborns will play with each other if they are in the same visual range. Where can you find another baby? Were you in a prenatal class? Have you found a drop-in center? Is there a new parents' support group nearby that you can attend with your baby? Did you share a hospital room with someone you liked? Do you walk in the park frequently? People with babies gravitate towards each other, and in this way you may find playmates for your baby—and for yourself.

Daily Exercise

One of the most enjoyable and beneficial activities you and your baby can perform is daily exercise. If you establish a daily routine, your baby will learn good movement and coordination skills and YOU will enjoy a more flexible and energized body. You will also have fun rolling around together and being silly.

Your routine can be as simple as turning on the TV to a yoga show, a flexibility stretch and strength class, or a full aerobic workout, depending on your interests. Place a quilt on the floor and have lots of open space in front of the TV. Place your baby in a comfortable position on the carpet and let him watch you. During commercials, do some of the "baby exercises" or movement games presented in this book.

Your routine can also be as complex as your own training and interests. One master badminton

player we know takes her baby and babysitter along to tournaments. Daycare is available at many health clubs. Your baby may also enjoy watching you swim or run around a squash court from the safety of his infant seat, and you can interrupt your activity if he needs attention. You can put your baby in a pouch carrier or a backpack and go walking, bicycling, or cross-country skiing once his neck muscles are strong enough to support his head. As he grows, your baby will want to participate more and more in the fun. Once he is sitting up he will love riding on a bicycle carrier wearing his helmet. Check with your doctor and your pediatrician concerning your exercise program. A new mother can usually resume her normal exercises by about the six-week check-up following her baby's birth.

The Daily Walk

It is important to get your baby of any age outdoors as frequently as possible. It is healthy to get outside. Fresh air mobilizes the metabolisms of both you and your baby, so that you both experience a surge of energy. Get outside with your baby every day. Dress appropriately for the weather.

Even a brisk 15-minute walk outside is good for you, and a longer walk is even better. Avoid having to run errands; use this time for relaxation with your baby, not for stressful necessities. If your baby is awake, make sure he has a view of the world. Start showing your baby all of nature's wonders.

While your baby is an infant, put him in a pouch-type baby carrier that supports his head and neck and leaves your hands free. As your baby grows older, a stroller is essential. When he reaches toddlerhood, a red wagon and a sleigh make your outdoor excursions even more fun. And soon, of course, he will walk and run everywhere.

Out in the World

S how your newborn his world. He is quite portable, so take him to lunch with your friends or
go for a swim or to a fitness class. Go on a shopping expedition together. Try to spend at least two
hours away from home together, at least once a
week. Take this opportunity to locate valuable
community resources—community centers with
baby swim programs, playgrounds for new parents
and babies, toy libraries, wading pools, petting
zoos, and interesting playgrounds. Go on long
walks together; both you and baby are happier out
in the world. Remember to sing and recite rhymes
as you walk along.

The Mini-Vacation

E very three or four weeks, plan a family mini-
vacation of at least half a day away from
home. Mini-vacations should be enjoyable for
everyone, so discuss your plans in advance and
make your preparations well ahead of time. Mini-
vacations can include:

- a picnic in the park
- a sporting event
- a visit to a lake or a beach
- a long, leisurely walk in the woods
- a trip to a farm, a zoo, or an aquarium
- tea at a fine hotel
- a ride on a ferryboat
- excursions to museums or art galleries

Make your own list according to your family's
interests and resources. Avoid long drives and
huge crowds on your mini-vacation. The idea is to
do exactly what you LIKE to do for a few hours,
and relax. When you experience joy, you share
that joy with your baby. The fun he has with his
whole family on these outings makes him feel
happy and very special. He knows that he is participating in something that makes you happy.

The Afternoon Nap

T here is no reason why your baby must always sleep in his crib. Let him nap outside,
dressed and sheltered according to the weather.
Place him in a carriage, out of the wind, or in a
sheltered spot, or go for a walk. Even in the
coldest, darkest January of a northern winter,
afternoon naps can be happily spent outside. In
the summer, cover your baby's carriage with
netting to prevent insect bites, and let him sleep
in the shade. Often he may just fall asleep in his
stroller on your long walks.

On the other hand, there is nothing more
relaxing for both you and your baby than taking
him into your arms for a nap in bed. Open the
window wide, wrap your baby in a warm
blanket, and place him in the fetal position. Give
your baby a breast or a bottle if he usually has
one at this time. You don't need to nap yourself
(but go ahead if you want to); just relax, breath-
ing in the fresh air, luxuriating in a relaxing
cuddle with your baby. Give yourself at least 15
minutes to unwind. Your baby will quickly fall
asleep and you will feel refreshed and full of
zest, ready to take advantage of the time you
have alone while your baby sleeps.

Outdoor Picnics

We all know that food tastes better outdoors. Because your baby is portable, and his feeding routine is simple, take him outside for picnics, even for his early breast or bottle feedings.

Thoma nursed Gabriel outside during her first winter. They would both bundle up and sit outside on the doorstep. Thoma threw a heavy shawl over both of them and they would snuggle away, toasty warm.

Picnics can be as simple or as complex as you like. They can be a simple sandwich or snack in the backyard, an exotic clam bake at the seashore, or a Texas-style barbecue. Make sure you have tasty baby or toddler foods along, according to your child's diet, and enjoy. Let your child experience the wonderful variety of foods cooked or eaten outdoors. Can you forget the wonderful taste of foods cooked over a campfire? Or the sensation of watermelon juice running down your chin? Even Pablum tastes better outside!

Dress Him for Play

Play is your baby's work. Make sure he wears his workclothes. A construction worker would look silly going to work in his best bib and tucker. Fussy baby clothes have a place for special pictures and special occasions, but they are not appropriate for his everyday "WORK." Could YOU crawl around effectively if you were tied up in your finery?

Visualize the Rewards of Parenting

Most daily chores have no long-lasting rewards, but parenting and playing with your child do. When daily pressures seem overwhelming, visualize the rewards. The rewards you are seeking are closeness with your child, and the joy of a happy child bringing you happiness as you bring him happiness. Visualize your child a year from now, two years from now, going off to school; visualize being together. See your child as happy, bright, caring—someone whose face warms your heart, whose life is an important addition to your own. Visualize a sense of wholeness and completeness for yourself, knowing that friendship and people are the champagne of life.

Living Each Day

You create reality! The freshness of childhood is a world of new magic. Within your child's soul is a new, unknown world in the making. When you live each day in the spirit of having fun and playing with your child, your "work" becomes "play." You can see, hear, and feel with your child's perspective. Playing with your child means being with your child, and experiencing your child's peace, love, and happiness. You feel close to another human being, who presents a fascinating new world. You become refreshed and you experience your world anew. You find joy on the faces of the world's children, and you become extremely happy.

A happy child feels right about the world and right about himself. Laughing together is the best way to raise a happy child. Your happiness is spontaneous, just as your creativity is spontaneous. Your play releases your happiness as well as your creativity. Love inspires play and love develops in play. Love is built on a history of the happy memories you build together.

Laughter makes you healthy. Cuddling, learning, and growing make you happy. These activities have their own inherent joy, because through them you and your baby grow.

C H A P T E R   O N E

So I've Hung the Mobile — Now What?

Birth to Three Months

You realize with wonder that your newborn is a completely functioning human being. She is not a stuffed china doll, she will not break when you touch her, and she is not, in the words of one new father, "The Slug" he expected. Her senses are functioning and maturing every day. During the first three months, she becomes acquainted with her new surroundings, the very important people in her life, and her own body. Both you and she are gaining confidence in your ability to handle your new relationship. She doesn't CARE if you don't know which end to diaper yet; she trusts you will learn sometime before she is toilet trained. She's right, chances are you will.

MOVEMENT

During the nine months your baby has been *in utero,* she has experienced movement. She has moved around on her own, doing her own set of exercises. She has felt her mother's walking, bending, and swaying motions. Rocking and swinging motions comfort her and provide that "back-to-the-womb" security.

Dancing

Dancing is a wonderful way to have fun with your newborn. She experiences rhythm, which is the basis for her later talking, walking, running, skipping, and hopping. Find some simple, happy, melodic tunes on the radio or stereo. Ask her, "May I have this dance?" and sing or croon a song in her ear. Hold her close, with one hand supporting her head and the other hand supporting her back. Rock and sway back and forth to the beat of the music. When the song is over, thank her for a lovely dance and return her to her seat.

The Elevator Game

At a quiet time when you are both awake and alert, play the "Elevator Game." You can start this game as soon as your baby can hold her head steadily. Lying on your back, lift her over your head and bring her down so you can kiss her on the cheek, saying, "I'm going to kiss you." Say, "You are going up and down like an elevator, and I'm going to kiss you when you come down to me." Lift her up and down as long as you and she want to play this game.

The Rocking Chair

Some babies love being held and rocked to sleep. Sing lullabies to your baby while you are rocking her. Rocking gently is a wonderful introduction to rhythmic movement.

HINT: Some babies don't like slow rocking, but prefer an increased tempo.

Baby Bird

As you lie on a floor or bed, gently lift your baby up and down. Hold your hands under her armpits or around her chest or midriff. Fly your baby forward, backward, and side to side. Gently dip her head, then her feet, moving her in all directions, slowly and gently, so that she is in a comfortable flight pattern. You can play this game as soon as she can hold her head up.

Eeezy-kneezies

Holding your baby's calves just below the knee, gently flex one leg so her thigh touches her tummy. Then gently stretch her leg out and down to a resting position. Repeat with the other leg.

Touch the Sky

Holding your baby's hands in your own, gently raise her arms up above her head. Then bring them back down to her sides. Say, "up, down, up we go, down we go, reach up, reach down, and let's touch the sky!"

Baby Hugs

Gently cross your baby's arms over her chest, letting her "hug" herself. Now gently stretch her arms out wide to hug the whole world, then bring them back to the crossed position.

CHANGING GAMES

Touching

Nothing develops your bond faster than tender stroking, cuddling, caressing, and touching. Of course, you will be holding your newborn as she eats, regardless of whether she is getting the breast or the bottle. Caress and stroke her, and talk or sing to her while she is feeding.

Some newborns enjoy being swaddled, held tightly, and rocked. Some want to be held and cuddled constantly. Other newborns don't like being restrained, and wiggle, squirm, and struggle whenever you hold them close. Both types of babies are entirely normal. Regardless of type, each newborn does want to be touched and stroked to feel your warmth and closeness. Rather than holding and rocking a "squirmer," dance around the room with her at more active times, and lie beside her on the floor or on the bed for some quieter touching games.

Dressing, Undressing, and Changing

Caress, stroke, tickle, or kiss your baby every time you change her. Blow gently on her tummy, caress her feet, pat her on the bottom, and tickle her hands. Use some changing rhymes such as the ones below whenever you have an extra minute or two to play.

Jeremiah

Jeremiah, blow the fire,
(Substitute your baby's name.)
Puff, puff, puff.
(Blow little puffs on baby's tummy;
First you blow it gently,
a sustained gentle blow, then
Then you blow it rough!
a big gust.)

(19th-century English music hall song)

Brandy Hill

As I went up the Brandy Hill
(Touch baby's tummy.)
I met my father with good will.
(Touch her mouth and smile.)
He had jewels, he had rings,
(Touch her fingers.)
He had many pretty things.
(Tickle her lightly.)
He'd a cat with nine tails,
(Pat her bottom.)
He'd a hammer wanting nails.
(Pat bottoms of her feet.)
Up Jock!
(Tickle up her body.)
Down Tom!
(Tickle down her body.)
Blow the bellows, old man.
(Puff gently on her tummy.)

(Traditional, United States)

I'm Gonna Get You!

When your baby is awake and alert, say, "I'm gonna get you! I'm gonna touch your nose. I'm gonna touch your cheeks. I'm gonna touch your forehead. I'm gonna touch your tummy. I'm gonna touch your legs. I'm gonna touch your back." Smile as you say this, and use a soft, high-pitched voice. Stroke her gently, if she enjoys this. Bend your face down to where she can see you when you touch her. Let her know you are there.

Changing "Peek" Games

Gain a few extra "peek-a-boos" when you are using a towel, or changing your baby's clothes, and say, "Ooooh—there you are!" You might like to play "This Little Baby." This tune and many others appearing in this book can be heard on *The Baby Record* by Bob McGrath and Katharine Smithrim, Kids' Records.

This Little Baby

This little baby rocked in the cradle.
(Wiggle one arm.)
This little baby jumped in bed.
(Wiggle the other.)
This little baby crawled on the carpet,
(Wiggle one leg.)
This little baby bumped her head.
(Wiggle the other.)
This little baby played hide 'n' seek.
(Put your face where baby can see it.)
Where's that little baby?
(Hide your eyes with your hands.)
Oo-oo-ooh, peek!
(Show your eyes and hide them.)
Oo-oo-ooh, peek!
(Show them again!).)

(Traditional, southern United States)

Pat Your Baby

Gently stroke your naked baby after she has had her bath or is being changed. Hold her in your arms against your body and rub her back and the back of her head. Lay her down on a warm, soft surface and kneel or sit beside her. Gently stroke her arms, starting at her shoulders. Speak or sing to her softly. Extend and pat her arms, body, and legs. Stroke her neck, and her head from top to chin. Gently rub her hands and feet between your hands. You may find this a perfect time to use a little baby oil.

Parts of her Body

In the first three months your newborn will find her hands, and maybe her feet. It is important that she has some undressed and unswaddled time every day so she can investigate her body. Let her splash and kick freely when she has her bath.

Play some finger and toe games to familiarize your newborn to her newly discovered hands and feet. She will play with her hands, looking at them, touching them, and learning about what they can do. Your first finger play will be "This Little Pig Went to Market."

This Little Pig Went to Market

This little pig went to market.
>   (Touch each toe or finger in succession, start-
>   ing with thumb or big toe.)

This little pig stayed home.
This little pig ate roast beef.
This little pig had none.
This little pig cried, "Wee, wee, wee!
I can't find my way home!"
>   (Tickle hand or foot.)

(Traditional, Great Britain, North America)

"The Booglie Wooglie Piggy," sung by Eric Nagler on *Fiddle up a tune*, Elephant Records, is a great rendition of the "This Little Pig" finger play.

This One's Old

(Starting with her big thumb or toe, touch each finger or toe in succession.)

This one's old.
This one's young.
This one has no meat.
This one's gone to buy some hay.
And this one's gone to the village.

(Traditional, China)

Pat Her Toes

Tap your baby's toes and pat her feet as you talk to her. Smile at her when she smiles at you. Say a few special "I Love You"s.

The Man in the Mune

(Say this rhyme while tapping the soles of your baby's feet.)

The man in the mune
Is making shune,
Tuppence a pair an'
They're a' dune.

(Traditional, Scotland)

Touching and Feeling

Provide pieces of interesting textures for your newborn to experience. Place her on a soft rug on the floor. Have her touch the dog or cat, or a stuffed animal. Say, "soft," "warm," "fuzzy," "furry." Then take a contrasting object, such as a pot lid, and say "hard," "metal," "cold," "smooth." Don't play this game with tiny objects that could be swallowed. Let her also experience feathers, fur, silk, a face cloth, wool, foil, corrugated cardboard, and a soft paint brush. You may want to use some of these textures to make a "touch book" or a "touch picture" for her room.

Smile Dance

Holding your baby tenderly, do a smile dance together. Move in and out of her visual range as you dance. As she smiles at you, go close to her and smile. Let her establish her own smiling rhythms and come and go as she pleases with her smiles. When she smiles, move close. When she stops smiling, move back.

MUSIC

Lullabies

A lullaby is ANY song that calms your baby. Some newborns prefer crooning and tender cuddles. Some prefer rollicking songs and dancing enthusiastically. Your baby may settle to different types of songs in different circumstances. Rock or dance the rhythm of the lullaby with your baby, whichever she prefers.

Faster Tempos

Almost any song with a quick beat is a lifesaver, and fun to boot, if you have to gallop around with a colicky baby. Try these old-timers: "The Band Played On," "Lullaby of Broadway," "Bicycle Built for Two," "Sidewalks of New York," "The Man on the Flying Trapeze," and "Hava Na Guila." An excellent record for galloping around to is *Bunyips, Bunnies and Brumbies* by Mike and Michelle Jackson, Elephant Records. Use lively old favorites when your baby seems bored.

I'se the B'y

I'se the b'y that builds the boat,
And I'se the b'y that sails her!
I'se the b'y that catches the fish and
Takes 'em home to Li-zer.

Chorus:
Hip yer partner, Sally Tibbo'!
Hip yer partner, Sally Brown!
Fogo, Twillingate, Morton's Harbour,
All around the circle.

Sods and rinds to cover your flake,
Cake and tea for supper,
Codfish in the spring of the year
Fried up in maggoty butter.

(Traditional, Newfoundland)

What'll I Do With My Baby-o?

(Here is a slightly quieter, but still energetic lullaby. Move your baby to the directions indicated.)

First verse and chorus:

What'll I do with my baby-o?
What'll I do with my baby-o?
What'll I do with my baby-o?
If she won't go to sleepy-o?

Wrap her up in calico,
Wrap her up in calico,
Wrap her up in calico,
And send her to her daddy-o [or mammy-o].

Wrap her up in a tablecloth,
Wrap her up in a tablecloth,
Wrap her up in a tablecloth,
And toss her up in the old hay loft.

Send her east and send her west,
Send her east and send her west,
Send her east and send her west,
Send her up to the old craw's nest.

Send her north and send her south,
Send her north and send her south,
Send her north and send her south,
And put a little moonshine in her mouth.

(Traditional, southern Appalachia, United States)

Quiet Times and Feeding Times

Perhaps the most wonderful playtimes are those quiet times spent cuddling, petting, nuzzling, crooning and talking softly with your baby. Perhaps the most enjoyable quiet time is feeding time. This time brought me feelings of incredible peace, contentment, and joy. I felt a basic, primitive connection to all mothers of all times as I held Baby Jenny in my arms while I sang her a lullaby.

Quieter Lullabies and Crooning

Crooning lullabies can be done while nursing or rocking to any soft song to the sounds of doo-doo, doo-doo-doo, or la-la, la-la-la, with made up words such as, "Poor little baby, can't go to sleep, what will we do?" Pat your newborn's back while rocking or cuddling.

Poor Adam

I feel so sorry for old Adam,
Just as sorry as can be;
For he never had no mammy
For to rock him on her knee.

(Traditional, Spiritual, United States)

Ho, Ho, Watanay

Ho, ho, watanay,
Ho, ho, watanay,
Ho, ho, watanay,
Ki yo ke na,
Ki yo ke na.

(Traditional, Iroquois lullaby)

Bye Baby Bunting

(Croon words over and over.)

Bye baby bunting, your daddy's gone a-hunting
For to catch a rabbit skin, to wrap the baby
   bunting in.
Bye baby bunting, your mammy's gone the other
   way
To beg a bowl of sour whey, for little baby
   bunting.

(Traditional, England)

Bed Is Too Small

Bed is too small for my tiredness,
Give me a hilltop with trees.

Chorus:
Tuck a cloud up under my chin,
Lord, a blow the moon out, please.

Rock me to sleep in a cradle of dreams,
Send me a lullaby of leaves.

(Traditional, Spiritual, United States)

The Heaven Is Bright

The heaven is bright,
The earth is bright,
I have a baby,
Crying all night.

(Traditional, China)

Hush-a-Bye

Hush-a-bye, don't you cry,
Go to sleep you little baby.
When you wake, you shall have
All the pretty little horses.
Dapples and greys, tans and bays,
All the pretty little horses.

(Traditional, southern United States)

Sleep Baby Sleep

Sleep baby sleep,
Your father tends the sheep.
Your mother shakes the dreamland tree,
Down falls a dream for thee.
Sleep baby sleep.

(Traditional, Great Britain)

Hush Little Baby

Hush little baby, don't say a word
Papa's gonna buy you a mocking bird.
If that mocking bird don't sing
Papa's gonna buy you a diamond ring.
If that diamond ring turns brass
Papa's gonna buy you a looking glass.
If that looking glass gets broke
Papa's gonna buy you a billy goat.
If that billy goat don't pull
Papa's gonna buy you a cart and bull.
If that cart and bull turn over
Papa's gonna buy you a dog named Rover.
If that dog named Rover don't bark
Papa's gonna buy you a horse and cart.
If that horse and cart fall down
You'll still be the sweetest little baby in town.

(Traditional, United States)

All Through the Night

Sleep my love and peace attend thee,
All through the night;
Guardian angels, God will send thee,
All through the night.
Soft the drowsy hours are creeping,
Hill and vale in slumber sleeping,
Love alone his watch is keeping,
All through the night.

While the moon her watch is keeping,
All through the night;
While the weary world is sleeping,
All through the night.
O'er thy spirit gently stealing,
Visions of delight revealing,
Breathes a pure and holy feeling,
All through the night.

(Traditional Welsh melody, words by Alfred Lord Tennyson)

A lovely version of this song can be heard on the *Peter, Paul and Mommy* record album by Peter, Paul and Mary, Warner Brothers Records.

WORD PLAY

Your baby is a listener. Your voice was a "womb sound" to her, and it is as reassuring as your heartbeat and the warmth of your cuddles. Your baby's hearing is almost completely developed at birth, and she is calmed by human voices, especially yours. She is soothed by soft, rhythmic sounds, such as a ticking clock. She likes melodic sounds, especially your singing. She may enjoy listening to music boxes.

Talk to Your Baby

There you are, looking into her bright little eyes. What do you say? After you've said, "I LOVE YOU, YOU'RE BEAUTIFUL" several hundred times, the conversation lacks a little "oomph." You coo, gurgle, make a few baby noises. . . and she responds. What then?

Immerse your baby in words. Tell her what you are doing. "I'm going to change your diaper now." "It's time for us to feed your fish." Give her a weather report. Read the newspaper to her out loud. Ask for her answers to the crossword puzzle. Report the stock market quotations and farm reports. Tell her how to make the salad or peel the potatoes. Talk about sorting the laundry. Sure, it's a little advanced for her right now, but you are doing two essential things: you are establishing the habit of talking to her, and you are treating her with respect.

Your child cannot learn to speak unless she hears her language spoken, so talk with her. Have fun with words you use, and discover the magic in nursery rhymes and poetry. Some words sound so different and some sound so alike. Have fun with the way the words can roll off your tongue.

Your baby will start to babble about the same time she starts to smile. She may string her sounds together into sentence sounds. Mirror her sounds back to her to establish a conversation.

Nursery Rhymes

You probably know more nursery rhymes than you realize. Just in case you don't remember, here are a few to jog your memory, and some you may not recognize to add to your repertoire.

Georgie, Porgie, Pudding and Pie

Georgie, Porgie, pudding and pie,
Kissed the girls and made them cry.
When the boys came out to play,
Georgie Porgie ran away.

(Traditional, England)

Hey Diddle Diddle, the Cat and the Fiddle

Hey diddle diddle, the cat and the fiddle,
The cow jumped over the moon.
The little dog laughed to see such sport
And the dish ran away with the spoon.

(Traditional, England)

Hark, Hark, The Dogs Do Bark

Hark, hark, the dogs do bark,
The beggars are coming to town.
Some in rags, and some in tags,
And one in a velvet gown.

(Traditional, England)

Curley Locks!

Curley locks, curley locks, wilt thou be mine?
Thou shalt not wash dishes, nor yet feed the swine;
But sit on a cushion and sew a fine seam,
And feed upon strawberries, sugar and cream.

(Traditional, England)

Nut Tree

I had a little nut tree,
Nothing would it bear
But a silver nutmeg
And a golden pear;

The King of Spain's daughter
Came to visit me,
And all for the sake
Of my little nut tree.

(Traditional, England)

Little Boy, Little Boy

Little boy, little boy, where were you born?
Up in the highlands, among the green corn.
Little boy, little boy, where did you sleep?
In the byre with kye, in the cot with the sheep.

(Traditional, Scotland)

Babylon

How many miles to Babylon?
Threescore miles and ten.
Can I get there by candlelight?
Yes, and back again.
If your heels are nimble and light,
You may get there by candlelight.

(Traditional, England)

Higglety, Pigglety, Pop!

Higglety, pigglety, pop!
The dog has eaten the mop;
The pig's in a hurry,
The cat's in a flurry,
Higglety, pigglety, pop!

(Samuel Griswold Goodrich, United States 1846)

Come, Let's to Bed

(Say this rhyme while giving a breast or bottle before your baby's nap.)

Come, let's to bed,
Says Sleepy-head;
Tarry a while, says Slow;
Put on the pan,
Says Greedy-Nan,
We'll sup before we go.

(Traditional, England)

Cobbler, Cobbler

Cobbler, Cobbler, mend my shoe.
(Wiggle one of baby's feet.)
Have it done by half-past two.
(Hammer lightly with your fist.)
Stitch it up and stitch it down.
(Make sewing motion on baby's foot.)
Now nail the heel all around.
(Hammer lightly on baby's heel.)

(Traditional, Great Britain, North America)

Rock-a-Bye Baby, Thy Cradle Is Green

Rock-a-bye baby, thy cradle is green;
Father's a nobleman, mother's a queen.
And Betty's a lady and wears a gold ring,
And Johnny's a drummer and drums for the king.

(Traditional, England)

Wine and Cakes for Gentlemen

Wine and cakes for gentlemen,
Hay and corn for horses,
A cup of ale for good old wives,
And kisses for young lasses.
(Give baby a kiss.)

(Traditional, England and Wales Harvest Song)

Little Miss Muffet

Little Miss Muffet
Sat on a tuffet,
Eating her curds and whey;
There came a great spider,
Who sat down beside her
And frightened Miss Muffet away.

(Traditional, Great Britain, North America)

QUIET TIMES

Visual Games

During the first month of life your newborn begins to coordinate her eyes. In the first few days she will fix her eyes on your face while you are holding her close. Eye-to-eye contact is rapidly, if not instantly, established. Very soon she will become quiet as soon as she sees your face. Sometimes she will stop eating to gaze into your eyes. Within six weeks or so she will smile with glee and respond to you with her whole body when she sees your face.

At birth your newborn's sharpest vision is between eight and twelve inches from her eyes—the distance from your chest to your face. By the time she is three months old, she sees as well as an average 40-year-old without glasses.

Your baby's preference is to look at faces, although she likes to look at patterns and moving objects as well. By one month, she can follow an object from side to side with her eyes. At three months, she will find her hands and maybe her feet, and try to grasp at them. She will also try to hit or grasp objects that interest her. She usually prefers to see something new rather than something she has seen before, unless it is YOU, of course.

Say "Hello"

When your baby's eyes are open, and she is looking at you, say "hello" or "hi" to her. Talk to her with the soft, high-pitched voice that she loves. Smile at her often during your talks.

Peek-a-Boo, While Rocking

The game is more "peek" than "boo" with your newborn. She has a visual memory of about two-and-a-half seconds, and the best distance between your faces is eight to twelve inches.

When your newborn has been fed and changed and is awake, move your face in and out of her focal range. This is easily done while you are rocking her and crooning a lullaby or saying a nursery rhyme, such as "Rock-a-Bye Baby." Or you may just want to say, "Hi there, sweetheart!" as you rock into her line of vision.

Rock-a-Bye Baby

(Hold her on your lap, facing you.)

Rock-a-bye baby, on the treetop,
When the wind blows, the cradle will rock.
When the bough breaks, the cradle will fall,
Down will come ———,
Cradle and all.

(Traditional, Great Britain, North America)

Hiding Peeks

A variation on the rocking peek can be done by covering your eyes with your hands, and then uncovering your eyes again. It is important to keep your newborn's attention by remembering her brief visual memory. You might want to do this when she has awakened from a sleep and isn't fussing when you pick her up. Just a few "peeks" will help her learn that you exist even when you can't be seen. A good hiding peek rhyme is "Peek-a-Boo, Peek-a-Boo."

Peek-a-Boo, Peek-a-Boo

(Uncover your eyes for every "peek.")

Peek-a-boo, peek-a-boo,
Who's that hiding there?
Peek-a-boo, peek-a-boo,
———'s behind the chair.

(Traditional, Great Britain)

Faces

Your newborn enjoys looking at faces more than anything else. She should have some toys with bright faces. Place pictures of faces from magazines where she can see them. Her stuffed animal that sleeps with her should have an interesting face with pronounced, if not exaggerated, features.

Making Faces

Is there another object in the universe with the wealth of expression of a human face? Think of a mime or an actor and present your newborn with the marvelous plasticity of the human face. She will be enthralled at the range of faces you can make at her. She will soon start to imitate you by sticking out her tongue and scrunching up her own face. During her third month she will begin to express her preferences by making faces at you.

Peer Friends

Your newborn is interested in looking at other babies, both her own age and slightly older. It is never too early to introduce her to playmates.

Mirror Games

A mirror is a world of wonder for your newborn. A stainless steel, nonbreakable mirror, fastened in your newborn's crib, provides endless delights. Find a mirror that will show her whole body, not just her head. Your newborn will soon realize that when she moves, so will the baby who lives in her mirror. Show your newborn the people who live in the mirror world: your cat, her bear, and all her important people. Use a mirror whenever you have a chance. If you have a full-length mirror, "park" her infant seat in front of it sometimes.

The Near and Far Game

When your two- or three-month-old baby is awake and alert, take a favorite doll or stuffed toy and move it close to her and then far away—a distance ranging between four or five inches and two or three feet away. As the object gets closer, your baby will reach for it with her newly developed coordination. Use facial expressions as well when you play this game.

Your Baby's Room

Your baby's room should be an interesting environment. Is it? What is on the ceiling, white nothingness? Can you put up some bright posters, colored paper kites, or pictures of babies from brightly colored magazines? Are the walls boring? Is the floor a comfortable, interesting, and safe place for your baby to explore as she gets older?

Change the position of her crib whenever you change her sheets so that she can have a new perspective and a different way of seeing her world. Even an inch or two will make a difference; you don't have to totally rearrange the furniture.

Does your baby have interesting objects hanging in her window? What is outside her window to catch her attention? Would some goldfish brighten up her room and give her something to look at?

The Mobile

Suspend mobiles within your newborn's line of vision. The best type of mobile is one that you can change every few days, because she gets bored looking at the same things day after day. Change the gizmos suspended from the mobile frequently. Hang mobiles over her change area,

over her crib, and any other place she spends time. Don't use anything on a mobile that could harm your newborn; make sure there are no tiny pieces that could be pulled off and swallowed. You can purchase elaborate and lovely mobiles, but they are also easy to make. A mobile can be as simple as a ribbon or a prism hung by a window where it can catch the breeze. Perhaps you can design a mobile that makes sounds as well as looks interesting. Hang mobiles where they can catch air currents.

Have Your Baby With You

Whenever possible, have your newborn with you, watching what you are doing. Place her special infant seat in your kitchen, and bring her along when the family congregates. Let her be a part of activities. Let her see what is going on in her world. Tie bright faces and interesting toys to her infant seat, stroller, and car seat. Your baby deserves to be entertained and involved when she is with you.

Sniffing Scents

Your newborn has a fully developed sense of smell. Let her experience a variety of smells. Perfume or aftershave lotion, shaving cream, vanilla extract, cinnamon, nutmeg, cloves, mint, and other spices and herbs all expand your newborn's knowledge of smell.

OUTDOORS

A Tree for Baby

If you have your own yard, you may want to plant a tree to celebrate your child's birth. The tree will grow along with your child. Make a visit to a reliable nursery to select a tree with your baby, and have her with you when you plant her tree. Be sure to take pictures! Talk to her about her tree, and as she grows older let her care for her

tree by watering and feeding it. If you buy a fruit
tree, she can enjoy picking the fruit later on. If you
live in an apartment, you can buy a big potted
plant instead. Many cities have programs where
commemorative trees can be planted in a public
park.

Decorate Her Tree

You may want to provide some decorations to
make her tree more interesting. You can hang
some solid outdoor wind chimes or tie some bright
ribbons or streamers onto her tree to blow in the
breeze. You could put some small hanging flower-
pots on some of the lower branches, and you could
also add some hanging bird feeders.

Another Tree

When your baby is awake and alert, let her sit
under a tree in a gentle breeze. Depending
on the season, she may see glints of light filtering
through the leaves; she may admire a multitude of
autumn colors and dancing leaves; she may see
bare branches swaying while clumps of snow drop
off in the wintertime; and she may watch spring
birds returning to emerging leaves and flowers.

The Music of the Wind

Hang some wind chimes made of brass, wood,
or glass out of your baby's reach but where
the sound can be heard. Brass bells from India
work well. It is wonderful to hear outdoor wind
chimes tinkling during a January blizzard.

C H A P T E R   T W O

I Know You Can't Crawl Yet, So How Did You Get Here?

Three to Six Months

Your baby is a social creature. He has gotten used to his new life, and now he wants to be with you. He smiles spontaneously and perhaps laughs at you and his family. He enjoys being with other people, although he may be a bit shy around strangers. He babbles away and some of his noises start to sound almost comprehensible. Your baby may sleep six or more hours at night, and he is awake, alert, and active for long periods during the day.

At five months he really does look like those charming pictures of babies. He has probably doubled his birth weight and is easy to handle. He has lost his newborn fragility. He now wants to explore his world and learn about being alive. He expresses boredom, hunger, and impatience when he wants to be changed. He discovers his feet, and is able to reach for and grasp what he sees. Your baby attempts to pick up and maybe discard small objects such as his rattle or toy keys. He is fascinated by his reflection in a mirror, and makes sounds for his own entertainment.

By the time he is six months old, your more "settled" baby is laughing, smiling, rolling over, and perhaps creeping. He is paying attention to his surroundings.

Because he is such a social being, he wants to be with you, and, assisted by his developing physical skills, he may try to get to where you are on his own. Make his world safe. Babyproof, babyproof, babyproof. And do it NOW!

MOVEMENT

Your baby is trying to gain a sense of control over his physical movements. Encourage him with lots of active games. Make sure you have a large open space in your house where you can play with your baby on days when you can't get outside. If necessary, rearrange the furniture.

There are several types of games that require a grownup's presence. Bouncing, knee rides, swinging baby, and lifts allow your baby to experience the feelings of "up", "down", and "surprise" with his total being. Get comfortable, and start to play active games that require a big person and a small person.

The Rug Rat

Let your baby have the run of his house. Place him on a pile carpet, a warm bathroom or kitchen floor, or fresh, soft, clean grass, and let him explore. Get down sometimes and join him as he creeps and crawls. Provide a variety of surfaces on which he can gain mastery of his body. He needs freedom to discover his own physical limits and abilities. The best part of his day should be spent OUT of his playpen. Install gates to establish boundaries.

Flying Baby

Be SURE he hasn't just eaten when you play this game. Once he is able to raise his head by himself, he is ready for this game. You lie down on the floor, feet flat and knees up. Holding your baby under his arms, facing you, fly him gently over your head and back down towards your knees. If he really likes it, add some wiggles, bounces and lifts. Talk to your baby as you are flying him. Make up a flight plan to describe where he is going. He doesn't have to know where Katmandu is to love being flown there.

Baby Sit-ups

Lay your baby on his back on a soft floor. Sit facing him. Gently lift your baby to a sitting position, holding onto his hands. Then slowly lower him back to a prone position. Repeat, saying, "Baby sits up, baby lies down." (Use your baby's name.)

Rolling Pin

Very gently roll your baby back and forth on a carpeted floor or on the bed. Repeat the motion, if he likes it. Tell him he's rolling out the cookies.

Knee Rides

Knee rides are a good way for your baby to get a good bounce. Have him sitting on your lap, facing you. Hold him under his arms and move your bottom forward until you are sitting on the edge of the chair. Lift your heels so your baby gets a good bounce while you recite some bouncing rhymes.

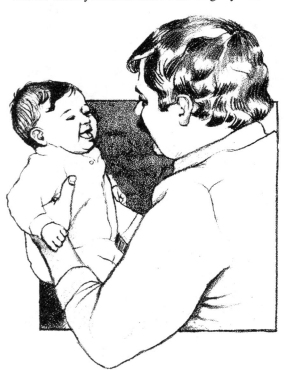

To Market, To Market

To market, to market, to buy a fat pig,
Home again, home again, jiggety jig.
To market, to market, to buy a fat hog,
Home again, home again, jiggity jog.
To market, to market, to buy a plum bun,
Home again, home again, marketing's done.

(Traditional, England)

I Had a Little Pony

I had a little pony
That trotted up and down.
I bridled him and saddled him
And trotted out of town.

(Traditional, England)

Mother and Father and Uncle Dick

Mother and Father and Uncle Dick
Went to London on a stick;
The stick broke and made a smoke
And stifled all the London folk.

(Traditional, England)

Galloping

Galloping around the room together is a wonderful way to burn off energy and experience rhythm. "Pop! Goes the Weasel" is an ideal galloping song because of the lively cadence and the anticipation of the "POP!" Both traditional versions are included here.

Round and Round the Cobbler's Bench

(Gallop around the room with your baby in your arms. When you sing "Pop!", lift him up quickly.)

Round and round the cobbler's bench
The monkey chased the weasel
The monkey thought 'twas all in fun
Pop! goes the weasel.

A penny for a spool of thread
A penny for a needle
That's the way the money goes
Pop! goes the weasel.

(Traditional, United States)

Up and Down the City Road

(Gallop around the room.
Lift him quickly on "pop!")

Up and down the City Road,
In and out the Eagle,
That's the way the money goes,
Pop! goes the weasel.

Half a pound of tuppenny rice,
Half a pound of treacle,
Mix it up and make it nice,
Pop! goes the weasel.

Every night when I go out,
The monkey's on the table;
Take a stick and knock it off,
Pop! goes the weasel!

(Traditional, British music hall song)

WATER PLAY

When your baby experiences water play and splashing he learns about his body. Besides getting clean, he also experiences volume with his whole body, which is essential for later math development.

The BIG Tub

Have you been using a baby bath until now? Why not take your baby with you into the BIG tub? Let him kick and splash away. Have a rubber duckie or two with you, and a chime ball or a "happy apple" that will ring when he kicks. Give him a sponge or face cloth so he can help you scrub.

Sponges

Buy a large package of sponges. Draw a shape on each—a circle, square, triangle, or hexagon. Or draw some animal shapes, such as a snail, dog, cat, cow, teddy bear, snake, or bird. Cut out the shape to make a simple two-piece puzzle. If you cut out two sponges of the same size and shape, but in different colors, you will have contrasting puzzles, and can give one to a friend. Find rhymes that match the shapes you have cut out, and say the rhymes as you are having your bath.

"Jacuzzi"

Use a hand-held shower attachment under water to spray on your baby for a relaxing "jacuzzi."

Wading

Hold your baby under his arms and place him in about three inches of water. Let him "walk" with your support from one end of the tub to the other.

Bath Rhymes

Say some bathtub or water rhymes when you give your baby his bath. Tickle rhymes are fun, too.

Rub-a-Dub-Dub

Rub-a-dub-dub,
Three men in a tub—
And who do you think they be?
The butcher, the baker,
The candlestick maker—
Turn 'em out,
Knaves all three!

(Traditional, England)

The Eensy, Weensy Spider

The eensy, weensy spider

> (Make climbing motion either by pivoting
> baby fingers or index fingers and the thumbs
> of the opposite hands, whichever is comfort-
> able for you.)

Climbed up the water spout.
Down came the rain and

> (Lower fingers as raindrops.)

Washed the spider out.

> (Push hands apart, making a splash.)

Out came the sun and

> (Place hands in circle over head.)

Dried up all the rain.

> (Sway arms back and forth.)

So the eensy, weensy spider

> (Make climbing motion with fingers.)

Climbed up the spout again.

(Traditional, Great Britain, North America)

This song may be the most popular song of the
century among the nursery set!

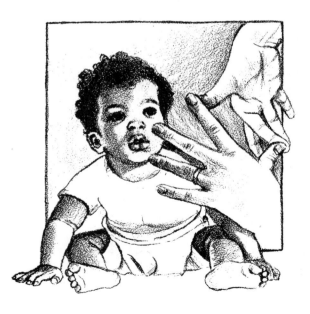

MUSIC

Sleepy Songs

Here are more sleepy-time and quiet-time
songs for your baby to enjoy for a long time
to come.

Wynken, Blynken and Nod

"Wynken, Blynken and Nod" is a beautiful,
gentle song that can be used either as a lullaby, or as a quiet, lulling poem. Fred Penner,
recording on Troubadour Records, has an enchanting version on *The Cat Came Back* album.

Wynken, Blynken and Nod one night
Sailed off in a wooden shoe—
Sailed on a river of crystal light
Into a sea of dew.
"Where are you going, and what do you wish?"
The old moon asked the three.
"We have come to fish for the herring fish
That live in this beautiful sea:
Nets of silver and gold have we!"
Said Wynken
Blynken
And Nod.

The old moon laughed and sang a song,
As they rocked in the wooden shoe,
And the wind that sped them all night long
Ruffled the waves of dew;
The little stars were the herring fish
That lived in that beautiful sea.
"Now cast your nets wherever you wish—
Never afeared are we";
So cried the stars to the fishermen three:
Wynken
Blynken
And Nod.

All night long their nets they threw
To the stars in the twinkling foam;
Then down from the skies came the wooden shoe,
Bringing the fishermen home.
'Twas all so pretty a sail it seemed
As if it could not be,
And some folks thought 'twas a dream they'd
dreamed
Of sailing that beautiful sea;
But I shall name you the fishermen three:
Wynken
Blynken
And Nod.

Wynken and Blynken are two little eyes,
And Nod is a little head;
And the wooden shoe that sailed the skies
Is a wee one's trundle-bed.
So shut your eyes while mother sings
Of wonderful sights that be,
And you shall see the beautiful things
As you rock in the misty sea,
Where the old shoe rocked the fishermen three:
Wynken
Blynken
And Nod.

(Eugene Field, United States, 1892)

Simple Gifts

'Tis a gift to be simple
'Tis a gift to be free
'Tis a gift to come down
Where we ought to be,
And when we find ourselves
In the place just right,
'Twill be in the valley
Of love and delight.

When true simplicity is gained
To bow and to bend we shan't be ashamed,
To turn, turn will be our delight
'Til by turning, turning we come round right.

(Traditional, Shaker, United States)

High There in the Deep Blue Sky

High there in the deep blue sky,
Down the Milky Way,
Rides a ship without a sail,
With no oars, they say.
White the ship, its only crew
Is a rabbit white.
Westward they're floating onward,
Quietly through the night.

(Traditional, Korea)

Dancing Songs

Two delightful songs to dance to are "Teddy Bear's Picnic" and "You Are My Sunshine." Both can be heard on a lovely children's record by Anne Murray called *There's a Hippo In My Tub* from Capitol Records. Another good dancing song is "The Bear Went Over the Mountain."

The Bear Went Over the Mountain

The bear went over the mountain
The bear went over the mountain
The bear went over the mountain
(Hold the mountain emphasis.)
To see what he could see.

And all that he could see
And all that he could see
Was the other side of the mountain
The other side of the mountain
The other side of the mountain
          (And hold mountain again.)
Was all that he could see.

(Traditional, United States)

Rock-a-My-Soul

Oh, a rock-a-my soul in the bosom of Abraham,
Rock-a-my soul in the bosom of Abraham,
Rock-a-my soul in the bosom of Abraham,
Oh, rock-a-my soul.

So high, you can't get over it,
So low, you can't get under it,
So wide, you can't get around it,
Oh, rock-a-my soul.

(Traditional, Spiritual, United States)

Sailing, Sailing

Sailing, sailing over the bounding main,
Many a stormy wind shall blow
Ere Jack comes home again.

Sailing, sailing over the bounding main,
For many a stormy wind shall blow
Ere Jack comes home again.

(Traditional, Sea Shanty, United States)

Get On Board

(This is a wonderful rocking song for babies.
Adapt as a "choo-choo" song for 30- to 36-
month-olds, sitting on the floor in a line, rocking
back and forth or holding hands leaning forward
and backwards.)

The gospel train is coming
I hear it close at hand
I hear the car-wheels moving
And rumbling through the land.

Chorus:
Get on board, little children,
Get on board, little children,
Get on board, little children,
There's room for many a-more.

The fare is cheap and all can go
The rich and poor are there
No second class aboard this train
No difference in the fare.

(Traditional, Spiritual, United States)

WORD PLAY

Babbling is essential to language development. Your baby is an observer, gaining an understanding of his language by watching how others communicate. He is learning that we communicate through language and that language is a powerful tool. He is learning how language stops and starts. He listens to the sounds we make with our tongues, lips, and palates. He is learning the cadences and rhythmic patterns of our language. When you talk to your baby and recite rhymes, enunciate well, showing your child how you use your lips, tongue, and palate to form words. Continue to use rhymes frequently.

Babbling

Imitate the sounds your baby makes. You may hear recognizable "ba," "ma," and "da" sounds. You can also show your baby how to wave "bye-bye"; and the word he produces may sound like "ba-ba." One of the reasons your baby's first words are likely to be "Ma-ma" or "Da-da" is that Mom and Dad wait anxiously for these sounds and often repeat them back to baby. Your child is making other sounds as well. Listen and repeat them to him. Form the habit of turning his sounds into words. "Ha" can become "happy" "ba ba" can become "baa baa black sheep," "da" can become an invitation to talk about when Dad is coming home, and "pa" can evoke a conversation about Grandpa or Papa.

At six months babbling turns into recognizable language sounds. During the three-to six-month period you merely want to establish that you're hearing what your baby is trying to say to you.

Record Baby's Sounds

Tape your baby's sounds and play them back to him. Your baby will have an animated conversation with himself! The tape also provides a priceless record of your baby's first sounds and words. Record your baby's voice every three months or so to keep a record of his verbal development.

Rhymes

It is important for you to continue to recite nursery rhymes so your baby hears the sounds and rhythms of his language.

Old King Cole

Old King Cole was a merry old soul,
A merry old soul was he.
He called for his pipe and
He called for his bowl and
He called for his fiddlers three.

(Traditional, England)

There Was a Crooked Man

There was a crooked man, and he walked a
*   crooked mile,*
He found a crooked sixpence against a crooked
*   stile;*
He bought a crooked cat, which caught a crooked
*   mouse,*
And they all lived together in a little crooked
*   house.*

(Traditional, England)

William and Mary

William and Mary,
George and Anne,
Four such children
Had never a man.

They put their father
To flight and shame
And called their brother
A shocking bad name.

(Traditional, England)

There Was an Old Woman

There was an old woman
Lived under a hill
And if she's not gone
She lives there still.

(Traditional, England)

My Mammy's Maid

Dingty, diddlety,
My mammy's maid,
She stole oranges,
I am afraid;

Some in her pocket,
Some in her sleeve,
She stole oranges,
I do believe.

(Traditional, England)

Eating Rhymes

At mealtime, when the entire family gets together and talks about the day's events, include your baby in the conversation by saying some rhymes.

The Man in the Moon

The man in the moon
Came down too soon
And asked his way to Norwich;
He went by the south
And burnt his mouth
With supping cold plum porridge.

(Traditional, England)

There Was an Old Woman, and What Do You Think?

There was an old woman, and what do you think?
She lived upon nothing but victuals and drink;
Victuals and drink were the chief of her diet,
And yet this old woman could never keep quiet.

(Traditional, England)

Nose, Nose, Jolly Red Nose

Nose, nose, jolly red nose
And who gave thee that jolly red nose?
Nutmeg and GINger, cinnamon and cloves
That's what gave me this jolly red nose.

(From "King Henry's Mirth," *The Knight of the Burning Pestle*, England, 1609)

INDOOR GAMES

Your baby wants to be with you constantly. He will begin to initiate play with you. Social games give him the opportunity to imitate your actions and reactions, as well as to develop his coordination. Many of the following games will become favorites as your baby matures.

Pat-a-Cake

Pat-a-cake, pat-a-cake,
Baker's man.
            (Clap hand lightly eight times.)
Bake me a cake
As quick as you can.
Pat it
            (Pat palms together.)
And prick it
            (Prick with imaginary fork.)
And mark it with a "B"
            (Draw "B" or baby's initial.)
And put it in the oven
            (Open imaginary oven door.)
For baby and me.
            (Give him a hug and kiss. Use
            your baby's name, if you like.)

(Traditional, Great Britain, North America)

Bat ta pâte, bat ta pâte, pâtissier.
Fais-moi une tartlette vite, sans délai;
Petris-la, perce-la, marque-la d'un "B,"
Puis met-la au four pour mon petit bébé.

(Traditional, French Canada)

Play "Pat-a-Cake" several times a day, holding your baby's hands to guide him through the actions. Play "Pat-a-Cake" with your baby's feet when you are changing him.

Where's Baby?

This is another version of "Peek-a-Boo." Hide your face and say "Where's Baby?" (or your child's name). Then say, "Where's Mommy?" "Where's Daddy?" "Where's Cat?" "Where's Grandma?" It won't be long before your baby starts reaching towards each person named. As he gets older he will start to creep or crawl toward the people named, and by a year he may be throwing himself in their laps.

Touch Me/Touch You

This game helps your baby realize that he is like you. Put your baby on a bed or a soft carpet, and kneel above him. Lower your face to his and say "face" while you touch his face. Then put his hands on your face. Add features—"nose," "mouth," "eyes," "chin" (or "chinny-chin-chin" if you prefer), "ears," "neck," "cheeks," "forehead," and, if he has some, "hair." Gently guide his hands over the different facial features, both his and yours. Also, do finger plays involving facial features.

Bumblebee

Bumblebee was in the barn
>   (Circle your finger in the air.)
Carrying dinner under his arm.
>   (Move finger closer to baby.)
Buzzzzzzzz-zz-z!
>   (Give him a gentle poke.)

(Traditional, United States)

Knock at the Door

Knock at the door.
>   (Tap baby's forehead.)
Peek in.
>   (Stare into his eyes.)
Lift the latch
>   (Touch end of his nose.)
And walk in.
>   (Walk your fingers from his chin to his mouth.)
Go way down in the cellar and eat
>   (Tickle downward and pat
Up all the apples (yum yum).
>   his tummy.)

(Traditional, Great Britain.)

Baby and I

Baby and I
Were baked in a pie.
The gravy was wonderful hot.
We had nothing to pay
To the baker that day
And so we crept out of the pot.
>   (Creep fingers slowly up baby's body.)

(Traditional, Great Britain)

Thumbkin, Pointer

Thumbkin, Pointer, Middleman big,
>   (Point to each of baby's fingers in turn.)
Silly Man, Wee Man,
Rig-a-jig-jig.
>   (Roll his hands around each other.)

(Traditional, England)

QUIET TIMES

Your baby is now more comfortable in his world, so he can pay more attention to both his body and his surroundings. He is learning through all of his senses.

Smells

Introduce your baby to fragrant plants and flowers. Talk about all sorts of smells—your cooking ingredients, outdoor smells, perfumes, the skunk that didn't quite make it across the highway...whatever it is that you smell.

Warm and Cool

When you dry your hair, use the hair dryer on your baby's skin. Use the warm and the cool settings, but never the hot.

Lighting Changes

Your child's perception of objects changes under different intensities of light, so use a three-way bulb or a dimmer switch to change the lighting in various rooms of your home.

Textures

Make a textured blanket for your baby so he can feel different kinds of cloth. For example, silk, corduroy, satin, wool, cotton, and velvet are all wonderful. Make a mural of interestingly textured papers and hang it near your baby's changing area. Use sandpaper, aluminum foil, tissue paper, corrugated cardboard, wallpaper samples, wrapping papers, and cloth. Introduce touch-and-feel books such as *pat the bunny* (Dorothy Kundhart, Golden Books).

Reading

Buy or make some simple books for your baby. They should be chewable—either heavy cardboard or the floating plastic variety—and a manageable size for his hands. Pictures should be bright, and words, if any, should be printed in large letters.

Sit your baby on your lap and say, "Let's read [baby's name]'s book. This is a book about a [dog]." Show him the pictures and if he points to something, say, "That is the [dog barking: woof, woof, woof!]." Be calm and quiet, but enthusiastic as well.

Mirror Game

When you look at your baby in the mirror, say, "See the happy face," "See the sad face," "See the angry face." Exaggerate your features and ham it up. Put your baby where he can often look at and touch the baby in the mirror. Show him what happens when he touches the baby in the mirror. It's great for his developing self-confidence.

OUTDOORS

Out in the Community

Show your baby his community and how he fits in. Talk about the fire engines, police cars, hospitals, ambulances, buses, trains, airplanes, schools, stores, libraries, parks, and playgrounds he sees. He will understand far more than you think even from his earliest days. He will also learn that there are people available to help him as he grows up.

Sit Outside

If weather permits, throw a blanket or a quilt on the grass, snow, leaves, or porch. Put out some of your baby's favorite toys and sit on the blanket with him. As you luxuriate let your baby set the pace for his own play and exploration.

Exploration

Place your baby on leaves, grass, or snow to discover what the world is all about. Be sure to check the area for animal feces and unsafe objects. Let him crawl about the yard or park at his own pace, to see what he can see. A little clean snow won't hurt him.

The Playground

Take your baby to the playground, no matter what the season. Let him experience the baby swings, if there are some, as soon as he can hold his head up. Push him gently. Let him slide down the slide with Mom or Dad holding him. Sit on a regular swing with your baby in his pouch carrier and swing away. As he grows, let your baby's stay in the swing run longer and longer. Have him "hang" from the climbers as you hold him. By the time he is two, he will be quite comfortable at the playground and may need only minimal assistance.

Make a Baby Swing

Make your baby a swing by using ropes or chains to secure a large plastic milk box— the kind you store record albums in—to a tree. Cut out and smooth some leg holes in one side of the container, and, if necessary, prop your baby up with small cushions or rolled baby blankets. Double check your hardware attachments regularly.

Action Games

Play some active movement games outside where you have plenty of space. Toss and jostle baby, and bounce him around.

Airplane Baby

This was Jenny's favorite game of all before her first birthday. Start this game when your baby can hold his head up securely. Pick him up, holding him firmly under his arms, face down, in a horizontal position. You need lots of room and a baby that loves action. Fly a circuit—take off, veer around in a left-handed square, and come in to land! Start the "airplane" with appropriate noises, spread out his arms for the wings and go roaring off. As your baby grows older, add loops, rolls, spins, stalls, and other aerobatic maneuvers. You will probably tire of this game faster than your baby will!

Swing Baby

As soon as he can hold his head up firmly, carefully pick up your baby by holding one of his wrists and the ankle on the same side in each of your hands. Gently swing him back and forth, then lower him gently. Alternate sides. He will probably love to play this game until he is too heavy to pick up this way. This was Gaby's favorite action game.

CHAPTER THREE

Here You Are, Under My Feet (the Creeper, Crawler, and Maybe Cruiser)

Six to Nine Months

Now is the time your baby gains mobility. She will creep, crawl, and perhaps pull herself to a standing position and move while holding onto furniture. As she becomes more and more physically active, babyproofing becomes more and more essential. Play your Silly Game for Grownups (p.2) over and over again. MOVE or REMOVE tippy furniture that could land on top of her as she pulls herself to a stand. Remember she will put EVERYTHING into her mouth, whether it's edible or not. Your crawler has a developing awareness of what she wants to do next, which makes it mandatory for YOU to know what she is doing—constantly.

Your baby is also learning to sit up by herself. She loves to sit in all sorts of exciting places: a grocery cart, her high chair, her car seat.

Most babies alternate between sitting and moving around. However, some babies seem to be in perpetual motion, while others want to sit still in one place. It is all part of your baby's individuality.

By the time she is nine months old, your baby will be able to pick up and drop objects with both hands. She will discover that she has a problem to solve when she has a toy in each hand, and wants a third.

MOVEMENT

Your baby is gaining increasing mastery over her body through movement. Here are some games you can play to enhance her physical competence.

Hide 'n' Seek

This simple "Hide 'n' Seek" is only a few steps away from "Peek-a-Boo." Partially hide yourself from your baby and let her come to you. Use furniture or hide behind doors. Partially hide behind a tree at the park. Play hiding games frequently, using your body and her toys. Call her, if necessary. Don't completely hide yourself; she still needs to see you to know you are there.

Under, Over, Around, and Through

Where can your baby hide? What will she fit under? (the table) What can she go over? (cushions) What can she get into? (closets) What can she get behind? (the sofa). This game will teach her about the size of her body, as well as provide some good places for her to "hide 'n' seek."

The Cushion Climb

Your baby needs to climb. Remove all the cushions from your sofas and chairs, heap them in a pile on the floor, and give her a chance to do some elementary mountaineering. Then set up some cushion "stairs" so she can begin to learn to climb stairs properly. This is a wonderful way to get your baby tired out for a nice long nap, and the cushions provide a cozy place to curl up. Hide her behind some cushions and play "Peek-a-Boo."

Baby Twirls

Lay your baby on her back on a smooth tile or hardwood floor and sit beside her. Gently raise her legs about three or four inches from the floor and hold her ankles together. Using her raised legs as a "handle," gently pivot her torso.

Leg Lifts

Slowly and gently, lift each of your baby's legs separately, up and down. Then lift both legs up and down. Lift her legs up and gently flex them over and onto her chest, without pushing or pulling. Permit her legs to flex naturally, never force them.

Rocking

A rocking toy to sit inside or a rocking chair may be fun for your baby, given her new sitting abilities. Make sure you support her on her rides until she gains good control of her body, or prop her up with cushions.

Ankle Rides

Sit on a straight-backed chair and cross your legs. Place your crawler on your upper ankle, facing you. Hold her hands or place your hands under her arms. Lift your leg up and down to the rhythm of some good bouncing rhymes, such as the ones below. If your baby doesn't like ankle rides, use these rhymes as knee bounces.

Grandfa' Grig

Grandfa' Grig
Had a pig
In a field of clover;
Piggy died,
Grandfa' cried
And all the fun was O-VER.

         (Tip your baby to one side on O.)

(Traditional, Great Britain)

Donkey, Donkey

Donkey, Donkey, do not bray,
Mend your pace and trot away;
Indeed, the market's almost done,
My butter's melting in the sun.

(Traditional, United States)

Tom, Tom

Tom, Tom, the piper's son,
Stole a pig and away he run;
The pig* was eat
And Tom was beat
And Tom went howling through the street.

*pig=a currant bun made in the shape of a pig

(Traditional, England)

If Wishes Were Horses

If wishes were horses, beggars would ride
If turnips were watches, I would wear one by my
   side.
And if "ifs" and "ands" were pots and pans
There'd be no work for tinkers!

(Traditional, England)

Riding on My Pony

Holding your baby in your arms, gallop around the room singing:

Riding on my pony,
My pony, my pony,
Riding on my pony,
Whoa! Whoa! Whoa!

(When you get to the last line, pull your baby in as you "stop" the pony for each whoa!).

(Traditional, Flanders, adapted)

Let's Take a Walk

Take a walk around the house together, as you sing:

Let's take a walk, take a walk, take a walk,
To see what we can see, now.
Let's take a walk, take a walk, take a walk,
To see what we can see, now.

(Traditional, United States)

When you take your walks around the house, say, "This is the stove," "This is the refrigerator," "This is the door," "This is the bathroom." Make up songs about the items you identify. Play "Let's Take a Walk" outside, too.

Action Games

Play lots of action games with your baby. Sit on the floor, feet flat, knees up. Place your baby on your knees, facing you, holding hands. Then play "Humpty Dumpty" and "One, Two, Three." These games provide a good sense of anticipation.

Humpty Dumpty

(Bounce baby up and down on your knees; quickly lower knees to floor on "fall," then bounce her again.)

Humpty Dumpty sat on a wall,
Humpty Dumpty had a great fa-a-a-ll.
All the king's horses and all the king's men
Couldn't put Humpty together again.

(Traditional, England)

One, Two, Three

One, two, three,
>   (Bounce your baby.)
Baby's on my knee.
>   (Do nothing.)
Rooster crows and
>   (Crow, "Cock-a-doodle-doo" enthusiastically.)
Away she go-o-o-o-es!
>   (Quickly lower your knees to the floor.)

(Traditional, United States)

Follow the Leader

Mimic your baby's movements. When she puts her head on one side, imitate her. Baby may see what's happening and initiate more movements, which you also mimic.

WATER PLAY

Bath time can be quite a challenge. Spread a bath towel on the bottom of the big tub to keep baby from slipping and let her splash away in two or three inches of water. She may lie back and kick furiously. Have a few extra towels handy so everyone and everything can dry off afterwards.

Bath Toys

It is now time to acquire a flotilla of bath toys to be used for years to come. Your baby will love boats, ducks, plastic floating books, and containers that float, pour, squirt, and spray water. A tub activity center is a worthwhile, long-lasting investment. Get one that flip-flops and squirts. Big people will enjoy it too.

Let Your Baby Help

Give your baby facecloths and sponges so she can help you wash her. She will probably suck water from the cloth or sponge, but it won't hurt her. Sing "This is the Way We Wash Our Face."

This Is the Way We Wash Our Face

(Tune: "Here We Go 'Round the Mulberry Bush")

This is the way we wash our face
Wash our face, wash our face
This is the way we wash our face
On a (day of the week) (morning or evening)

(Other verses can include: wash our toes, wash our arms, scrub our feet, tickle our tum.)

(Traditional, England, adapted)

When the Ducks Get Up in the Morning

While your baby is having her bath, sing songs to her rubber duckies, such as:

When the ducks get up in the morning
They always say "Quack, quack."
When the ducks get up in the morning
They always say "Quack, quack."

(Traditional, United States)

Superduck

Hold one of your baby's rubber duckies under the water and let it go quickly so it will pop up out of the water. (It helps to apply lots of pressure while the duck is under water.)

Rain Is Falling Down

(While your baby sits in her bath, wiggle and lower her fingers until they SPLASH into the water. Clap her hands lightly for the "pitter patters.")

Rain is falling down—splash!
Rain is falling down—splash!
Pitter patter,
Pitter patter,
Rain is falling down—splash!

(Traditional, United States)

Tickle Games

Continue to play tickle games with your baby, both in the tub and while she is getting dressed. Here are two tickle games that babies of this age enjoy:

These Are Baby's Fingers

These are baby's fingers,
                    (Use your baby's name.)
These are baby's toes.
                    (Touch her finger, toes,
This is baby's tummy button,
                    and belly button.)
Round and round it goes.
                    (Draw circles on her tummy.)

(Traditional, England)

Round and Round the Garden

Round and round the garden
                    (Circle her tummy.)
Goes the teddy bear.
One step... two steps...
                    (Walk fingers up her chest.)
Tickle her under there!
                    (Tickle her under arms or chin.)

(Traditional, England)

"Round and Round the Garden" can also be done as a finger tickle, by drawing circles on baby's hand, "stepping" your fingers up her arm, and tickling under her chin.

CHANGING GAMES

Continue to play changing games with your baby and show her her fingers and toes.

The Pettitoes

The pettitoes are little feet,
                    (Tap her feet together.)
And the little feet not big.
Great feet belong to the grunting hog
                    (Make a hog's snuffing sounds.)
And the pettitoes to the little pig.
                    (Make "wee, wee, wee" sounds.)

(Traditional, England)

Shoe the Old Horse

Shoe the old horse,
                    (Wiggle one foot
Shoe the old mare.
                    and then the other.)
But let the little pony run
                    (Tap her feet together lightly
Bare, bare, bare.
                    to the end of the rhyme.)

(Traditional, England)

Leg Over Leg

As you turn your baby over while she is being changed, say this rhyme:

Leg over leg as the dog went to Dover.
When he came to a stile—
Whoop!

(Turn her over on whoop!)

He went over.

(Traditional, England)

Let's Go to the Wood

"Let's go to the wood," said this little pig.
"What to do there," said this little pig.

(Wiggle each wrist.)

"Find our mother," said this little pig.
"What to DO with her?" said this little pig.

(Then each ankle.)

"Kiss her all over," said this little pig.

(Kiss and hug your baby.)

(Traditional, England)

MUSIC

Your baby now responds physically to music. Dancing and bouncing are ideal introductions to music, because they combine a song or a rhyme with stimulating physical activity. Your baby may move her whole body in response to music, perhaps for some songs more than others. She may express in her babbling the beat of the music she is hearing. A favorite song for your baby will be "As I Was Walking to Town."

As I Was Walking to Town

As I was walking to town one day,
I met a — upon the way
And what do you think that ——— did say?
———, ———, ———.

(Traditional, North America, adapted)

When you sing this song, leave a slight musical pause after, "I met a ———." Between 12 and 15 months your baby may indicate her choice of animal, either by name... "cat"... or noise... "meow"...

This song can have all sorts of variations. Dogs bark, cats meow, cows moo, horses neigh, ducks quack, birds cheep, chickens cluck, and turkeys gobble. As your baby grows older, you can add lions that ROARR-R-R, alligators that snap, donkeys that hee-haw, mice that squeak, and elephants that trumpet. The possibilities are endless.

Instruments

Your baby is developing the coordination to bang on a drum, or shake a rattle. You and she can make or find some simple instruments to play. Tap the beat gently while you sing your songs and say your rhymes.

Drums

Banging is a natural activity for your baby. A pot is a drum and a wooden spoon the drumstick. An inverted plastic ice cream container makes a quieter drum. Show her the beat of some of her familiar nursery rhymes, such as "Baa, Baa, Black Sheep" and "Little Miss Muffett." Here are some more drum songs:

Fee, Fie, Foe, Fum

Fee, fie, foe, fum
Big giant here I come
Fee, fie, foe, fum
BIG GIANT HERE I COME!!!

(Traditional, Great Britain)

Let's Play Our Drums

Let's play our drums together
Let's play our drums together
Let's play our drums together
Because it's fun to do.

(Traditional, Great Britain)

Adapt and sing this song as you tap your sticks, ring your bells, and shake your shakers together.

Bathtub Drums

Give your baby a large plastic ice cream container to use in the bathtub. Show her how to play her drum songs with splashing effects.

Bells

Lace dime store bells together with a shoelace or a strip of leather, or tie the bells to a stick for baby to hold and shake.

Ride a Cock Horse

Ride a cock horse to Banbury Cross
                 (Shake bells rhythmically.)
To see a fine lady
Upon a white horse.
With rings on her fingers
                 (Tap bells on your baby's fingers
And bells on her toes
         and her toes.)
She shall have music wherever she goes.

(Traditional, England)

Shakers

A rattle makes a good musical instrument. You can make your own shaker by putting some rice, unpopped popcorn, or dried grain in a plastic container of manageable size and sealing the top. As baby shakes her rattle, say familiar rhymes such as "Hey Diddle Diddle" or "Jack Sprat."

Rhythm Sticks

Rhythm sticks are two pieces of 3/4-inch dowelling, six inches long. Commercial rhythm sticks, at 14 inches, are too long for small children to manage, although you can cut them in half to make a pair for baby and a pair for you. Recite or sing familiar nursery rhymes, such as "Hark, Hark, the Dogs Do Bark," and emphasize the rhymes with the tapping of the sticks.

WORD PLAY

Your crawling baby is a talker, babbling constantly — to her toys, to people, to her fish. Her babbles change, however, depending on the audience. It is as if she knows that people will respond to words while toys won't. Her babbles start to resemble language forms. You will hear the intonations of questions and commands as well as descriptions in her vocalizations.

Morning Chatterbox

Listen to your baby's spontaneous, cheerful morning chatter, and her incredible range of sounds. Relax and have your morning cup of tea or coffee as you listen to your baby's conversation with you.

Word Games

Lie down with your baby and start repeating her sounds. She loves to communicate and will find a special joy in having you LISTEN to what she has to say. Here's a typical conversation:

Baby: Hee!
You: Hee!
Baby: Ha!
You: Ha!
Baby: Who?
You: Who?

Repeat the sounds without reference to specific words unless your baby spontaneously produces some. Enjoy your conversation and bask in the sounds.

Sounds most likely to occur at this stage are: ha, he, ba, be, me, ah, da, ma, oh, ka, pa ("t" and "s" sounds are difficult).

Putting the "Bop" in the "Bop du Wop"

When your baby begins to actively use sounds, such as "ba ba " and "da da," sing the backgrounds to your favorite '50s, '60s and '70s rock 'n' roll songs. For example, your baby can learn the words to "Barbara Ann" in the same amount of time as it takes to learn "Baa baa black sheep." Dance with your baby while singing the background music.

Poetry

Your child will delight in the intricacies of language when you read poetry to her, no matter how good or how bad. Victorian parlour poetry by Edward Lear and Lewis Carroll, for instance, is wonderful, as are the works of Dr. Seuss and Dennis Lee. Let the words roll forth from your mouth. Find and recite some lovely nonsense verse, or recite some of your favorite songs as poetry. Give your best possible dramatic performance.

Jabberwocky

'Twas brillig, and the slithy toves
Did gyre and gimble in the wabe:
All mimsy were the borogoves,
And the mome raths outgrabe.

"Beware the Jabberwock, my son!
The jaws that bite, the claws that catch!
Beware the Jubjub bird, and shun
The frumious Bandersnatch!"

He took his vorpal sword in hand:
Long time the manxome foe he sought —
So rested he by the Tumtum tree,
And stood awhile in thought.

And, as in uffish thought he stood,
The Jabberwock, with eyes of flame,
Came whiffling through the tulgey wood,
And burbled as it came!

One, two! One, two! And through and through
The vorpal blade went snicker-snack!
He left it dead, and with its head
He went galumphing back.

"And hast thou slain the Jabberwock?
Come to my arms, my beamish boy!
O frabjous day! Callooh! Callay!"
He chortled in his joy.

'Twas brillig, and the slithy toves
Did gyre and gimble in the wabe:
All mimsy were the borogoves,
And the mome raths outgrabe.

(Lewis Carroll, *Through the Looking Glass,* England, 1872)

Books

Read a variety of books to your baby. Start with bright picture books with one word per page, such as those by Dick Bruna and Jan Pienkowski. Add books with complex pictures, so you and she can identify several items in one picture. Also, read rhyming books, such as *Jelly Belly* by Dennis Lee or *Dr. Seuss' ABC*. Read longer stories as well, according to her attention span.

KITCHEN PLAY

A babyproofed kitchen is a wonderful place for your baby. Pull up your baby's high chair or let her sit in her infant seat, where she can watch and participate. Talk to her—she's a great companion. Give her a drawer or a cupboard of her own for kitchen toys.

Pot and Lid

Give your baby her own pot and lid. Show her how to bang them together to make noise. Turn the pot over to make a drum and give her wooden spoons for drumsticks. You can soften the sound by padding the ends of the wooden-spoon drumsticks with electrical tape or bandages.

Baking

Let your baby play with some flour or corn meal and a sifter or strainer when you are baking. Put her down on the floor on some newspapers and give her a quarter of a cup of flour to play with in her sifter.

Finger Painting

When your baby is sitting up at a table or high chair, put a bit of yoghurt, ketchup, a squirt of whipped cream, or a dollop of her cereal onto her tray and let her "fingerpaint" with the goop. Let her feel the texture, and spread it about.

You can save a painting she does this way by adding some non-toxic paint or food color to the cereal. Place a sheet of paper over her painting to transfer the design onto the paper, and *voila!* her first masterpiece, suitable for framing. Make sure the cereal is mixed with water, not milk, if you want to save the painting.

Ooshy, Squeezing

If your baby is drinking juices, take a bit of her fruit juice and add some unflavored gelatin and let it set to make jello. Put some of her jello in a plastic bag and tie the top. Let her squeeze it and experiment with what happens when it is pushed, poked, prodded and banged. Make sure the plastic doesn't go into her mouth. When she has finished

with the bag, pour the jello out so she can continue to play with it and eat it with her fingers.

Eating Fun

As your pediatrician introduces solid foods to your baby's diet, let her feed herself using her hands, at least some of the time. Finger foods such as bread, cheese, carrots, bits of meat, banana, pieces of cooked pasta, dry cereal, are all wonderful for experimenting and learning about the textures of the different foods people eat.

INDOOR GAMES

Your baby may be starting to cut teeth. It helps to distract her from her sore gums by playing interesting games.

Which Hand?

Put a small toy in one of your hands and ask your baby to select the hand with the toy in it. Be obvious when you "hide" the toy, so she can easily select the correct hand. Say, "What a clever baby, you found it!" You can say a rhyme, such as "Handy Dandy" when you play this game.

Handy Dandy

(Hide a toy in one hand and let your baby select the hand she wants.)

Handy dandy,
Riddledy ro.
Which hand will you have,
High or low?

(Traditional, England)

Ice

Use an unbreakable cup and ice. When you are waiting, anywhere, at an airport, in a restaurant, at home, give her her ice in an unbreakable cup. "Pretend" you are drinking with her, and teach her to go "cheers" with her glass. The bonus is there is little mess, because the ice that doesn't get consumed melts. Ice and a plastic cup has kept one small international traveller amused for at least a half hour at a time!

Where's (Kitty)?

A good way to distract a teething baby is to give her a task. Say, "Let's go find the cat..." and go on a search. Variations can include: "Let's go see the moon..."; "Let's watch the sun come up..."; "Let's watch the garbage collectors take away the garbage..."; "Let's go get the mail...," and so on.

Hiding Toys

P artially hide a toy under a diaper or blanket and let your baby find it. She is learning to find objects that have "disappeared". She knows that objects are real, even when they can't be seen, as long as they are hidden in an obvious manner.

Hide a small plastic toy, a ping-pong ball, or a teething ring in pockets or purses for baby to find as a special treat.

Paintbrushes

C ollect some large, soft paintbrushes for your baby's future art work, and use them occasionally for tickles now.

Texture Walks

T ake your baby on a walk around the house so she can feel an assortment of textures. You might run her hands over heating vents, wallpaper or paint surfaces, floor surfaces, and bathroom tiles. Look carefully around your house for textured objects to feel, such as the wavy ridge texture of an old-fashioned washboard or corrugated cardboard. Give her a chance to touch interesting surfaces.

HINT: Say "bye-bye" and wave every time you leave your baby's sight. This way she learns that you will always come back.

QUIET TIMES

Sounds

Y our baby notices and responds to the important sounds in her life. The sound of your voice will reassure her that you are there, even when she can't see you. She is curious about the sounds she hears, and where they come from. She will look for a dog when she hears barking, she will look up for the sounds of an airplane or a helicopter, she will search for a fire truck when she hears a siren, and she will look at the telephone when it rings.

Talk to her about all the sounds she hears, both inside and outside. Talk about voices, footsteps, animal noises, bird sounds, a toilet flushing, the vacuum cleaner, the coffee grinder, the blender, the washer, the dryer, and the sounds her stroller makes as she travels over different surfaces.

Soft Lullabies and Poetry

C ontinue to sing lullabies and recite soft poetry with your baby. Take her into your arms before a nap and recite or sing long gentle poems.

Can You Make Me a Cambric Shirt

Can you make me a cambric shirt,
Parsley, sage, rosemary, and thyme,
Without any seam or needlework?
And you shall be a true lover of mine.

Can you wash it in yonder well,
Parsley, sage, rosemary, and thyme,
Where never sprung water, nor rain ever fell?
And you shall be a true lover of mine.

Can you dry it on yonder thorn,
Parsley, sage, rosemary, and thyme,
Which never bore blossom since Adam was born?
And you shall be a true lover of mine.

Now you've asked me questions three,
Parsley, sage, rosemary, and thyme,
I hope you'll answer as many for me,
And you shall be a true lover of mine.

Can you find me an acre of land,
Parsley, sage, rosemary, and thyme,
Between the salt water and the sea sand?
And you shall be a true lover of mine.

Can you plough it with a ram's horn,
Parsley, sage, rosemary, and thyme,
And sow it all over with one peppercorn?
And you shall be a true lover of mine.

Can you reap it with a sickle of leather,
Parsley, sage, rosemary, and thyme,
And bind it up with a peacock's feather?
And you shall be a true lover of mine.

When you have done and finished your work,
Parsley, sage, rosemary, and thyme,
Then come to me for your cambric shirt,
And you shall be a true lover of mine.

(Traditional, English courting song)

Piping Down the Valleys Wild

Piping down the valleys wild
Piping songs of pleasant glee
On a cloud I saw a child,
And he laughing said to me,

"Pipe a song about a Lamb";
So I piped with merry chear;
"Piper pipe that song again"—
So I piped, he wept to hear.

"Drop thy pipe thy happy pipe
Sing thy songs of happy chear";
So I sung the same again
While he wept with joy to hear.

"Piper sit thee down and write
In a book that all may read"—
So he vanish'd from my sight.
And I pluck'd a hollow reed,

And I made a rural pen,
And I stain'd the water clear,
And I wrote my happy songs
Every child may joy to hear.

(William Blake, *Songs of Innocence*, Great Britain 1789)

OUTDOORS

Continue to get outside as often and for as long as possible. The world outdoors is a fascinating place. Play ball with your baby as soon as she can sit up properly. Balls are one of the most basic toys of all times. They come in all colors, sizes, and weights. Make sure your baby has plenty, from soft cloth balls she can grasp easily, to highly visible, hard-to-grab beachballs. Balls are fun to use outdoors where they can do less damage and can go farther. Play lots of action games as you include your baby in your own outdoor life.

The Beachball

As soon as your baby is crawling, inflate a beachball and roll it towards your baby. Then crawl after her, pushing the ball just out of her reach so she has to move to get to it.

Grocery Shopping

Grocery shopping with a baby is fun when you make a game of it. Go at times when there are no crowds. As soon as she can sit up securely, let her ride around the store in a grocery cart. Talk, think out loud, and discuss your options. Show her the big, bright pictures and letters on boxes and packages. Take her into the produce department and name the fruits and vegetables. Many of the items you will purchase are for her, so let her help make the choices. She can indicate what kind of cereal she wants, and whether she wants bananas or apples. Let her throw the non-perishable, unbreakable items into the cart herself. Very young children absorb information at a rapid rate. Use the supermarket to provide your child with hundreds of "bits" of information for later use.

Piggy Back

Some children love piggy back, others hate it. There seems to be no middle ground. A "piggy back" helps your baby develop her balance up on Mom's or Dad's shoulders. It also lets her see the world the way a big person does, one that's even taller than Mom or Dad. Have her legs over your shoulders, hold onto her hands. Say some rhymes and move to the rhythm of the words as you play "piggy back." The following is a good rhyme to use because the rhythm intensifies with each verse.

A Paris, à Paris

A Paris, à Paris,
Sur un petit cheval gris.

> (Walking rhythm.)

A Rouen, à Rouen,
Sur en petit cheval blanc.

> (Trotting rhythm.)

A Québec, à Québec,
Sur la queue d'une belette.

> (Galloping rhythm.)

(Traditional, France, French Canada)

Build a Snowman

Build snow people as part of your winter ritual whenever weather permits. Your baby will love her snowman.

Use sticky snow, roll balls and stack them up. Dress the snowman with a hat, scarf, and castoff clothing. Insert the traditional carrot nose and two eyes made out of coal (use charcoal left over from the summer barbecue season).

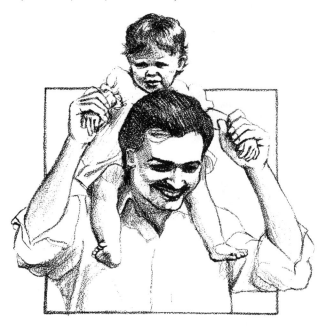

C H A P T E R   F O U R

How Did You Get Up There All By Yourself?

Nine to Twelve Months

Your mobile baby now goes into overdrive in his climbing, crawling, cruising, and, possibly walking. His most basic needs are to move and explore. His curiosity is insatiable; he wants to investigate everything. He is learning to climb everything and has the mental ability to figure out how to move furniture to climb even higher. He may often find himself in impossible situations. He has a short attention span and no sense of danger. Therefore, he needs a vigilant adult with him on his explorations.

Your mobile baby is also gaining dexterity as his fingers become more flexible. He is learning to drop his toys. He likes to drop and play with small toys. Hinges fascinate him. Boxes that open, nesting toys, and the doors on kitchen cupboards mesmerize him. He loves to open packages. Everything goes in his mouth.

It is important to talk directly to your baby about everything in his world, and to provide names for everything. He is imitating language and some of his sounds are actually intelligible. He's starting to recognize and use meaningfully, the rhythms, inflections, and facial expressions of language.

Your baby is dependent on you, your partner, and close relatives. Although he may be shy around strangers and in strange places, he loves his special people dearly, and has lots of smiles, hugs, and kisses for them. He is especially dependent upon his mother, and makes continual requests of her. He learns the meaning of "no" and begins to protest and assert himself. He also seeks your approval and tries to please you.

MOVEMENT

Locomotion now takes on an entirely different meaning. Your baby is gaining competence in two types of movement—the vertical, standing and cruising; and the horizontal, climbing and crawling. He needs to experience both types of movement. He is also interested in balancing. He will try to mimic all your movements.

The Stair Climb

Babies like to climb. Teach your baby to climb stairs and come down again safely. To teach him to climb place a toy a step or two higher than he is. He will work to reach the toy. To teach him to descend, place the toy on a lower step. Your baby faces into the steps and slides down on his tummy, feet first. Show him how to lower his bottom and legs to the next step. Even when he improves at this game, keep your stairs gated. Supervise all climbing activities until he is at least two years old.

Boo!

This is a game in which timing is essential. The game is the "Boo" part of "Peek-a-Boo." Get down to your baby's level by lying on the floor, couch, bed, or chair. Say to your baby, "Come and get me," and when he does, say, "Oooh — you GOT me! Let's do it again." When another person is present, send the baby to "get" that person, who, in turn, acts startled. Send the baby back and forth between the two of you, or on to another person.

Hide 'n' Seek

Continue to play "Boo!" but start hiding in slightly less obvious although still visible, places. Your baby may look for you in the place in which you hid previously, even when you are in plain view.

Leg Lifts

Once your baby is cruising comfortably, put a straight-backed chair in the middle of the room for balance for both of you as you do some leg lifts. You hold onto a corner of the chair back, facing the side of it. Have your baby hold onto the corner of the chair seat facing you. Slowly kick lift your outside foot about 18 inches, to the front, to the side, and to the back. Hold the other corner of the chair and lift your other leg. Have your baby mimic you.

Foot Flex

Still holding onto the chair, lift one leg off the floor and point the toe, then flex the foot, then point the toe again. Change legs. Have your baby mimic you.

Knee Bends

Stand beside the chair, spine straight, with your heels together and your toes pointed out slightly. Slowly bend your knees and lower your body, trying to keep your knees over your toes. Straighten your legs and repeat. Have your baby copy your movements.

Movement Games

Do lots of your baby's favorite knee rides, ankle rides, action games, and bouncing games. Add these games to your collection:

Dickery, Dickery, Dare

Dickery, dickery, dare,
> (Bounce him, facing you.)

The pig flew up in the air.
> (Lift him high on "up.")

The man in brown
> (Bounce him again.)

Soon brought him down,
> (Hold still on "down,"

Dickery, dickery, dare.
> then bounce again.)

(Traditional, England, United States)

Tommy Trot, a Man of Law

(Quickly bounce your baby.)

Tommy Trot, a man of law
Sold his bed and lay upon straw;
Sold the straw and slept on grass
To buy his wife a looking glass.

(Traditional, England)

Old Boniface*, He Loved Good Cheer

(Bounce your baby to the beat.)

Old Boniface, he loved good cheer,
*And took his glass of Burton**,*
And when the nights grew sultry hot
He slept without his shirt on.

Boniface — the innkeeper in Beaux' Strategem,
1707
**Burton—brown ale*

(Traditional, England)

Jack 'n' Jill

(Sit on floor, legs straight, baby on your knees, facing you. Knees up on UP. Baby to lying position on back on DOWN, touch his head on CROWN and tickle up legs for last line.)

Jack 'n' Jill went UP the hill
To fetch a pail of water
Jack fell DOWN
And broke his crown
And Jill came tumbling after.

(Traditional England, probably from Medieval Norse)

Matthew, Mark, Luke and John

(Have your baby ride on your knee.)

Matthew, Mark, Luke and John
Hold my horse 'till I leap on
Hold him steady, hold him sure
And I'll get over the misty moor.

(Traditional, England)

Come Up, My Horse

(This can be a knee, ankle, or piggyback ride.)

Come up, my horse, to Budleigh Fair.
What shall we have when we get there?
Sugar and figs and elecampane*;
Home again,
Home again,
Master and dame.

*Elecampane—an herb used to flavor candy

(Traditional, England)

This Is the Way the Ladies Ride

(Sit on the edge of a hard chair.)

This is the way the ladies ride,
nim, nim, nim.

(Baby sits sidesaddle on your knee.
Slowly bounce him.)

This is the way the gentlemen ride,
trim, trim, trim.

(Baby faces forward, bouncing on both
your knees, to a trotting rhythm.)

This is the way the farmers ride,
tr-ot, tr-ot, tr-ot, tr-ot.

(With baby on both your knees, lift one
heel at a time to jostle-bounce.)

This is the way the hunters ride,
gallop, a-gallop, a-gallop, a-gallop.

(Quick, energetic, galloping bounce.)

And this is the way the astronauts ride,
Whoosh!!!!!

(With baby on his feet, hold him
under the arms and whoosh him up.)

(Traditional, Great Britain, adapted)

Ride Baby Ride

Ride baby ride
> (Bounce your baby alternately up and down
ch-ch, ch-ch, ch-ch,
>> and side to side.)
Ride that horsey ride
> (Up and down
ch-ch, ch-ch, ch-ch...etc.
>> side to side.)
WHOA-A-A!
> (Pull in for a hug.)

(Traditional, United States)

A Froggie Sat on a Log

(Sitting on a chair, knee bounce, with your baby facing you. Open your legs and lower baby between your knees on FELL. Support his head and neck.)

A froggie sat on a log,
A-weeping for his daughter,
His eyes were red,
His tears he shed.
And he FELL right into the water.

(Traditional, United States)

Ride, Ride, Ride, Mr. Dobbin

(Have baby ride on your knee or ankle.)

Ride, ride, ride, Mr. Dobbin
Keep that carriage a bobbin'
Oh, I won't be late
'Cause it's our first date,
And we have to take —— to the ball.
> (Use your baby's name.)

(Traditional, United States)

WATER PLAY

Washing Hands

Sit your baby on the kitchen counter so he can reach into the sink and start to wash his own hands. Talk to him about clean/dirty, before/after, all done/not all done, wet/dry, bubbles/no bubbles, soap, and SPLASH! Make sure he doesn't have a chance to turn on the hot water tap, but do let him splash away.

Tub Toys

Add an inflated ring tube or a ball to your baby's bath. Talk about what floats and what doesn't. Provide a small plastic strainer or sieve and a ladle for him to play with. Give him a set of plastic nesting measuring cups as well, so he can pick up and dump water.

Catch the Ducks

Show him how to catch and pick up his ducks, as they swim past. Continue to sing songs to his ducks.

Bathtub Rain

Punch holes in the bottom of a plastic container (yogurt, cottage cheese, or ice cream) and fill it with his bath water. Hold up for the container to make rain. If he enjoys it, let him be caught in a rain shower.

Ice

Have a plastic cup filled with ice cubes ready at bathtime. Drop the ice cubes into the tub and have baby catch them with his cup.

Wash Baby

Give baby a small rubber or plastic doll to bathe while you are washing him. He may squirm around just a little bit less if he is busy.

Wash the Tub

Show baby how to wipe the tub with his sponge. Show him how to go in circles, zig-zags, up and down, and back and forth.

Michaud

(This is a good drying-off or changing game.)

Michaud est monté dans un pommier.
> (Wipe baby upwards from toes to head.)

Michaud est monté dans un pommier.
> (Turn him over and wipe the other side.)

La branche a cassé (Snap).
> (Flick towel or clap hands—well away from your baby.)

Michaud est tombé. (BOOMP!)
> (Tap his bottom lightly.)

Où donc est Michaud?
> (Open hands and shrug shoulders.)

Michaud est su'l dos!
> (Rub his back.)

Ah, relève, relève, relève,
> (Wipe his back with the towel.)

Ah, relève, relève Michaud.

(Traditional, France, French Canada)

CHANGING GAMES

Does your baby dislike having his shirts pulled over his head? "Little Man in a Coal Pit" may help.

Little Man in a Coal Pit

Little man in a coal pit
> (Take baby's arms out of sleeves. Hold shirt up ready to pull.)

Goes knock, knock, knock;
> (Tap his head gently three times through shirt.)

Up he comes, up he comes,
> (Pull shirt off, saying, "There

Out at the top.
> you are!")

(Traditional, Great Britain)

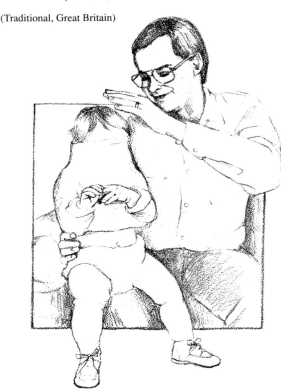

Head and Shoulders

(Tune: "London Bridge")

Head and shoulders, knees and toes,
> (Touch the body parts named.)

Knees and toes, knees and toes.
> (Show your baby where to touch.)

Head and shoulders, knees and toes,
Eyes, ears, mouth and nose.

(Traditional, Great Britain)

"Head and Shoulders" can also be sung to the tune of "There is a Tavern in the Town."

Head and shoulders knees and toes, knees and
toes
Head and shoulders knees and toes, knees and
toes.
Head and shoulders knees and toes,
Eyes and ears and mouth and nose, mouth and
nose.

(Traditional, United States)

MUSIC

Continue to bounce your baby to the rhythm of the music he hears. At this age he attempts to imitate the sounds he hears, and high and low pitches of music. Sing songs in which sounds, words, noises, and phrases recur.

Ham up your performance with as many hand gestures, facial and verbal expressions as you can conjure up. Quack and waddle around the room for a duck, bow-wow and wag your tail for a dog. Wave your trunk and trumpet for an elephant. (Why can't Farmer McDonald keep an elephant on the farm, or a dinosaur, for that matter?)

Reward your baby's responses to the song, with "What a great dog," or "What a good job!" It won't be long before the "E-I-E-I-O's" start.

Old McDonald Had a Farm

Old McDonald had a farm, E-I-E-I-O!
And on this farm he had a ———
> (The farmer can, of course, be "she".)

E-I-E-I-O!
With a ———, ——— here and
A ———, ——— there.
Here a ———, there a ———
Everywhere a ———, ———.
Old McDonald had a farm,
E-I-E-I-O!

Substitute crazy animals if you get bored with the usual ones. Some animal sounds you can use are: dog—*woof, woof,* cat—*meow, meow,* sheep—*baa, baa,* cow—*moo, moo,* horse—*neigh, neigh,* duck—*quack, quack,* donkey—*hee-haw, hee-haw,* kangaroo—*boing-boing,* lion—*roar, roarrrrr!*

(Traditional, Unknown)

Three Little Pigs

A jolly old sow once lived in a sty,
And three little piggies had she;
And she waddled about, saying: 'Umph! umph!
umph!'
While the little ones said: 'Wee! wee!'
'My dear little brothers,' said one of the brats,
'My dear little piggies,' said he;
'Let us all for the future say: "Umph! umph!
umph!"
'Tis so childish to say "Wee! wee!"'

Then these little pigs grew skinny and lean
And lean they might very well be;
For somehow they couldn't say: 'Umph! umph!
umph!'
And they wouldn't say: 'Wee! wee! wee!'

So after a time these little pigs died,
*They all died of felo-de-se; ***
From trying too hard to say: 'Umph! umph!
umph!'
When they only could say: 'Wee! wee!'

A moral there is to this little song,
A moral that's easy to see;
Don't try while yet young to say: 'Umph! umph!
    umph!'
For you only can say: 'Wee! wee!'
* Felo-de-se—self-destruction

(Alfred Scott-Gatty, 1870, United States)

Musical Instruments

H ave your child continue to play his musical
instruments. Make clear to him that music is
more than noise, chaos and banging. Add singing,
chanting, or marching to his drumming. Sit down
and play instruments with him. Let him have his
bursts of energetic participation, but do provide direction. His instruments should be treated as instruments, not as toys. Music is more than
cacophony, it has structure and purpose which
satisfies the soul.

This Is the Way We Play Our Drums

(Tune: "Here we go 'Round the Mulberry Bush.")
(Tap drums in time to the music.)

This is the way we play our drums
Play our drums, play our drums
This is the way we play our drums
Let's play our drums together.

(Traditional, England, adapted)

Also play "This Is the Way We Shake Our
Shakers," "This Is the Way We Ring Our Bells,"
and "This Is the Way We Tap Our Sticks."

Jingle Bells

(Ring bells in time to the music.)

Jingle bells, jingle bells,
Jingle all the way.
Oh what fun it is to ride
In a one-horse open sleigh.
(Repeat)

(Traditional, unknown)

Twinkle, Twinkle Little Star

(Ring bells in time to music.)

Twinkle, twinkle, little star
How I wonder what you are!
Up above the world so high,
Like a diamond in the sky.
Twinkle, twinkle, little star
How I wonder what you are!

(Jane Taylor, England 1806)

ART

Making His Marks   (Scribbling)

N ow is the time for your child to start to scribble. When he is seated comfortably, give him
some paper and a big, fat crayon. Use pieces of
masking tape so his paper won't scrunch up. Show
him how to make his first tentative marks on the
paper. Then watch him go!

Make a Blackboard

H ang a blackboard in your kitchen within your
child's reach. Let him sit and scribble with
pretty, colored chalk or wipe-off water pastels.
Paint a low wall with blackboard paint. It's cheap
and can be painted over when your child is older,
or used as a family information center for years to
come.

Save Baby's Art

S ave some pieces of your child's artwork.
Label them on the back with his name and
age. Some of his work may be worth framing
when you use good materials. Don't forget to hang
some of his pieces on the refrigerator. By displaying his work, you show him that you value what
he does.

Baby's Art Book

Put some plain white paper in a three-ring binder to make a portfolio for your baby's scribbling. You can take the binder in the car, or on public transit. It will prevent the paper from being crumpled and it will provide you with a permanent record of your baby's artistic ability. Tie a couple of non-toxic felt pens to the rings so his art book is ready for immediate use. Keep a small packet of crayons in your pocket or diaper bag.

Jello Painting

Make two or three separate bowls of jello in different colors. Place pieces of paper in front of your baby and put globs of jello on each sheet. Encourage him to spread and swirl his finger paint. Use different textures of paper if you like, such as butcher's paper or waxed paper. Of course, no harm is done if he eats his finger paint!

WORD PLAY

Your baby's interest in and understanding of words is growing quickly. He can understand and follow simple directions. He will answer to his name. He will look at people who call his name, play "Pat-a-Cake," wave, say "bye-bye." and throw a kiss when asked to. Continue to recite nonsense verse and complex rhymes so he hears the richness of his language.

Repeat After Me

This game helps to increase your baby's spoken vocabulary. You say a word, such as "water" and your baby repeats the word, which may sound like "Wawa." You say, "Great!" and hug your baby, then say "water," properly. He'll say "Wawa" for some time yet, but eventually he will say "water" properly. Easy words for your baby to repeat are baby, daddy, mommy, lamb, man, apple, puppy, diaper, cow, cat, moo, and bye-bye.

Impressing Grandparents

When you know that grandparents are coming to visit, you can prime your child to be a star for them. Train him to say a special word for Grandpa (perhaps "bumpa") and Grandma (perhaps "nana"). Rehearse the words by playing "Repeat After Me" a week before the grandparents' visit. Coaching will give the desired results and your mother-in-law will think your baby in a genius and you are a marvel. Success with this game can begin any time between eight and 18 months. As you play the game, enjoy the blossoming of a wonderful skill—your child's ability to speak our language.

Tongue Twisters

Let the words roll off your tongue as you say some tongue twisters so your baby hears some complex language patterns.

Moses Supposes

(Touch baby's toes.)

Moses supposes his toeses are roses,
But Moses supposes erroneously;
For nobody's toeses are posies of roses
As Moses supposes his toeses to be.

(Traditional, England)

Peter Piper Picked a Peck of Pickled Peppers

Peter Piper picked a peck of pickled peppers;
A peck of pickled peppers Peter Piper picked.
If Peter Piper picked a peck of pickled peppers,
Where's the peck of pickled peppers Peter Piper
*   picked?*

(Traditional, England)

KITCHEN PLAY

The kitchen is a fascinating place for your baby. One of his favorite toys is probably a cupboard door that he can swing back and forth.

Kitchen Blocks

Give your baby empty food containers to use as building blocks. Cardboard boxes, plastic tubs, egg cartons, paper towel rolls, and cans all make entertaining blocks to build with, sort out, and knock over. Putting things away in his cupboard is half the fun.

Coffee Can/Oatmeal Box

Give your child a cylindrical oatmeal box or a coffee can with a lid and some old-fashioned clothes pegs (the kind without the spring) to put into his special container. These materials can show him the concepts of "in" and "out." He can drop his pegs into the container, and then with the lid on, shake them like a rattle.

Dinnertime Rhymes

Continue to say occasional nursery rhymes at dinnertime, especially when the rhymes relate to the food being eaten.

The Muffin Man

Oh, have you seen the Muffin Man,
The Muffin Man, the Muffin Man:
Oh, have you seen the Muffin Man
That lives in Drury Lane?

Oh, yes I've seen the Muffin Man,
The Muffin Man, the Muffin Man:
Oh yes I've seen the Muffin Man
That lives in Drury Lane.

(Traditional, England)

Jack Sprat

Jack Sprat could eat no fat,
His wife could eat no lean,
And so between them both, you see,
They licked the platter clean.

(Traditional, England)

Charley Barley

Charley Barley, butter and eggs,
Sold his wife for three duck eggs.
When the ducks began to lay,
Charley Barley flew away.

(Traditional, England)

Little Tommy Tucker

Little Tommy Tucker
Sings for his supper:
What shall we give him?
White bread and butter.
How shall he cut it
Without e'er a knife?
How will he be married
Without e'er a wife?

(Traditional, England)

INDOOR GAMES

As your baby's manipulative skills grow, give him opportunities to find out what his hands can do. Get an assortment of small plastic toys for him to play with and investigate.

Big Box

One of your baby's favorite toys will be a big box (such as a diaper box) that he can hide toys in. Cut a hole in the side of the box and use a short piece of rope, knotted at both ends, so he can pull the box after him as he crawls around.

Hide the Toy

Continue to hide a small toy in one of your hands and have baby "guess" where the toy is. You might want to introduce the concept of one hand being "right" and the other being "left." Which hand has the toy should be obvious.

Handy, Dandy, Prickly, Prandy

Handy, dandy, prickly, prandy,
Which hand will you have?

(Great Britain, 1598)

Feeling Textures

As your baby's hands become more flexible, discuss the textures and the qualities of the objects he touches. Talk about all kinds of differ-ences. Say, "This is a smooth red ball," "This is a soft, fuzzy bear," "This is a hard, wooden block." Let him hear descriptions of his world.

Cardboard Trumpet

Hum, talk, or sing into an empty paper towel or toilet paper tube. Then give your baby the tube so he can try to make the noises, too.

Simple Commands

Use simple commands as a way of having fun with your baby. Say, "Show me your toes," "Where is your belly button?" "Throw Daddy a kiss," "Play Pat-a-Cake with Mommy"....

Newspaper Crumble

Rub your baby's hand across an old newspaper and say, "Smooth." Rip the paper, saying, "Listen." Crumble the paper and again say, "Listen." Give the paper to your baby, saying, "Rough." Tear pieces of the paper into shreds and bits. Give another piece of paper to your baby and say, "Now you do it."

Stop-and-Start Dancing

As you dance with your baby, have someone else stop and start the music and dance together accordingly. This is a wonderful way to develop your baby's sense of anticipation.

Animal Sounds

Now is the time to introduce your baby to all kinds of animals. Make a trip to a zoo or farm, if possible. Introduce songs such as "Old McDonald Had a Farm" (p. 49) (your baby may pipe in on the "E-I-E-I-Os"), "Three Little Pigs" (p. 49), and "I Had a Rooster" (p. 79).

Your baby probably has a collection of stuffed animals. Sit beside all of them on the floor with your baby. Talk about each animal. "This is an orangutan. He doesn't have a tail and he eats fruit, just like you." "This is a gorilla. He is the largest primate" (beat your chest and make King Kong noises). "This is a lion. He goes Roarrrrrr!" "This is a lamb. His wool is cut off to make your coat and he goes baa...."

Have the animals "talk" to your baby. Have the elephant trumpet at him. Tell him the animals' names and the noises they make. Say, "I'm a tiger [roar] and I'm going to EAT you!" Be silly and make chomping noises. Nuzzle your baby, give him a few tickles and hugs, and give a BIG burp. Say, "Oh, that tasted good!" Then say, "I'm a bumblebee. If you're not careful, I'm going to STING you!" Buzzzz-zz-zz-z! Use your finger like a divebombing bee.

The toys you use don't have to be expensive plush ones; plastic is fine. You can also make animals out of shoe boxes, corn cobs, sticks, paper, hamburger containers, and anything else you have around the house.

Cut out bright pictures of animals to make your baby's own animal book. Make animal noises with him every time you play with his animals. Say lots of rhymes about animals, including their noises.

The Cock's on the Wood Pile

The cock's on the wood pile
Blowing his horn,
    (Crow "Cock-a-doodle-doo!")
The bull's in the barn
    (Snort and paw the ground.)
A-threshing the corn.
The maids in the meadow
Are making the hay
The ducks in the river
Are swimming away.
    (Quack and make swimming movements.)

(Traditional, England)

The Little Black Dog Ran Round the House

The little black dog ran round the house
    (Bark, "Arf, arf, arf!")
And set the bull a-roaring,
    (Roar like a bull.)
And drove the monkey in the boat,
    (Jump up and down, scratching.)
Who set the oars a-rowing,
    (Row an imaginary boat.)
And scared the cock upon the rock,
Who cracked his throat with crowing.
    (Crow like a rooster.)

(Traditional, England)

QUIET TIMES

Read stories and nursery rhymes as part of your baby's bedtime routine. Reading together gives him security, comfort, companionship, pleasure, entertainment, pretty pictures, and your undivided attention. Show your baby how pages turn, how words are read from left to right, how stories begin at the front and go to the back, and how lines of print are read from top to bottom.

Jemima

There was a little girl, who had a little curl
Right in the middle of her forehead,
And when she was good she was very, very
    good,
But when she was bad she was horrid.

She stood on her head, on her little truckle-bed,
With nobody by for to hinder;
She screamed and she squalled, she yelled and she
    bawled,
And drummed her little heels against the winder.

Her mother heard the noise, and thought it was
    the boys
Playing in the empty attic,
She rushed upstairs, and caught her unawares,
And spanked her, most emphatic.

(Attributed to H. W. Longfellow, United States)

Arthour Knycht

Arthour knycht he raid on nycht,
Vith gyltin spur and candil lycht.

(The Complaynt of Scotlande, 1549)

Six Little Mice

Six little mice sat down to spin.
Pussy passed by and she peeped in.
What are you doing, my little men?
Weaving coats for gentlemen.

Shall I come in, to cut off your threads?
No, no Mistress Pussy, you'd bite off our heads.
Oh, no, I'll not; I'll help you spin.
That may be so, but you can't come in.

(Traditional, England)

Snail, Snail

(Make a fist, thumb tucked inside. Lift little finger
and index finger to make horns.)

Snail, snail, put out your horns
And I'll give you bread and barley corns.

(Traditional, England)

A Wise Old Owl

A wise old owl sat in an oak,
The more he heard the less he spoke.
The less he spoke the more he heard.
Why aren't we all like that wise old bird?

(Traditional, United States)

My Mother Said

My mother said that I never should
Play with gypsies in the wood,
If I did she would say,
Naughty girl to disobey.

Your hair shan't curl, your shoes shan't shine,
You naughty girl, you shan't be mine.
My father said that if I did,
He'd bang my head with a teapot lid.

The wood was dark, the grass was green,
Up comes Sally with a tambourine;
Alpaca frock, new scarf-shawl,
White straw bonnet, and a pink parasol.

I went to the river—no ship to get across,
I paid ten shillings, for an old blind horse;
I up on his back, and off in a crack,
Sally tell my mother, I shall never come back.

(Traditional, Great Britain, North America)

OUTDOORS

Your baby's movements become more directed as his coordination improves. When you are outside, play lots of action games. Don't forget to play ball with him frequently.

Tug of War

"Tug of War" is fun anytime, especially in the snow. Use a scarf or a piece of cloth. You hold one end and have your baby hold the other. Pull the scarf gently and wait for him to pull you back. Tumble over when he gives you a good tug. You can play this game as soon as your baby can sit up by himself.

Handwalk

When your baby is crawling securely, play "Handwalk" (wheelbarrow) outside on the lawn. Pick up his legs, a few inches from the ground, and encourage him to walk on his hands. Try to flip him over gently after he has grown used to this game.

Roughhouse

Crawl around together in the grass, snow, or leaves. Add some bouncing, lifting, jostling, light pushing, and tickles. Be gentle as you roll and tumble with your baby. Let him climb on you.

Gotcha!

Walk up behind your baby in an exaggerated way and say "Gotcha!" Don't completely startle him, and don't play this game if he is "off" in any way. Say in a big, deep voice, "I'm a big giant and I'm going to eat you ALL up... Gotcha!... Yum, yum!" Then give him some hugs and tickles and giggles. Sometime after imaginative play begins to develop, your baby will start to get YOU, and you'll be amazed at how startled you are.

Ways to Get Around

Talk to your child about all the ways of getting around in the world. He can walk, run, glide on his bicycle seat with Mom or Dad, ride in his car seat, go up in elevators and escalators, and take a subway, streetcar, bus, train, or boat. He can fly in an airplane, or ride in a wagon. Later, he will have his own tricycle and pedal toys. Let your baby experience all the forms of transportation that are easily available to you.

Ball Rolling

As soon as your baby can sit up comfortably, sit with him facing you, in a straddle position. Chant "Roll the Ball to Me" to teach him to listen and release the ball at the right moment. Start with a beach ball, and as his expertise grows, switch to smaller balls. When he rolls the ball to you, hug him and say, "What a clever baby! What a good job! Let's do it again!" The game might develop into a rolling "catch." You can grow into bounce the ball and throw the ball. To create fun and confusion once the game is well established, have two or three balls of different sizes roll around at once.

Roll the Ball to Me

(Chant. Gesture baby to roll the ball towards you.)

Roll the ball,
Roll the ball,
ROLL the ball to me.
Roll the ball,
Roll the ball,
ROLL the ball to me.

(Traditional, North America)

Retriever

Once your baby can understand simple instructions and can crawl well, have him retrieve balls bounced off a wall. This is a good way to tire him out, and get lots of fresh air, just before a nap.

Feeding the Birds (Squirrels, Raccoons, and Other Small Animals)

Your baby will love to feed his leftovers to birds and squirrels, in his backyard. When he is about a year old, he can gather his bread crumbs, crackers, cookie bits, and teething biscuits in a cottage cheese container. Place his container in the refrigerator, and when you have cooking fats from meat, pour them over the breadcrumb mixture. Add some birdseed, if you wish. When you have a full, solid container, turn the contents onto your birdfeeder. You can cut surplus fats off your meat before cooking it, and put them outside for the birds as well.

When your child is about 18 months old, he will be delighted to spread pine cones with peanut butter to hang out for the birds. He can also roll the peanut-butter-covered surface in birdseed.

Get the best bird book you can afford to identify the various birds that come to your feeder. Show your baby a picture of the bird at his feeder, tell him the name of the bird, and add to his appreciation of the vast array of wildlife all around us. Take your bird book along on trips to the country, picnics, and vacations.

Birds and squirrels can also be fed at the park. Your toddler will delight in tossing bits of stale bread to all the birds he sees.

HINT: It is not fair to attract birds with food if you or your neighbors have a hunter-type cat roaming about.

Don't forget to recite rhymes about the birds your baby sees.

Robin the Bobbin*

Robin the Bobbin, the big-bellied Ben,
He ate more meat than fourscore men;
He ate a cow, he ate a calf,
He ate a butcher and a half,
He ate a church, he ate a steeple,
He ate the priest and all the people!
A cow and a calf,
An ox and a half,
A church and a steeple,
And all the good people,
And yet he complained that his stomach wasn't
    full.

*Supposed to refer to Henry VIII of England.

(Traditional, England)

Two Little Blackbirds

Two little blackbirds
            (Index fingers up in air.)
Sitting on a hill
One named Jack
            (Put one hand forward
And one named Jill
            and the other forward.)
Fly away Jack
            (Fly fingers of one hand behind back,
Fly away Jill
            and the other hand.)
Come back Jack
            (Bring one hand forward
Come back Jill.
            and the other hand.)

(Traditional, England)

CHAPTER FIVE

Wibble Wobble, Wibble Wobble, To and Fro

Twelve to Fifteen Months

Your baby is developing a sense of humor. She adores having an audience and performs for the sake of applause, not for the performance itself. Give her lots of applause. She knows and expresses her likes and dislikes. She understands when you scold her. She may scream when she is frustrated, which is usually when you are doing something for her that she wants to do herself, such as holding her cup or spoon.

She imitates everything; it's how she learns. She loves to follow you around as you work, so give her a small version of your "tools": a brush and dustpan, a plastic hammer, a cloth so she can wipe, too. She also imitates others socially and is establishing her own ways of relating to people. She tries to signal her wishes to you without crying, by bringing you her sweater when she wants to go out, or a toy that she wants for her play.

Your baby likes to somersault and roll around so show her how. She is learning to stoop down to pick up toys. She stands, sits, and climbs up and down by herself. She loves to bounce around to rhymes and music and she loves to listen to rhymes. She also loves to color spontaneously.

It is impossible to keep her neat and tidy so don't bother to try. "Messy" is important to her, so just give her a bath at the end of the day.

She loves to chatter away to herself and to listen to words, so keep talking to her about EVERYTHING. She now knows the names of her family members, her special friends, and her special toys.

MOVEMENT

Your baby is now creeping, crawling, sitting, pivoting, cruising, standing, and probably walking. She also loves to climb. She can stack two or more blocks, and can judge distance when reaching for a toy she wants. Play lots and lots of bouncing games with her.

Row, Row, Row Your Boat

(Sit on floor, legs apart in a straddle position. With baby facing you, hold hands. Rock back and forth to music. Repeat song quickly, then slowly.)

Row, row, row your boat
Gently down the stream,
Merrily, merrily, merrily, merrily,
Life is but a dream.

(Traditional, Great Britain, North America)

I Know a Little Pony

I know a little pony
            (Knee ride with baby facing forward.)
Her name is Dapple Grey
She lives down in a meadow
Not very far away
She goes nimble, nimble, nimble...and
            (Quick bounce.)
Trot, trot, trot...and
            (Jostling bounce from side to side.)
Then she stops and waits a bit...
            (No movement.)
Gallop, gallop, gallop, HEY!!
            (Quick gallop, swing her up on HEY.)

(Traditional, England)

Baby a Go Go

(Start with your baby on your lap, turn knees from side to side while bouncing baby. Lift her up on Hey ah!)

Baby a go go hey ah!
Baby a go go hey ah!
Baby a go-o-o
Baby a go, go, go.

(Traditional, United States)

Trot, Trot, Trot

Trot, trot, trot to London,
> (Bounce your baby on your knees, facing you.)

Trot, trot, trot to Dover.
Look out, ———
> (Use your baby's name.)

Or you might fall O-VER!
> (Tip her to one side.)

Trot, trot, trot to Boston,
> (Knee-bounce baby again.)

Trot, trot, trot to Lynn.
> (Support her waist and neck firmly with your hands.)

Look out, ———
Or you might fall IN!
> (Open your knees and let her "fall" backwards until her head is by your ankles on "in!."
> As she gets used to the game
> and gets older hold her hands, instead
> of supporting her body.)

(Traditional, England)

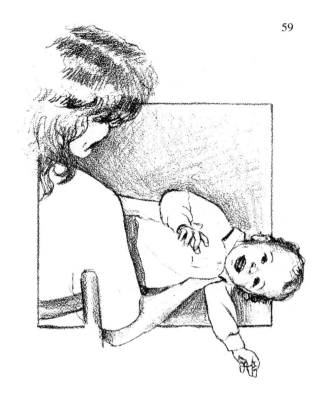

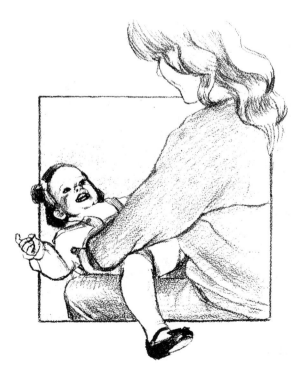

Obstacle Course

Set up an obstacle course where your baby can climb, crawl, and cruise. Get down on the floor and show her the route. After a few trial runs, have a race, which she, of course, wins.

Toe Touches

Stand straight, lift your arms over your head, then, keeping them stretched out, lower them slowly. Bend your body from the waist and touch your hands to your toes (if they reach). Encourage your baby to do the same. After a few toe touches, raise your arms and touch your head, shoulders, chest, waist, and hips slowly. Then bend over to touch thighs, knees, ankles, and toes. Name each part of the body as you and she bend and touch. You can sing "Head and Shoulders, Knees and Toes" as you play this game (see page 49).

WATER PLAY

Continue to play bath games. You may want to establish some basic tub rules, such as: "Don't touch the HOT tap"; "Don't stand up in the tub;" "Don't throw water on the floor." Because your baby gets so messy as she plays, you may have her splash around in the kitchen sink or in an outdoor wading pool through the day. Provide some unbreakable water toys to use in places other than the tub—a plastic container punched with holes, measuring cups and spoons, a strainer, a plastic eyedropper, flexible plastic tubing, straws, and funnels.

Blow Some Bubbles

Blow bubbles with your baby and ask her to show you the big ones and the small ones. Talk about the iridescent colors and the shapes of the bubbles (spheres, globes, circles). She'll be excited to see big bubbles and surprised when she touches one. Ooops!

Let Her Wash Herself

Let your baby wash herself. Say, "wash your toes now; wash your hands; wash your tummy; wash your elbows." This is a good way for her to learn all the parts of her body as well as get clean. Give her a small sponge or facecloth and let her scrub away.

Wrap Her Toys

Wrap up small toys in your baby's washcloth and then let her unwrap her "gifts." Soon she'll be wrapping up "presents" for you!

Mother, May I Go Out to Swim?

Mother, may I go out to swim?
Yes, my darling daughter.
Hang your clothes on a hickory limb
But don't go near the water.

(Traditional, United States)

Straws

Show her how to make bubbles by blowing through a straw when she has her juice or milk. By now she may be ready to drink from a straw, as well as blow.

CHANGING GAMES

Baby Dressing Baby

Your baby may now be quite wiggly when she is being changed. Give her a doll to play with while you are changing her. If her hands are busy, her bottom half will be less active.

Dressing Routine

Talk about the clothes you are putting on her. Say "Diaper on bottom," "tights over diaper," "pants over tights," "undershirt over top of body," "shirt over undershirt," "snowsuit to keep you warm and dry," "hat on head," "scarf keeps neck warm," "mitts keep your hands warm," "boots keep feet dry," "zipper keeps snowsuit zipped," and so on. Make it clear why you are putting her clothes on, and what they do.

Let's Get Dressed

(Tune: "Here We Go 'Round the Mulberry Bush")

Let's put on your special pants,
Your special pants, your special pants.
Let's put on your special pants,
Let's put the pants on you.
(...your special shirt, socks, shoes, boots, coat, hat, mitts, scarf...)

(Traditional, adapted)

Here Sits the Lord Mayor

Here sits the Lord Mayor
                    (Touch her forehead
Here sits his men
                    and her eyes.)
Here sits the cockadoodle
                    (Right cheek.)
Here sits the hen
                    (Left cheek.)
Here sit the little chickens
                    (Tap teeth.)
Here they run in
                    (Mouth.)
Chin chopper, chin chopper
Chin chopper chin.
                    (Tickle under her chin.)

(Traditional, England)

Tommy Thumbs

Tommy Thumbs up and
                    (Thumbs up sign, both hands
Tommy Thumbs down
                    thumbs down.)
Tommy Thumbs dancing
                    (Thumbs up and bounce them from right to
All around the town.
                    left in front of you.)
Dance 'em on your shoulders
                    (Bounce them on shoulders
Dance 'em on your head
                    and on head
Dance 'em on your knees and
                    and on knees.)
Tuck them into bed.
                    (Fold arms, hiding hands.)
...Peter Pointer Up and Peter Pointer Down
                    (Repeat using index fingers.)
...Finger family up and finger family down....
                    (Use all fingers.)

(For older children, Toby Tall for middle finger, Ring Man for ring finger, and Baby Fingers for little finger.)

(Traditional, England)

MUSIC

Alouette!

Alouette, gentille Alouette,
Alouette, je t'y plu-me-rai.
Je t'y plu-me-rai la tête,
       Je t'y plu-me-rai la tête, (echo)
Et la tête.
       Et la tête. (echo)
Alouette.
       Alouette. (echo)
OH...

(In each stanza after the first, the words of the preceding verses are repeated in reverse order. The final verse would be:)

Et la queue
       et la queue
Et le dos
       et le dos
Et le cou
       et le cou
Et les yeux
       et les yeux
Et le nez
       et le nez
Et le bec
       et le bec
Et la tête
       et la tête
Alouette
       Alouette
Oh...
Alouette, gentille Alouette,
Alouette, je t'y plu-me-rai.

(Traditional, French Canada)

Instruments

I Can Play My Drum

I can play my drum very softly,
    (Play drum lightly.)
But I can play my drum very loudly.
    (Loudly.)
I can play my drum very softly,
    (Lightly.)
But I can play my drum very loudly.
    (Very loudly.)

(Katharine Smithrim)

Loudly/Softly/Slowly/Quickly

(Do each action in the song.)

Loudly, loudly, play our drums,
Softly, softly, play our drums.
Slowly, slowly, play our drums,
Quickly, quickly, play our drums.

(Katharine Smithrim)

High/Low

(Using a shaker, do each action in the song.)

Shake it, shake it, shake it high,
Shake it, shake it, shake it low,
Shake it, shake it on your tum,
Shake it, shake it on your toe.

(Katharine Smithrim)

Jack Be Nimble

Jack be nimble,
    (Tap sicks to beat.)
Jack be quick,
Jack jumped over the candlestick.
Jack jumped up high,
    (Tap sticks up over head.)
Jack jumped down low,
    (Tap sticks on floor.)
Jack jumped over and burnt his toe.
    (Tap sticks on baby's toe.)
Oo-oo-ow!

(Traditional, England)

Hickory, Dickory, Dock

Hickory, dickory, dock
    (Tap sticks to the beat.)
The mouse ran up the clock
    (Double time running up clock.)
The clock struck one
    (Back to regular beat.)
The mouse ran down
Hickory, dickory, dock.

(Traditional, England)

Mary, Mary, Quite Contrary

(Ring bells on the beat.)

Mary, Mary, quite contrary,
How does your garden grow?
With silver bells and cockle shells,
And pretty maids all in a row.

(Traditional, England)

Frère Jacques/Are You Sleeping?

(Tap bells on hand.)

Frère Jacques, Frère Jacques
Dormez-vous? Dormez-vous?
Sonnez les matines, sonnez les matines,
Din, din, don!
Din, din, don!

(Traditional, France)

Are you sleeping? Are you sleeping?
Brother John, Brother John
Morning bells are ringing,
    (Shake bells vigorously.)
Morning bells are ringing,
Ding, ding, dong!
Ding, ding, dong!

(Traditional, England)

Mary Had a Little Lamb

(Tap sticks to the beat)

Mary had a little lamb, little lamb, little
 lamb
Mary had a little lamb, it's fleece was white as
 snow.
Everywhere that Mary went, Mary went, Mary
 went
Everywhere that Mary went the lamb was sure to
 go.

(Sarah Josepha Hale, United States, 1830)

ART

Don't try to draw your reality into your child's artwork. The concept of "what it is" is inconceivable to her—she is doing a process. Let her learn, grow, and develop with her materials at her own pace. Don't interrupt her scribblings and drawings. Instead, let her discover her own abilities.

Crayons

Crayons are an ideal medium for children because they are immediate. They provide your budding Picasso, who wants to make her mark quickly, with a medium that promotes energy and enthusiasm. They do not require water, and no final stage is required, like waiting to dry. Crayons are not messy and can be used on a wide variety of papers. They are easy to carry, care for, and store. They can be pointed to produce a fine line or used sideways to color large areas. Colors can be easily blended, and added over each other. Crayon pictures can be rubbed with a soft cloth to enhance the colors. Give her a BIG box of crayons—and use them, with lots of plain paper.

Scribbling

Why give your baby pencils, chalk, crayons, paint, or markers when she only scribbles, jabs, and pokes at the paper? Because scribbling helps develop the hand-eye coordination needed later for her drawing, painting, and printing letters. Her first marks are made by swinging her arms back and forth, up and down, and by jabs and pokes at the paper. These random jottings will eventually evolve into more controlled arcs in one direction, and then into straight lines, circles, triangles, and, soon, whatever she wants to record on paper.

Provide plenty of paper at this stage and get to know your local art supply store. Your child will enjoy scribbling until the age of four, so buy lots of crayons, paints, brushes, markers by the dozens and various types of paper. Establish an art drawer or shelf in your baby's room, and fill it with art goodies, magazine cut-outs, scraps of papers, and other materials that will come in handy later. Organize a suitable table or desk and chair for your child to use for her workspace.

Early Scribbling

Let your baby use one material at a time: a felt pen, a pencil, a water crayon, a crayon, or a piece of chalk. Always use non-toxic materials. Let her experience contrasts in paper surfaces and use a chalkboard if you have one. By the time she is three, your child may spend 20 or 30 minutes (or longer) per activity, when a new or exciting material is being used.

Use contrasting materials. Try black crayon on white paper, red felt marker on white paper, or black felt pen on yellow paper, white chalk or bright water crayons on a chalkboard.

Don't introduce paints for a few months yet, because they flow so easily.

HINT: Does a school near you offer art classes? Find out where the students buy their materials; they usually know where to find the best at the most reasonable prices.

WORD PLAY

Your baby learns to communicate through language sounds before she learns to talk. Respond constantly to her sounds, but never use baby talk with her. Discuss things non-stop: about the world, about what she's doing, your daily routines, where you are going. Expose her to other languages, and tell her other people speak different languages. Say a variety of morning greetings: "Hi, bonjour, good morning, ciao, hello, buenos dias." Recite complicated poems and rhymes to her so she hears the magic of her language. If her attention span permits, recite longer nursery rhymes. Use her toys to dramatize the longer rhymes.

Little Bo-Peep

Little Bo-Peep has lost her sheep,
And doesn't know where to find them;
Leave them alone, and they'll come home,
Wagging their tails behind them.

Little Bo-Peep fell fast asleep,
And dreamt she heard them bleating;
But when she awoke, she found it a joke,
For they were still a-fleeting.

Then up she took her little crook,
Determined for to find them;
She'd found them indeed, but it made her heart bleed,
For they'd left their tails behind them.

It happened one day, as Bo-Peep did stray
Into a meadow close by,
There she espied their tails side by side,
All hung on a tree to dry.

She heaved a sigh, and wiped her eye,
And over the hillocks went rambling,
And tried what she could, as a shepherdess should,
To tack again each to its lambkin.

(Traditional, England)

O Dear What Can the Matter Be?

Oh dear, what can the matter be
Dear, dear, what can the matter be?
Oh dear, what can the matter be?
————'s so long at the fair.

(Use your child's name.)

He promised he'd buy me a fairing should please
*   me,*
And then for a kiss, oh! he vowed he would tease
*   me,*
He promised he'd bring me a bunch of blue
*   ribbons*
To tie up my bonny brown hair.

(Traditional, Great Britain, North America)

Swan Swam Over the Sea

Swan swam over the sea,
Swim, swan, swim!
Swan swam back again,
Well swum swan!

(Traditional, England, United States)

Theophilus Thistle

Theophilus Thistle, the successful thistle sifter,
In sifting a sieve full of unsifted thistles,
Thrust three thousand thistles through the thick of
*   his thumb.*
If Theophilus Thistle, the successful thistle sifter,
Can thrust three thousand thistles through the
*   thick of his thumb,*
See thou, in sifting a sieve full of unsifted thistles,
Thrust not three thousand thistles through the
*   thick of your thumb.*

(Traditional, England, United States)

Upon Paul's Steeple* Stands a Tree

Upon Paul's steeple stands a tree,
As full of apples as may be;
The little boys of London town
They run with hooks to pull them down;
And then they run from hedge to hedge,
Until they come to London Bridge.

*The steeple on St. Paul's Cathedral was
destroyed June 4, 1561 by lightning.

(Traditional, England)

Magnetic Letters

Start accumulating magnetic letters to be used for several years to come. Buy both upper-case and lower-case letters, if possible in different type styles. Stick them on any metal surfaces in your house. Spell "hot" on the stove and "cold" on the refrigerator. Display your baby's name in all the places you can. Spell other words in her world—"DOG," "CAT," "MOMMY," "DADDY," "BABY." You are showing your baby that our language is coded and that the code is understandable. She may learn her letters earlier than you EVER thought possible, through simple exposure to how our language works. If her letters come with a plastic holder, they are a good puzzle. The letters are perfect for hanging artwork on the refrigerator.

Books, Books, Books, Books

Make your own personal books using magazines, photos, and odds and ends. Other useful materials are construction paper, decorative wallpaper, glue or glue sticks, scissors, pencils, crayons, magic tape, and felt markers. Buy a blank book, or lace together pieces of cardboard (shirt cards from the laundry are perfect), or use notebooks or photo albums to assemble your story. There is nothing more special for your baby than a story in which she is the central character.

HINT: Photo albums can be bought cheaply right after Christmas at most discount stores.

Stock up every year, both for your photos and to make special storybooks.

Picture Books

Picture books with large bright personal pictures are wonderful and will enthrall your baby. Pictures can be cut out of magazines and cut out from some of your not quite reasonable photos.

One of the loveliest books I've seen was made by baby Sarah's mommy that combined the alphabet with bits of pictures of Sarah's life, pictures from magazines, and letters cut from a newspaper. The "G" page had a girl, a picture of Grandma, her other grampa, a giggling person, a giraffe, and a picture of friend Gillian.

Touch and Feel Books

Make your own touch and feel books from scraps you have around the house. Plastic bubble packaging, corrugated cardboard, aluminum foil, tissue paper, terry towelling, and all sorts of fabrics, suede, fur, and leather can provide a variety of textures and contrasts. Use a glue stick or white glue to adhere your material to the cardboard.

KITCHEN PLAY

Mealtime Sounds of Food

Listen to and talk about the various sounds that foods can make. The crunch of a cracker, the sizzle of broiling meat, the whistle of the tea kettle, the popping of the toaster, squeaky cheese like mozzarella, the slurp of soup and the fizz of soft drinks will all entrance your baby.

Baby Chef

Let your baby help make her own sandwich. Spread a slice of bread with cheese spread or cream cheese. Give the bread to your baby and let her poke in some raisins, dry cereal, bits of soft fruit, or any of her favorite foods.

Dough Words

When you bake with a heavy type of dough (for bread, biscuits, or dinner rolls) make your baby some special "word loaves" of her own. Shape the letters of your baby's name and bake them into her bread. Then add other words she knows or learns as time goes by.

Peel the Label

While you are preparing dinner with your baby, have her try to peel the labels off any tins or packages you plan to use. But don't give her general access to your tinned goods, or you won't have any idea what's in them! She loves removing labels!

Your Child's Drawer or Cupboard

Your child should have her exclusive drawer or cupboard in the kitchen filled with plastic containers, empty boxes, toys, junk mail, safe kitchen utensils, a child-sized rolling pin, and cookie cutters. She will soon use many of these items in her cooking and art activities.

Eating Rhymes

Continue to include references to food in nursery rhymes. The more your baby hears about new foods, the more willing she may be to try them.

Simple Simon

*Simple Simon met a pieman
Going to the fair;
Said Simple Simon to the pieman,
"Let me taste your ware."*

*Says the pieman to Simple Simon,
"Show me first your penny."
Says Simple Simon to the pieman
"Indeed I have not any."*

*Simple Simon went a-fishing,
For to catch a whale;
All the water he had got
Was in his mother's pail.*

*Simple Simon went to look
If plums grew on a thistle;
He pricked his fingers very much,
Which made poor Simon whistle.*

*He went for water in a sieve
But soon it all fell through;
And now poor Simple Simon
Bids you all adieu.*

(Traditional, England)

Old Mother Hubbard

*Old Mother Hubbard
Went to the cupboard
To fetch her poor dog a bone;
But when she got there
The cupboard was bare
And so the poor dog had none.*

*She went to the baker's
To buy him some bread;
But when she came back
The poor dog was dead.*

*She went to the undertaker's
To buy him a coffin;
But when she came back
The poor dog was laughing.*

*She took a clean dish
To get him some tripe;
But when she came back
He was smoking a pipe.*

*She went to the fishmonger's
To buy him some fish;
But when she came back
He was licking a dish.*

*She went to the alehouse
To get him some beer;
But when she came back
The dog sat in a chair.*

*She went to the tavern
For white wine and red;
But when she came back
The dog stood on his head.*

*She went to the fruiterer's
To buy him some fruit;
But when she came back
He was playing the flute.*

*She went to the tailor's
To buy him a coat;
But when she came back
He was riding a goat.*

*She went to the hatter's
To buy him a hat;
But when she came back
He was feeding the cat.*

*She went to the barber's
To buy him a wig;
But when she came back
He was dancing a jig.*

*She went to the cobbler's
To buy him some shoes;
But when she came back
He was reading the news.*

*She went to the seamstress
To buy him some linen;
But when she came back
The dog was a-spinning.*

She went to the hosier's
To buy him some hose;
But when she came back
He was dressed in his clothes.

The dame made a curtsey,
The dog made a bow;
The dame said, "Your servant,"
The dog said, "Bow-wow."

(Sarah Catherine Martin, England 1805)

INDOOR GAMES

Let Your Baby Help

Your baby learns through imitation and she wants to do what you are doing. Let her assist you when it is safe. Sort the laundry with her help. Ask her to bring you the red sock. Talk about how and why you are separating the clothes. Sorting is a skill she can learn now. She can also help you in the kitchen, by stirring, or wiping up crumbs and spills, helping at the sink, sweeping. Give her a plastic hammer and screwdriver when you do home repairs.

Sing and Dance

Let loose when you sing and dance with your baby—it's so much fun! Have her stand up, hold hands, and sway back and forth to your favorite records. Sing all her favorite songs and dance or bounce to them. One of the greatest blessings your child will bring you is the freedom to sing, move and enjoy.

Blow Out the Flashlight

Show your baby how a flashlight shines in the dark and point out her toys with it. Show her how to "blow" it out: when she goes "puff," snap off the light.

QUIET TIMES

Here are some classic lullabies to add to your collection. Don't forget to include lots of "good-night" rhymes in your baby's go-to-bed routine.

Oranges and Lemons

Gay go up and gay go down to ring the bells of
*　　London Town.*
Oranges and lemons, say the bells of
*　　St. Clement's.*
Bull's eyes and targets, say the bells of
*　　St. Marg'ret's.*
Brickbats and tiles, say the bells of St. Giles'.
Pancakes and fritters, say the bells of St. Peter's.
Two sticks and an apple, say the bells at
*　　Whitechapel.*
Old Father Baldpate, say the slow bells at
*　　Aldgate,*
Maids in white aprons, say the bells at
*　　St. Catherine's.*
Pokers and tongs, say the bells at St. John's.
Kettles and pans, say the bells at St. Anne's.
You owe me five farthings, say the bells of
*　　St. Martin's.*
When will you pay me? Say the bells of Old
*　　Bailey.*
When I grow rich, say the bells of Shoreditch.
Pray when will that be? Say the bells of Stepney.
I'm sure I don't know, says the great bell at Bow.

Here comes a candle to light you to bed,
He comes a chopper to chop off your head.

(Traditional, England)

There Was an Old Woman Tossed Up in a Basket

There was an old woman tossed up in a basket,
Seventeen times as high as the moon;
Where she was going I couldn't but ask it,
For in her hand she carried a broom.
"Old woman, old woman, old woman," quoth I,
"Where are you going to up so high?"
"To brush the cobwebs off the sky!"
"May I go with you?"
"Aye, by-and-by."

(Traditional, England)

Go to Bed Late

Go to bed late,
Stay very small
Go to bed early
Grow very tall.

(Traditional, United States)

Down With the Lambs

Down with the lambs
Up with the lark
Run to bed children
Before it gets dark.

(Traditional, United States)

OUTDOORS

Sand and Water Play

Sand play and water play are essential for your child. As she learns to pour, she also learns about quantity and how to measure. Some educators feel that without adequate play with sand and water at the toddler stage, a child will have trouble learning mathematics. Let your child experience water in the great outdoors, as well as in her bathtub.

Swimming

Take your baby swimming with you at the beach or pool, to experience jumping and splashing in large quantities of water. You may wish to enroll in a parent-and-tot swim class.

Wading

You can have as much fun at a wading pool as swimming at a beach. Consider also an inflatable wading pool for your yard. Collect toys that can be used in water—spray bottles (from window cleaner), squirt bottles (from liquid dish detergent), floating balls, and plastic containers. Punch holes in a large plastic container, such as a clean empty bleach bottle, to make a sprinkler. Get in and splash too! Never leave a wading pool unsupervised.

Ice Blocks

Use non-toxic water colors or food coloring to make colored ice blocks. Use these as regular "blocks" outside in the winter, or pop them into your toddler's wading pool in the summer.

The Sandbox

If you have the space in your yard, build a big sandbox. Make an easy-to-remove cover to keep out animals. If you don't have yard space, make sure you take your child to a playground with a big sandbox whenever the weather permits. A pail, shovel and sieves are essential.

Animals

Take a trip to a farm, a zoo, or a pet store. Talk about the names of the animals, the noises they make, where and how they live, how they move, whether they swim in water, walk on land, or fly in the air. What do they look like? What color are they? Do they have scales? Feathers? Skin? Shell? Fur? Stripes? Spots? A long neck? Your toddler may not remember it all, but she will take in more than you think. Add the noises the animals make. Take your toddler to a petting zoo, where she can touch a fuzzy sheep, scratch goats, and get to know and touch the animals.

Hide 'n' Seek

Introduce hide 'n' seek games after your baby's first birthday. Take turns hiding and seeking. Say, "Where's [baby's name], where could she be? THERE she is!" and give her a hug. Even when she is obvious, search in a few extra places, saying, "I wonder where [baby's name] IS? Not behind the tree, not under the chair, not lost in the woods... " When it is your turn to hide, be obvious about where you are, and say, "What a good job, you FOUND me; aren't you a clever baby!"

C H A P T E R S I X

So Much to Do and So Little Time

Fifteen to Eighteen Months

Your baby has become a toddler. His energy is boundless! He suddenly recognizes that it is HIS action that has caused his toy to move.

Your toddler will begin activities by himself, but he needs help to carry them through. He doesn't want interference from you, but he does depend on your being there for support and encouragement. It is time to step back and to learn to be a creative stage manager and director. Encourage fun and safe play activities and discourage and actively eliminate opportunities for dangerous or harmful ones. Present appealing options. When he has a choice he can begin to understand the results of his actions in a safe environment.

Although your toddler is learning that he is a separate person from you, he still wants to be with you and to copy you. Your work is his play. He wants to be like you and be with you constantly. He loves you totally and you are his hero. At the same time, he wants the freedom to experiment on his own. It is a very exciting but sometimes frustrating time for everyone.

The worst frustration occurs when your toddler becomes over-tired, overstimulated, or hungry. Naps, quiet times, and snacks become crucial for everyone's well-being. Often he will seem to "pass out" from exhaustion, and nap times may arrive earlier than expected. At other times, however, he may be totally unwilling to leave the excitement of play for a nap. Develop a transition period of quiet play to help your toddler wind down for his much-needed nap.

MOVEMENT

In the past three months your baby has gone from being a "wobbler" to being frenetically mobile, going in all directions simultaneously. In this next three-month period, he will gain great mastery of this mobility. It's as though he has invented walking, running, jumping, and climbing ALL BY HIMSELF!

Here are some games that will channel some of his boundless energy and enthusiasm.

Ring Around a Rosy

(Circle around holding hands. On "down," fall to the floor or ground.)

Ring around a rosy,
A pocket full of posies,
Husha-husha,
We all fall down.

(Sitting down, pretend to pull up flowers. Stand on "up.")

Pulling up the daisies,
Pulling up the daisies,
Husha-husha,
We all stand up.

(Fold hands like a church and steeple, then, waving arms, pretend to fly around the room to a designated spot.)

The robin in the steeple,
Is singing to the people,
Husha-husha,
We all fly home.

(With a partner, walk around the room as though carrying a pail full of water. On "down," place pail on floor and sit down.)

The king has sent his daughter,
To fetch a pail of water,
Husha-husha,
We all put it down.

(Have your toddler lie face down and pat his back. Clap your hands for thunder and lightning. Stand on "up.")

Cows are in the meadow,
Lying fast asleep,
Thunder, lightning,
They all stand up.

(Traditional, Great Britain, North America)

One Is a Giant

One is a giant who stomps his feet
> (Stomp feet around room.)

Two is a fairy so light and neat
> (Flit around the room, arms flapping.)

Three is a mouse that crouches small
> (Crouch low, face down.)

And four is a great big bouncing
> *ball!*
> (Jump up and down, clapping hands.)

(Traditional, England)

Jack in the Box

(Crouch low, hide head with hands. Pause slightly just before you jump on yes.)

Jack in the box
Sits so still
Won't you come out?
...yes, I WILL.

(Traditional, United States)

Mother and Father and Uncle John

(Give a knee-ride, with your toddler facing forward.)

Mother and Father and Uncle John
Went to town, one by one.
Mother fell off!
> (Tip him to one side.)

Father fell off!
> (And to the other side.)

But Uncle John went on and on and
> *on and on and on...*
> (Back to center and increase bouncing until the end.)

(Traditional, England)

Trot, Trot to Boston Town

Trot, trot to Boston Town
> (A knee- or ankle-ride)

To get a stick of candy.
One for me and one for you
And one for Dicky Dandy.
> (Tip your toddler to one side.)

(Traditional, United States)

Tommy O'Flynn

(Give a knee-ride, with your toddler facing you. Put your hands behind his neck and waist for support. Open your knees so he lowers back between them on "down." Bring him back up. Open your legs again for "in." Bounce him to end of rhyme.)

Tommy O'Flynn and his old grey mare
Went off to see the country fair
The bridge fell down
And the bridge fell in
And that was the end of
Tommy O'Flynn, O'Flynn, O'Flynn...

(Traditional, Scotland, adapted)

Rickety, Rickety

(Hold your toddler on knees, facing you. Jog one knee at a time so he gets a bumpy ride. On whoa! pull him in for a hug.)

Rickety, rickety rocking horse,
Over the fields we go.
Rickety, rickety rocking horse,
Giddy up, giddy up, whoa!

(Traditional, United States, adapted)

Ah, Si Mon Moine Voulait Danser

Ah! si mon moine voulait danser,
Ah! si mon moine voulait danser,
Up capuchon je lui donnerais,
Up capuchon je lui donnerais.
Danse, mon moine, danse.

Tu n' entends pas la danse.
Tu n' entends pas la danse.
Tu n' entends pas mon moulin lon-la!
Tu n' entends pas mon moulin marcher.

(Traditional, French Canada)

Dance to this happy song with your toddler in your arms. When older children sing the song, have them hold hands and spin around. This song can be heard on the *In the Schoolyard* record or tape by Sharon, Lois & Bram, Elephant Records.

Look Around

Sitting cross-legged on the floor with your baby, show him how to gently and slowly rotate his head forward, to the side, backward, to the other side, and forward again. Reverse directions and repeat. Say, "Look at the floor, look at that side of the room, look at the ceiling, look at the other side of the room, look back at the floor."

Down by the Station

(As you sit on the floor in a straddle position, hold hands with your child, rocking back and forth to the beat while singing this song. Increase the tempo for a verse, then decrease as the train comes into the station. Use "Toot, toot, chug, chug, home they come" for the last line.)

Down by the station, early in the morning
See the little puffer bellies all in a row
See the engine driver, pull the little handles
Toot, toot, chug, chug, off they go.

(Traditional, Great Britain, North America)

WATER PLAY

Water is magic for your toddler. It comes in plain and colored, using non-toxic water or food colors. It can be hot, warm, cold, frozen, and sometimes bubbly. It soaks clothes, it's cold and icy. It pours, splashes, and comes out of taps. It rains down and makes puddles to splash. It forms when ice or snow melts. Toys float in it, toys sink in it. Sugar dissolves in it. It will leak through some containers, but can be carried in others. And nothing can beat a bubble bath!

Bubbles

Bubbles are magic for your toddler. Blow bubbles for your toddler until he is older. Explain that bubble solution tastes "yucky" even though it is non-toxic, and warn everyone to be careful about getting bubbles or bubble solution in the eyes. We blow "superbubbles" in the kitchen or bathroom all year round, just before the floor gets washed.

Superbubbles

Bubble solution is inexpensive, but may be available only seasonally. Home-made "superbubbles" are inexpensive to prepare, and make huge bubbles, especially when you blow them slowly.

¼ cup clear liquid dishwashing detergent
¼ cup glycerine (from drugstore)
¾ cup water
1 Tbs. sugar

Add more glycerine to make the bubbles even stronger, if you like. To make enormous bubbles, dip the large end of a plastic kitchen funnel into the solution and blow through the small end. You can also bend thin coat hangers to make large bubble rings. A large bubble string is commercially available for humongous outdoor bubbles.

Blow the Bubble

S how your toddler how to keep a bubble aloft as long as possible by blowing it from underneath. If your toddler has older sibs or friends, you could have them try a "bubble race" to see who can blow the bubble (intact) across a predetermined finish line.

Catch the Bubble

W et your toddler's hands and have him try to catch bubbles as you blow them. Try using dry hands, too.

Stomp the Bubble

T HIS IS NOT A BATHTUB GAME! Have your toddler try to stomp on the bubbles and break them as they land on the grass or floor. Have him break it, rather than allowing it to break naturally. This is great to help develop his coordination.

Clap the Bubble

H ave your toddler try to break the bubble by clapping his hands together. Lots of small bubbles made from a store-bought solution make this a challenge. Play some music and have him clap to the beat as he tries to break the bubbles.

Poke the Bubble

H ave your toddler try to break the bubble by poking it with his finger in mid-air. With superbubbles, this can be tricky if your toddler's hands are wet. He may end up with bubbles stuck on his fingers.

The Superbath

F ill up your bathtub with water that is a comfortable temperature, with mild bubblebath solution added. Both you and your toddler climb in for a long, luxurious bath. Include liquid bubble solution and a bubble ring, bubbly stuff to drink (club soda, mineral water, ginger ale), and relaxing music, such as Handel's *Water Music*.

Blow bubbles at your child, avoiding his eyes. Enjoy your liquid refreshment in non-breakable glasses, going "clink" and "cheers" in a toast. This is an excellent stress reducer. It makes a child with chickenpox feel almost human, as long as you add baking soda to the bath, if your pediatrician says baths are okay.

Glug Glug

Glug glug went the little green frog one day
> (Make frog noises.)

Glug glug went the little green frog.
Glug glug went the little green frog one day,
And his eyes went gloink, gloink, gloink.
> (Blink your eyes.)

(Traditional, United States)

CHANGING GAMES

Your toddler loves to make a game of getting dressed and undressed. He will help by raising his arms or bottom, giving you his foot—in fact, doing almost everything you ask. At change time, sing, "I'm gonna take that sock right offa your foot," or "I'm gonna take that arm right out of that sleeve" to the tune of "I'm Gonna Wash That Man Right Out Of My Hair" from *South Pacific.*

Dressing Up

Clothes and dressing up may be important to your toddler. This isn't the imaginative, "being other people" dressing up that comes between 2 and 3. Instead, he wants to experiment in order to find out what this person "ME" is all about. You can begin to assemble a treasure trove of costume jewelry, wigs, hats, and soft, shiny, or textured fabrics by raiding attics, garage sales, and thrift stores. Dressing up may be a major part of play for years to come.

Tickle Games

Tickle games become especially important as your toddler starts to recognize the parts of his own body. He will giggle every time you touch his belly button. These games can be used in your changing routines, at bathtime, while waiting for

your pediatrician, or while travelling. You can also add more scientific names for the body parts; who knows, medical school could be somewhere in your toddler's future.

There Was a Little Man

There was a little man who had a little crumb,
> (Touch corner of your toddler's mouth.)

And over the mountain he did run,
> (Walk fingers over the top of his head.)

With a belly full of fat,
> (Tap his tummy lightly with both hands.)

And a big tall hat,
> (Raise your hands over his head.)

And a pancake stuck to his bum, bum, bum.
> (Tap his bottom.)

(Traditional, Great Britain, North America)

This Little Pig

This little pig had a rub-a-dub-dub.
> (Scrub one of your toddler's legs,

This little pig had a scrub-a-scrub-scrub.
> then the other.)

This little pig-a-wig ran upstairs.
> (Run fingers up one arm.)

This little pig-a-wig called out bears!
> (Call out "bears!")

Down came the jar with a great big slam!
> (Slap hands on knee or in water.)

And this little piggy ate all the jam. Yum, yum.
> (Rub your toddler's tummy.)

(Traditional, England)

Clap, Clap, Clap Your Hands

Clap, clap, clap your hands
As slowly as you can
Clap, clap, clap your hands
As quickly as you can.

Shake, shake, shake your hands...
Roll, roll, roll your hands...
Rub, rub, rub your hands...
Wiggle, wiggle, wiggle your fingers...
Pound, pound, pound your fists...
Kick, kick, kick your feet...

(Traditional, North America)

MUSIC

Music is becoming increasingly important to your toddler. If you are uncomfortable with your own musical skills you may want to consider enrolling in a parent/child music class. Check your local paper, or ask your local library or nursery school if a class is available. If not, arrange a group with a musical Mom or Dad as a leader. More and more, your toddler will enjoy listening to children's records and tapes. Use your library to test children's music before buying.

Instruments

The beat of music may cause a new response in your toddler—jumping and wiggling. He enjoys playing rudimentary instruments—banging a spoon on a pot, drumming on empty ice-cream containers, shaking shakers or ringing bells laced together. Show him how to play whatever musical instrument is attracting his attention.

Baa, Baa Black Sheep

(Tap drums to the beat.)

Baa, baa, black sheep, have you any wool?
Yes, sir, yes, sir, three bags full:
One for my master,
One for my dame,
And one for little ———
Who lives down the lane.

(Traditional, England)

This Old Man

This old man, he played one,
>   (Tap drums for this verse.)
He played knick-knack on my drum.
With a knick-knack, paddy wack,
Give your dog a bone,
This old man came rolling home.

This old man
>   (Tap sticks for this verse.)

This old man, he played six
He played knick-knack on my sticks
With a knick-knack, paddy wack
Give your dog a bone
This old man came rolling home.

The other verses can go:

one—drum
two—shoe
three—knee
four—door
five—hive
six—sticks
seven—heaven
eight—gate
nine—line
ten—once again

(Traditional, Great Britain, North America)

One, Two, Buckle My Shoe

(Tap sticks)

One, two, buckle my shoe
>   (Touch shoe with one stick.)
Three, four, shut the door
Five, six, pick up sticks
>   (Click sticks high in the air.)
Seven, eight, lay them straight
>   (Place sticks parallel in front of your toddler.)
Nine, ten, a big fat hen
>   (Flap arms folded for wings and "cluck, cluck, cluck".)

(Traditional, England)

ART ACTIVITIES

Continue to have your toddler scribble. Give him lots of opportunity to make his marks in the world with crayons and newsprint.

Painting and Pasting

Painting and pasting are messy activities, so do them outdoors, when weather permits, or in an easily cleaned area. Use masking tape to hold paper securely. Non-toxic, water-soluble finger paints and markers are lots of fun in the bathtub. Poster paints, glue, and paste should all be non-toxic and water soluble as well. Show your toddler how to rub a glue stick on his paper and add materials to the sticky area. Supervise carefully.

Finger Paint

Mix 2 cups of cold water and ½ cup flour in a pot. All-purpose flour is fine, but whole wheat or rye flour will add texture. Stirring constantly, bring to a simmer on the stove. Add to the hot mixture a paste of 2 Tbsps cornstarch mixed with 4 Tbsps cold water. Allow to cool. Add color to small amounts of the paint, using food colors, water colors or bits of water crayons.

Finger Painting

This is one type of painting that is ESSENTIAL for your toddler. It is just as "mucky" as playing with sand, dirt, and water, but it comes in wonderful colors.

Sit your toddler at a table or on the floor where you can oversee the painting. Spread out plastic or newspapers to catch the drips. Dampen some finger paint paper, or use some shiny, clean butcher's paper. Put a few globs of paint on the paper and show him how the paints can be swirled, pushed, shoved, and moved around. At first, limit the number of colors to two. Show the different effects produced by using knuckles, thumbs, fingers, heel of hand, fingertips, fingernails....

First Playdough

This first playdough recipe is good for very young children because it is very soft. Mix 3 cups of flour, ½ cup salad oil, and enough water to bind—approximately ½ cup. Knead well. If you like, add a bit of food coloring. Allow your toddler to push, poke, prod, bang, and manipulate his playdough. There's no harm if he eats a bit of it, but it won't taste very good.

Macaroni/Pasta

Dried macaroni and pasta is a wonderful medium for your artist. Pasta can be glued, strung, colored, painted, or stuck in playdough. And even picky eaters can be swayed when you throw a handful of alphabet letters into the soup stock, or into a cheese sauce.

Pasta comes in bead shapes (get the very large sizes for your toddler), shells, elbows, alphabets, numbers, and spirals. Buy an assortment of small, medium, and large sizes of dried pasta when you do your grocery shopping. Save some of each type in the artwork drawer.

Stringing Beads

Stringing beads is wonderful for developing hand-eye coordination. Your toddler will love putting canneloni or manicotti onto shoestrings. As his hand-eye coordination improves, switch to a medium-sized canneloni or ziti bead. By the time he is three, he will be competent with ditalini, macaroni elbows, and tubettini strung on narrow ribbon.

Colored Pasta

You can color smaller pasta shapes, such as tubettini, ditalini, elbows, and alphabet letters, by shaking 2-3 Tbsps dried pasta together with a few drops of food coloring. Use the pasta to make necklaces, or add to playdough or baker's clay. Larger pieces, or irregularly-shaped pieces such as spirals, can be painted with watercolor paints and allowed to dry.

WORD PLAY

Your toddler may not be expressing himself verbally yet, but his understanding of words is growing daily. It is more important than ever to talk to your toddler about everything going on around him. He imitates all that he hears, and although you may not recognize everything he says, he is developing his own communication style.

Fast Words/Slow Words

You can make a fun game out of words if you say them first very fast, and then very slowly, stretching out each syllable. Use this technique with words most familiar to your child. You can use any word to make a surprise sound—just say it suddenly and unexpectedly.

Reading

Children will fall in love with books forever if they have pleasant early experiences with them. Your toddler should have his very own books to handle and manipulate. Well-loved and often-read books instill a desire to learn to read later on.

Read to your toddler for brief periods only, because his attention span is very short. Use an appealing, expressive voice. He should have a clear view of the book you are reading. Don't rush to tell him a story or a plot. At this stage, your toddler is probably more interested in the pictures than in the story. Let your toddler have lots of time to look at everything very carefully and DON'T RUSH.

Point out details in the pictures and talk to him about those details. To start stories, show your child the book and maybe read the first page—or read until his attention starts to fade, then switch to talking about the pictures. Gradually add more of the story, perhaps one page at a time. Show enthusiasm for any response your child makes to either the story or the pictures.

Favorite Books

Our favorite reading books of the toddler period were actually delightfully silly rhymes rather than stories. *Hop on Pop* and *The Foot Book*, by Dr. Seuss, and *Alligator Pie* by Dennis Lee, were special favorites. What we enjoyed most of all were the wonderful picture books by Jan Pienkowski and Dick Bruna, especially Dick Bruna's *B is for Bear*. Don't hesitate to read well-loved books over and over and over again.

Make Your Own Books

Create your own books with your child. Your toddler will love his books because he can remember the fun and pleasure of making them, and they tell HIS story. Books you could make with your toddler include: *Animals I Know* (based on animals he recognizes or family pets), *My Recipe Book, My Things That Are Small, My Things That Are Large, Flowers, Bugs, Birds, My Trip to...* (grandmother's, the doctor, a place visited on vacation), *Types of Weather, Numbers, Letters, My Relatives, My Friends*, and any other topic that interests him. Include his favorite rhymes in his story.

Animal Sounds

Your toddler is starting to recognize and to have a keen interest in animals. If you have a family pet, a special relationship may have developed between your toddler and the pet. He starts to recognize animals he sees on TV. Animal noises provide a great deal of fun. A perfect book for your toddler is *Gobble, Growl, Grunt* by Peter Spier, a compilation of animal pictures and animal noises to be read either in brief segments or until you both tire.

Songs featuring animal sounds include "Old McDonald," (p. 49), "I Had a Rooster," and "As I Was Walking to Town" (p. 37). Substitute all kinds of animal sounds, but make sure you also do your child's favorites.

I Had a Rooster

I had a rooster and my rooster pleased me.
I fed my rooster 'neath the green willow tree.
And my old rooster went cock-a-doodle-doo,
De-doodle, de-doodle, de-doodle, de-doo.

I had a cat and my cat pleased me.
I fed my cat 'neath the green willow tree.
And my old cat went me-ow,
And my old rooster went cock-a-doodle-doo,
De-doodle, de-doodle, de-doodle, de-doo.

For each verse, add a new animal and a new
sound:

mouse—squeak
lion—roar
dog—woof, woof
elephant—trumpet sounds
sheep—baa
cow—moo
horse—neigh
dinosaur ...
dragon ...

(Traditional, North America)

You can hear a fun version of this song on Fred Penner's *The Cat Came Back* album, Troubadour Records.

KITCHEN PLAY

Let's face it, we all spend a great deal of time in our kitchens preparing meals and cleaning up. Your toddler wants to, and can, help you in the kitchen, so make it safe for him. Ensure that all cleaning materials and knives are placed far out of his reach.

Kitchen Helper

Your toddler is interested in feeling, touching, and tasting just about everything. Let him sample a wide variety of textures and tastes from the ingredients you are using that are on his diet. Make sure his "samples" are easy to digest, and won't get stuck in his mouth or throat. Develop a "cooking chatter" about what you're doing, how ingredients mix together, what they taste like, smell like, and what happens when everything is combined and cooked.

Sous Chef

When you have food that is easy to prepare, take the time to show your baby how to correctly help. Whether it is opening a packet to put into a microwave or more complex washing carrots or potatoes, tearing lettuce, kneading dough, rolling cookies, shaking bottles, stirring two or more things together, your 15-month-old has the competence to help when you take the little bit of extra time necessary to teach him how. A few minutes well spent now may save you days of your life over your next eighteen or so years when somebody else is present who CAN wash the potatoes and lettuce. You are also enhancing his future culinary development.

Simplicity of directions and repetition are the keys to success in teaching your child. Allow yourself extra time in the kitchen when neither you nor your toddler feels pressured. If you are feeling harassed, postpone it. Just put in a few short sessions when you can relax and enjoy it. Use the old reinforcement standbys of praise, praise, praise and hug, hug, hug. Celebrate partial successes. Your child will be overjoyed to help with some of the "real" cooking.

Baby's Chicken Soup

Have your child wash two large potatoes, two red or green peppers, an onion, some cabbage (about two cups), two or three stalks of celery, and two or three carrots. Peel, seed, and chop the vegetables into chunks your toddler can handle. Have him help you put approximately 3 lbs. of chicken, either whole or in pieces, into a large pot. He can then add the vegetables.

Cover everything with water, put a lid on the pot, put it on the stove, and bring to a boil. Then turn down and let simmer for about two hours.

Add salt, pepper, and herbs to taste (thyme, garlic, parsley, cardamom, coriander, ...). Add a few fresh or tinned tomatoes. Taste and adjust seasonings, if necessary. Cook for 10 or 15 minutes longer, until the tomatoes soften, and then serve. This soup freezes well. (You can substitute beef bones, if you prefer.) Your toddler will be proud of his culinary contribution!

Baking Bread

S how your toddler that bread doesn't always come from a store-bought, plastic package, but can be made from simple household ingredients. If you have the time and the inclination, make some yeast bread that must rise in a warm place. If you don't have much time, bake some biscuits instead. Turn on the oven light and show the change. Bread dough makes great playdough. You can talk about the science of carbon dioxide and warmth, combining with yeast, flour and water.

Baking Powder Biscuits

Preheat oven to 450°F. Sift together in a large bowl:

1 ¾ cups pre-sifted all-purpose flour
½ tsp salt
3 tsps baking powder
Cut 5 Tbsps chilled butter or shortening into flour mixture. Add, all at once, ¾ cup milk or buttermilk.

Stir the dough until it comes away from the sides of the bowl, then turn it out onto a lightly floured board. Sift a tiny bit of flour over the top and pat down until the dough is desired thickness. Cut dough with a biscuit cutter or favorite cookie cutter dipped into a little flour sprinkled on the side of the board. Brush the tops of the biscuits with melted butter. (Have your toddler help you measure, sift, stir, cut, and paint with the melted butter.)

Place the biscuits on an ungreased baking sheet and bake until lightly browned—12 to 15 minutes.

Make Some Butter For His Bread

H ave your toddler help you whip cream to make homemade butter. Use heavy cream (35% butterfat) at room temperature. Help him whip the cream using hand beaters or cheat and use a food processor (he switches "on"). Drain the butter through a cheesecloth and chill. As the butter gets quite stiff, you may have to do the last of the whipping by yourself. A plastic whipped cream shaker can also be used to make butter. As your child shakes it, he can sing "Going to Kentucky" (p. 107).

Betty Botter

Betty Botter bought some butter.
"But," she said, "this butter's bitter.
If I put it in my batter,
It will make my batter bitter.
But a bit of better butter
Will make my batter better."

So she bought a bit of butter,
Better than her bitter butter
And she put it in her batter.
And it made her batter better.
So 'twas better Betty Botter
Bought a bit of better butter.

(Traditional, England)

Muffins

M uffins are a perfect snack for active toddlers. They're nutritious and just the right shape for holding and munching. You can experiment with endless combinations of healthy ingredients. Your toddler is not growing as fast as he was, so make sure you load his snacks with lots of healthy foods. He will love helping you make his cookies and muffins as much as he loves a food that he can carry around with him.

Banana Oatmeal Muffins   **375°F**

Combine
> *1 cup rolled oats*
> *1 cup unbleached or whole wheat flour*
> *½ tsp. salt,*
> *1 tsp. baking powder*

Mix together in a separate bowl
> *2 tbsp. brown sugar*
> *2 egg yolks, beaten*
> *½ cup warm milk*
> *⅓ cup salad oil*

Add dry mixture to wet mixture and stir well. Add 1 cup mashed banana, or 1 cup applesauce, or 1 cup cooked mashed carrots, or 1 cup shredded zucchini, or 1 cup cooked mashed pumpkin. Beat two egg whites until stiff and fold into the muffin mixture. Fill oiled muffin tins ⅔ full. Bake approximately 30 minutes, and cool. If desired, chopped dried apricots, raisins, cut dates, blueberries, or other fruit can be added, about ½ cup in total.

Note: Do not make this recipe until he has had his rubella innoculation so he doesn't have an allergic reaction to the albumin-based serum.

Washing Dishes

Pull a chair up to the sink and let your toddler help you wash the unbreakable dishes. Place plastic containers, lids, cups, non-sharp and non-breakable utensils and dishes in the sink. Partially fill with warm water and lots of suds. Let him splash away to his heart's content. Have towels, sponges, a mop, and whatever else is necessary on hand to absorb the spills and splashes.

INDOOR GAMES

Nothing is safe from your toddler's prying, peeping, and poking—he LOVES investigating his world. Toddlerproof one area completely so he can have total freedom in at least part of his indoor environment. You want to encourage and support your toddler as much as possible, not frustrate him in his play.

Growing Seeds

Planting and growing seeds teaches your toddler the idea that events occur over time. Alfalfa, mung beans, lentils, brassica, radish seeds, cress, and mustard greens can all be sprouted quickly indoors. Using a bean sprouter or a glass jar covered with cheesecloth, you can grow your own "crop" in a few days. Soak the seeds in cool water overnight, then drain. Place the seeds in your jar or sprouter. Place the seeds in a dark cupboard and rinse them off twice a day. Your toddler will love to help you rinse, and this gives you an opportunity to talk about how plants grow.

Note: Make sure that the seeds you use are intended for sprouting and that they have NOT been treated with chemical preservatives.

Pouring Dry Materials

Make sure your toddler has a chance to play with "sand" all year round. Make a small indoor "sandbox" area containing cornmeal, puffed wheat, or puffed rice. You can use a small, covered plastic tub or pail, or an outgrown baby bath. An old suitcase also works nicely. Supply strainers, funnels, sieves, containers, pails, and shovels for many hours of low-cost entertainment. If you buy a package of bulk cereal on sale, your toddler can safely eat his "sand." It is important that he pour and manipulate quantities of materials so that math skills will emerge later on.

Caves and Dens

You can make a special secret hiding place for your toddler by draping a blanket over a couple of chairs to make a "tent" or by placing a long tablecloth on a small table. A huge cardboard packing crate designed for a major appliance makes a great hiding spot. A pup tent in the back yard is fun, too.

Roughhouse

On a large, soft, carpeted area, have a (gentle) wrestling, tickling, hugging, "catch you," "chase you" match with your toddler. Let him win most of the time. Add some "hide 'n' seek" and "follow the leader."

QUIET TIMES

When naptime comes, you may occasionally find your toddler already asleep on the floor. More often, however, you may find him absolutely unwilling to "give in" to being tired. At these times you need to do some quiet, relaxing activities with your child. Read a book, or lie down and have a cuddle together, and relax yourself. Continue to recite longer, quiet, relaxing poetry as you and your baby cuddle.

Cards

Now is the time to start your toddler with cards: it may go on for life. You will need a deck of cards—it need not be new, or even complete. Take the time to show your toddler how to sort, separate, organize, and categorize the cards. These are important life skills that he can learn now. At his age red and black is probably the most differentiation you can expect, but as familiarity and experience grows you can ask for the ones with pictures, the women cards and the men cards, and the different suits as shape recognition comes. With number recognition comes sorting by numbers. By age four you will have a "fish" player, ready to go.

Close Investigation

Take the time to closely investigate a piece of fruit with your toddler. An orange, pomegranate, or grapefruit are recommended. Show him and talk about the color and texture of the skin, the smell outside, the surface, the oil in the skin. Peel it and open it, open the membrane slowly and show the juice sacs and seeds, smell the inside and then taste it. If you have a magnifying glass, use it for your investigations. Let him experience his food with all his senses.

Mirror Magic

Your toddler is beginning to differentiate himself from other people, so mirrors are important. Try to set up a variety of mirrors—for example, full-length, head-and-shoulder, square-tiled, and magnifying ones so he can discover himself in various ways.

When outside, point to his reflection whenever and wherever you encounter mirrors. Search for three-way and five-way mirrors in department stores. Mirrors that face each other and reflect images into infinity are especially intriguing.

The Owl and the Pussy-Cat

The Owl and the Pussy-cat went to sea
In a beautiful pea-green boat:
They took some honey, and plenty of money
Wrapped up in a five-pound note.
The Owl looked up to the stars above,
And sang to a small guitar,
"O lovely Pussy, O Pussy my love,
What a beautiful Pussy you are,
*   You are, you are!*
What a beautiful Pussy you are."

Pussy said to the Owl, "You elegant fowl,
How charmingly sweet you sing!
Oh! let us be married; too long we have tarried:
But what shall we do for a ring?"
They sailed away, for a year and a day,
To the land where the bong-tree grows;
And there in the wood a Piggy-wig stood,
With a ring at the end of his nose,
*   His nose, his nose!*
With a ring at the end of his nose.

"Dear Pig, are you willing to sell for one shilling
Your ring?" Said the Piggy, "I will."
So they took it away, and were married next day
By the turkey who lives on the hill.
They dined on mince and slices of quince,
Which they ate with a runcible spoon:
And hand in hand, on the edge of the sand,
They danced by the light of the moon,
*   The moon, the moon!*
They danced by the light of the moon.

(Edward Lear, Great Britain, 1846)

OUTDOORS

It is important to get your toddler of ANY age outside as frequently as possible, as long as you are both comfortably dressed. It is far easier to burn off excess energy outside, even on rainy days. And a toddler loves to be out in his community, looking all around.

Tumble in the Leaves

On a dry autumn day find or rake up a huge pile of leaves. Roughhouse together in the leaves; throw them all over each other, roll around, tickle, hug, and be generally silly.

Sand and Mud Play

Imagine the poor toddler who never makes mud pies, and never mixes sand and water! Ooey, gooey stuff is great fun for kids of all ages. If Mommy or Daddy get involved, it can be hilarious. How about a game of "Let's cover Mommy or Daddy up with sand" at a lake or beach in the summertime? How about a gentle roll-and-tumble in some nice, wet dirt? Mud wrestlers seem to enjoy themselves—maybe kids can show us something we've forgotten about getting dirty.

Wet Sand

Make sure your toddler has a chance to experience damp and wet sand, as well as dry sand. Use his pail and show him how to pack it full of moist sand, and tip it over to build a sand castle. Build large sand castles at the beach.

Washing the Car

When it's time to wash the car, assemble buckets of soapy water, sponges, and a hose with a spray. Have your toddler help you suds, scrub, and rinse off the car. He feels important when he helps with real chores, and he loves playing in suds. When you've finished the car, you can help him wash his wagon or other important toy.

Ice and Snow

Let your toddler experience other forms of water. Help him walk on slippery, icy surfaces, perhaps at a skating rink when it isn't busy, and let him roll in the snow. He can play in the snow with some of his sand toys.

Catch Snowflakes

Catch some snowflakes on your mittens and show your child how each snowflake has a unique shape. Use a magnifying glass if you have one. Let him catch snowflakes on his tongue as they fall. Show him that snowflakes soon melt if they contact a warm surface.

Frozen Bubbles

When you blow bubbles outside on a very cold day, they freeze almost instantly. If you're careful, you can poke holes in them without having the bubble disintegrate. Make some frozen superbubbles (See p. 73.) as well.

What Can You See?

Play this game while out walking or riding in the car. Ask your toddler to tell you what he sees. Talk about those things in either a silly or a serious way. If he sees a flock of birds, ask him where the birds are going, and talk generally about the birds. Even if all you get is "ba" or "birds fly home" it's a real win. You then make up your own version of what he said, for instance, "Yes, the birds are flying home. They are flying south because winter is coming and it is going to be cold here. Down south it is warm and there is no snow." Don't talk too much, just keep the conversation moving about what he has seen, and add your own imaginative words. Recite some rhymes or sing some songs about what he is seeing and talking about.

Elaborate His Experience

As your baby reaches toddlerhood, he spots all sorts of interesting things on his daily walks. He sees the gingerbread cookies in the bakery window, and wants one. He wants to investigate fire hydrants, mail boxes, and bus shelters.

Respond to and elaborate upon everything he notices. At a mailbox talk about letters, stamps, post offices, mail trucks, and mail delivery, and getting a letter. When you see a fire hydrant, discuss how the fire fighters put out fires with hoses that they attach to the hydrants. You can also arrange a visit to a fire station to visit the fire engines. Call up your community relations officer and go to visit the police station. Enrich and elaborate all of his interests.

I Spy

I Spy is an ideal game to play when out walking, driving, or waiting somewhere. Incorporate all the words your toddler knows. Say, for example, "I spy with my little eye something that is round, tastes good, has a peel, and makes juice. What is it?" "Orange." Add or subtract clues as necessary when you play this game.

"I spy with my little eye someone who gets off the train every day and loves you." "Daddy."

"I spy with my little eye something that is red." "Fire Engine." I Spy is a wonderful way to point out details of his world when you are out on your walks. You will play "I Spy" for years to come.

Stroller Walks With Toddlers

Your toddler may rebel against riding in his stroller. He now wants to walk and toddle everywhere, usually taking forever. Let him help you push the stroller until he tires out and wants a ride. Let him drag a pull toy along the sidewalk while he rides in his stroller. He'll love the extra noise.

Riding Toys

Riding in a red wagon or a sled can be fun for a toddler tired from walking. Sing songs such as "Bumpin' Up and Down In My Little Red Wagon," as you pull the wagon along.

Bumpin' Up and Down

Bumpin' up and down in my little red wagon,
Bumpin' up and down in my little red wagon,
Bumpin' up and down in my little red wagon,
Won't you be my darlin'?

Wheel fell off and the axle's broken,
Wheel fell off and the axle's broken,
Wheel fell off and the axle's broken,
Won't you be my darlin'?

————'s gonna fix it with his hammer,
————'s gonna fix it with his hammer,
————'s gonna fix it with his hammer,
Won't you be my darlin'?

Bumpin' up and down in my little red wagon,
Bumpin' up and down in my little red wagon,
Bumpin' up and down in my little red wagon,
Won't you be my darlin'?

(Traditional, North America)

This song is recorded on Raffi's *Singable Songs for the Very Young* (Troubadour) or Bob McGrath's *If You're Happy and You Know It Sing Along With Bob* (Kids' Records) albums. It can also be done as a knee- or ankle-ride with your toddler. Give him a knee-ride for the first verse, and hug him on "Won't you be my darlin'?" For the second verse, tip him over to alternate sides on "broken," and pull him in again for a hug. To fix the wagon, pound your fist as though hammering. The last verse is a repeat of the first verse.

As he learns to love this song, talk about the different parts of a wagon—the wheel, the axle, what happens when the axle breaks, and how to fix a broken wagon.

C H A P T E R   S E V E N

Mommy, What's That? Mommy, What's That? Mommy, ...

Eighteen to Twenty-four Months

Your older toddler will turn into a small child by the time she is twenty-four months old. She is not a baby anymore. She is getting very good at walking and she is adding running, a few tiptoe steps, walking backwards, and jumping—perhaps even more than once without falling down.

She is learning to control events and to organize her world. Her curiosity is insatiable. She CANNOT share her toys with other children. Her best playmates are children older than she is. She trusts adults, and expresses her feelings, wishes, and interests to them.

Names are important to her. Her vocabulary is increasing daily. She wants to know the name of everything. Be sure she knows her full name, and maybe her full address. She is starting to use words to make her needs known. By the time she is 24 months old her favorite, and most used, words will be "NO" and "MINE."

She enjoys active games with older children like "tag," "Ring Around a Rosy," and "B-I-N-G-O." She has lots of energy and needs lots of moving around.

MOVEMENT

Your older toddler just loves to move. Give her lots of opportunities to run around and to try out her new skills. Make sure she has plenty of playground time for climbing, swinging, and sliding. To improve her balance and coordination, have her hold your hand as she walks along low walls or curbs.

Action Songs

Your toddler loves to perform the actions of songs she sings. Although she probably will not be singing all the words, she will join in on her favorite chorus or phrases, such as "E-I-E-I-O" or "Skinnimarinky Doo." Introduce her to simple game songs like "London Bridge," "Hokey Pokey," "B-I-N-G-O," and "Looby Loo."

London Bridge

Play this as a party game with a group of both children and adults. Choose two of the tallest to make a bridge by facing each other and joining hands high. A name is chosen for each, for instance, "orange" and "lemon." During the song, the other children walk under the bridge and, on "My fair lady-o" one child is captured in the lowered arms of the two children forming the bridge. The child captured whispers a choice of "orange" or "lemon" to one of the bridge, and holds the back of the person selected. When all the children have been captured, the oranges and lemons have a tug of war.

London Bridge

London Bridge is falling down,
Falling down, falling down.
London Bridge is falling down,
My fair lady-o.

Build it up with iron bars,
Iron bars, iron bars.
Build it up with iron bars,
My fair lady-o.

Iron bars will bend and break...
Build it up with gold and silver...
Gold and silver will be stolen away...
Build it up with sticks and stones...
Sticks and stones will wash away...
Build it up with bricks and clay...
Bricks and clay will wear away...

(Traditional, England)

B-I-N-G-O

Farmer Brown he had a dog
> (Walk in a circle, holding hands.)

And Bingo was his name-o,
B-I-N-G-O, B-I-N-G-O, B-I-N-G-O,
> (Stamp feet for each letter.)

And Bingo was his name-o.
> (Stand still.)

B-I-N-G-...O-O-O-O-O!
> (As you slowly whisper "B-I-N-G," take small steps to the center of the circle. On "O-O-O-O-O," move back quickly to form a circle again.)

(Traditional, Great Britain, North America)

Hokey Pokey

(Follow the song directions. To do the Hokey Pokey, hands and index fingers point upwards, wiggle your body from side to side. Following verses: right hand, left foot, right foot, whole self.)

You put your left hand in
You put your left hand out
You put your left hand in
And you shake it all about
You do the Hokey Pokey and
You turn yourself around
That's what it's all about. HEY.

(Traditional, North America)

Looby Loo

(Hold hands and skip in a circle. Do as the song says.)

Chorus:

Here we go looby loo,
Here we go looby light.
Here we go looby loo,
All on a Saturday night.

You put your right hand in,
You put your right hand out.
You give your hand a shake, shake, shake,
And turn yourself about.

You put your left hand in...
You put your right foot in...
You put your left foot in...
You put your right arm in...
You put your left arm in...
You put your right leg in...
You put your left leg in...
You put your head in...
You put your whole self in...

(Traditional, Great Britain, North America)

Did You Ever See a Lassie (Laddie)?

(Mimic the actions of the leader.)

Did you ever see a lassie
A lassie, a lassie
Did you ever see a lassie
Go this way and that?
Go this way and that way
Go this way and that way
Did you ever see a lassie
Go this way and that?

(Traditional, Great Britain, North America)

Let's Tap Our Legs Together

(Sit down in a circle. Do what the words say.)

Let's tap our legs together
Let's tap our legs together
Let's tap our legs together
Because it's fun to do.
(...hit the floor,
...clap our hands,
...touch our noses,
...wiggle our ears,
...blink our eyes,
...all stand up,
...all sit down.)

(Traditional, North America)

Clap Your Hands, Little Sally

(Do what the words say. For subsequent verses,
stomp your feet, gallop around, turn around, hit
the floor...)

Clap your hands, Little Sally
Clap your hands, Little Sally Brown
Clap your hands, Little Sally
Clap 'em Sally Brown.

(Traditional, United States)

Draw a Pail of Water

(Have your child stand in your lap. Hold her
hands, and rock her back and forth. On three,
gently lower her between your knees.)

Draw a pail of water,
For the farmer's daughter,
One a-pumpa,
Two a-pumpa,
Three way down in the water.

(Traditional, Great Britain, North America)

Follow the Leader

Have your toddler mimic you as you walk, march, shuffle, tramp and tiptoe around, clapping your hands, touching your eyes, wiggling ears, tapping the floor, touching your nose...

Side Bends

Stand with your arms stretched out straight from your shoulders. Slowly bend to the left side; try to stretch your left arm to the floor, right arm reaches high to the sky. Arise to your beginning position, then bend to the right side, right arm stretching toward the floor, left arm up to sky. Repeat. Tell your toddler to play "Follow the Leader."

Splits

Sit on the floor with your legs out to the sides— as far as they will go in a straddle position. Lift your arms and stretch them out straight. Bend your torso to the left, touching your left hand to your left foot and arching your right arm over your torso. Come back up to the straight position. Bend and stretch over to the right. Repeat. Have your child mimic your actions.

WATER PLAY

Encourage her to play with water. Food coloring, soapy water, melting snow, sponges, cloths, funnels, sieves, dolls, plastic bottles, cups, spoons, floating and sinking objects, boats, straws, plastic tubes, shaving cream, bubble bath, plastic spray bottles, and plastic squirt bottles—all make marvelous water toys, inside or out.

Warm/Hot/Cold

Fill one container with cold water or ice, another with warm water, and a third with (comfortably) hot water. Have your child touch the water in all three containers, and talk with her about the dangers and uses of hot and cold water. Blindfold her and ask her to guess which one is which.

Bubbles

Continue to play with bubbles frequently. To make another simple bubble solution, mix ¾ cup clear liquid dishwashing soap, ¼ cup sugar and 2 quarts tap water.

Paint the House With Water

Give your child a large, soft paintbrush and a small pail of water, and show her how to "paint" the house. Talk about the differences in color when water is painted over the surface. Show her where you want her to paint.

CHANGING GAMES

Your child is learning more and more about her body, so continue to play all her favorite finger plays and changing games.

Hot Water, Cold Water

Hot water,
> (Tap your child's shoulders rhythmically.)

Cold water,
Running down your back water.
> (Tickle down her back.)

(Traditional, unknown)

Criss, Cross, Applesauce

Criss, cross,
> (Draw a large "X" on her back.)

Applesauce,
> (Tap shoulders to rhythm of words.)

Spiders climbing up your back.
> (Tickle up her back.)

Cool breeze,
> (Blow softly on the back of her neck.)

Tight squeeze,
> (Give her a hug.)

And now you've got the SHIVERS!
> (Tickle her all over.)

(Traditional, unknown)

Grandma's Glasses

Here are Grandma's glasses,
> (Make circles with thumbs and index fingers.)

And here is Grandma's hat.
> (Join fingertips and place on head.)

Here's the way she folds her hands,
> (Fold hands.)

And puts them in her lap.
> (Place in lap.)

Here are Grandpa's glasses,
> (Hold larger "glasses" to eyes.)

And here is Grandpa's hat.
> (Make larger "hat" with hands.)

Here's the way he folds his arms,
> (Fold arms with vigor.)

And has his little nap.
> (Close eyes and snore....)

(Traditional, Great Britain, North America)

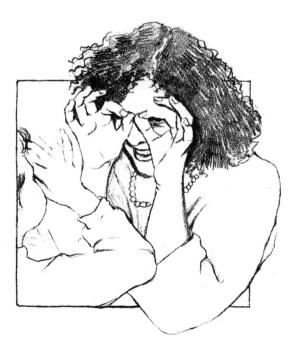

This Is My Right Hand

This is my right hand.
> (Show right hand.)

I'll hold it high.
> (Hold right hand high over head.)

This is my left hand.
> (Show left hand.)

I'll touch the sky.
> (Hold left hand high over head.)

Right hand,
> (Show right hand.)

Left hand,
> (Show left hand.)

Roll them around.
> (Roll hands around each other.)

Left hand,
> (Show left hand.)

Right hand,
> (Show right hand.)

Pound, pound, pound.
> (Pound fists together.)

(Traditional, Great Britain, North America)

Where Is Thumbkin?

(Tune: "Are You Sleeping?/Frère Jacques")

Where is Thumbkin?
> (Hide hands behind back.)

Where is Thumbkin?
Here I am, here I am!
> (Show hands, thumbs up.)

How are you today, sir?
> (Shake hands.)

Very well, I thank you.
Run and hide, run and hide.
> (Hide hands behind back.)

Where is Pointer (index finger)...
Where is Tall Man (middle finger)...
Where is Ringer (ring finger)...
Where is Baby (little finger)...
Where is everybody (all fingers)...
Where is left foot...
Where is right foot...
Where is left hand...

Where is right hand...
Where is your head...
Where are shoulders...
Where is your body...

(Traditional, Great Britain, North America)

MUSIC

When you play instruments with your child, add slightly longer songs with more verses. Blindfold your toddler and ask her to tell you which instrument you are playing as you make different sounds. For instance, "shake," "boom," "ring," "click."

HINT: Some children like to be blindfolded for games, but others dislike being unable to see. Your child may be more willing to be blindfolded if you show her that she can pull the blindfold off quickly; pull a scarf, a hat or a tea cosy loosely over her eyes so that she can remove it herself. Alternatively, ask her to cover her eyes with her hands and turn around.

Aikendrum

(Tap drums as you sing the song.)

There was a man lived in the moon,
In the moon, in the moon.
There was a man lived in the moon,
And his name was Aikendrum.

He played upon a ladle,
a ladle, a ladle.
He played upon a ladle,
And his name was Aikendrum.

His hair was made of spaghetti,
spaghetti, spaghetti.
His hair was made of spaghetti,
And his name was Aikendrum.

His eyes were made of meatballs...
His coat was make of roast beef...
His stomach was made of pizza...
His ——— was made of ———...
> (Use your child's favorite foods.)

(Traditional, Scotland)

Aikendrum has a friend named Willy Wood who eats up all the different parts of Aikendrum's silly body, if the song continues. Willy Wood plays a razor as a musical instrument, and lives in another town. It helps to make sure you know what Aikendrum was made of, so Willy Wood can eat him all up. Simply substitute Willy's name for Aikendrum's. The verses would go "He ate up all the spaghetti..."

Alphabet Song

(Play drums to the beat.)

A, B, C, D, E, F, G,
H, I, J, K,
L, M, N, O, P,
Q, R, S, T, U, V,
W, X, Y, and Z.
Now I know my ABCs
Next time won't you sing with me?

(Traditional, North America)

French Alphabet Song

A, B, C, D, E, F, G,
H, I, J, K, L, M, N, O, P,
Q, R, S, et T, U, V,
Double V, et X, Y, et Z.
Heureux, Heureux, j'aime chanter.
Je connais mon A, B, C.

(Traditional, French Canada)

Wee Willie Winkie

(Tap sticks to beat.)
Wee Willie Winkie
Runs through the town,
Upstairs and downstairs
In his night-gown.

Rapping at the windows,
Crying through the lock:
"Are the children all in bed
For now it's eight o'clock?"

(William Miller, Scotland, 1841)

One, Two, Three, Four

(Ring bells to beat)

One, two, three, four
Jingle at the cottage door.
Five, six, seven, eight
Jingle at the cottage gate.

(Traditional, England, adapted)

ART

Provide a comfortable table or desk and chair, an easel, or a high chair for your child's art activities. Do art at quieter times; don't try to force her attention when she wants to run around. Her work will not be "ART" as representation, but art as a process. Don't ask her what she is creating, but offer constructive comments, such as, "I like this patch of blue," "These lines are interesting," or "I like your red zig-zags." Enjoy the spontaneous beauty she creates. Keep art materials handy and be free with them. Don't expect her art play to last longer than 15 to 30 minutes, although if she is intensely interested, it may last much longer.

Selection of Art Materials

Set aside a separate shelf or drawer in which to store your child's art materials. When choosing an art material, ask yourself these questions:

- Is it non-toxic?
- Can it be easily stored?
- Can she use it with minimal assistance?
- Can she control the material?

Buy good-quality paper, good-quality paint, and good-quality brushes. The slight differences in price will pay dividends.

Art Materials to Accumulate

B esides being non-toxic, art materials should
contain no solvents. Water-soluble felt
markers making both thin and thick lines, crayons,
water pastels, tempera paints, finger paints, chalk,
white glue, glue sticks, and playdough are all lots
of fun for her.

HINT: Try putting playdough through your garlic press to make "hair" for her creations.

Over time, accumulate the following materials
for use in paintings, collages, sculptures, cut-outs,
and other art projects:

- acorns • aluminum foil • apple seeds
- ballpoint pens (biro) • beads • bobby pins
- bottle caps • broken toy parts • candy wrappers
- carbon paper • cardboard • candles
- cellophane • chalk • charcoal • checkers
- chestnuts • clean bones • clothespins • cloves
- coins • confetti • conté • costume jewelry
- cotton balls • cotton batting • dominoes
- dried beans • driftwood • dried pasta
- dried weeds • dry cereals • egg cartons
- egg shells • emery boards • empty pill bottles
- faucet washers • feathers • felt
- film cartridges • fishing lures—without hooks
- food colors • fur • gift wrap • glitter
- gold and silver thread • google eyes
- graph paper • gravel • gummed paper
- gummed stars • kleenex • lace
- leather scraps • magnets • metallic papers
- milkweed pods • orange pits
- paint sample chips • paper • paper clips
- paper fasteners • paper muffin cup liners
- paper punch • paper tubes • paste
- pastels (chalk or oil) • pebbles • pine cones
- pipe cleaners • pinking shears • popcorn
- rickrack • ribbon • ruler • sand • sandpaper
- scissors • seeds, nuts • sequins • shoe strings
- silver dragées • soap • sponges • spools
- stapler • stickers • straw • string • styrofoam
- tape • thread • tongue depressors • toothpicks
- tree bark • velvet/velveteen scraps • vermiculite
- watercolors • white glue • wine corks
- wooden skewers • yarns • other "junk"

Glue Collage

U sing glue sticks, diluted white glue or home-
made glue, have your toddler glue various
bits and pieces to each other, onto paper or a large
cardboard surface. What to glue? Start with paper
bits, junk mail, paper bags, styrofoam bits, greet-
ing cards, string or yarn, wrapping paper, fabric
bits, salt, rice, cornmeal, lentils, and anything else
you can think of.

Note: Do NOT allow your child to use rubber cement, airplane glue, or contact cement as they all
contain dangerous solvents.

Glue

B ring to a full, rolling boil ¾ cup water, 2
Tbsps corn syrup, and 1 tsp white vinegar.
Mix together separately ½ cup cornstarch mixed
with ¾ cup cold water. Stirring constantly, add
this mixture slowly to the hot mixture. Let stand
overnight before using.

More About Pastes and Glues

T he most satisfactory and safe glues for your
toddler are library paste, commercial paste,
mucilage, diluted white glue, glue sticks, and
wallpaper paste. If you are using flimsy papers,
such as rice paper or tissue paper, liquid starch
makes good paste.

Foot Painting

Spread large sheets of butcher or finger paint paper on a floor covered with newspapers. Add about ½ tsp liquid tempera paint to about ¼ cup buttermilk. Pour onto the glossy side of the paper. Remove your child's shoes and socks and encourage her to walk, stamp, and slide her feet through the paint to make different effects. This will be SLIPPERY, so hold her hands! Have a pail of warm, soapy water and a towel ready to clean her feet.

Finger Paint

1 cup lump laundry starch dissolved in cold
   water
1 quart boiling water
1 cup pure white soap flakes (not detergent) or
powder
   (Flakes are preferable.)
Poster paint, water crayons, or food coloring, for
   colors*

Add the boiling water to the starch and cold water mixture and boil until thick. Remove from heat and stir in the soap. Divide into small containers and add colors as desired.

*Cornstarch or 1 cup liquid starch can be substituted for the lump starch, but the result isn't quite as good.

Finger Painting

Use finger paint paper, the shiny side of butcher's paper, waxed paper, or any other smooth-surfaced paper. If you don't have finger paints available, substitute toothpaste, cold cream, hand lotion, liquid soap, salad oil, vaseline, tomato paste, or finely textured cereal.

Challenge Your Child

Give your child the freedom to let her imagination soar when she uses her art materials. Vary the kinds, shapes, sizes, and proportions of the materials that you provide.

Challenge her with variety. Make holes in some of the pieces of paper you give her. Make circles, triangles, squares, diamonds, ovals, free forms, hexagons, regular and irregular shapes to paint or color. Vary the colors she uses.

Goop

Goop can be pressed, rolled, punched, pinched, poked, prodded, and manipulated in every way. Your toddler NEEDS to play with goop. It can be potter's clay, plasticine, play dough, baker's clay or dough. She needs to use her goop spontaneously. Show her the different textures and effects that can be made using hands, elbow, fingers, knees, knuckles and toes. Rolling pins and cookie cutters can also be used occasionally, but encourage her to find other ways to handle the material. Goop provides great satisfaction as it is squeezed, banged, and pulled into different shapes.

Pat-a-Cake (Baker's Clay)

Mix thoroughly 4 cups all-purpose flour and 1 cup salt. Add 1 ½ cups cold water and mix well. Knead for at least ten minutes, or process with a steel blade in a food processor. This ensures that the mixture will bind and not fall apart when it is being worked. Form shapes as though the mixture were clay. Add pasta, acorns, or other art materials if you wish. Allow to air-dry, or bake in a 200-225° F oven for 2 to 3 hours until thoroughly dry. Paint the finished articles with bright colors. If you want a hole in the object, make the hole while the dough is still soft.

Baker's clay is great for making Christmas tree ornaments. Cut out the dough with cookie cutters and use a straw to make a hole for the string. This dough keeps well in a sealed plastic bag, and can be frozen and defrosted. It is best if made a day in advance and allowed to sit in a sealed package.

Heavenly Playdough

Boil ½ cup salt in 2 cups water until the salt dissolves. Add food coloring, tempera powder, or water crayon for color. Add 2 Tbsps salad oil, 2 cups sifted all-purpose flour, and 2 Tbsps alum (available at your drugstore). Knead or process until an even consistency results. Keep in an airtight container or a plastic bag. The dough will last two months or longer.

(You can substitute cornmeal or whole wheat flour for the all-purpose flour to achieve a different consistency.)

WORD PLAY

Reading is becoming more and more important as she grows. Although she still loves her old favorites, now is the time to gradually introduce more sophisticated books to her library. Select books with large type and add books with more words than pictures. Try the Babar books in the "I Can Read It Myself" series by Random House. Even though your child is probably not talking much yet, she is growing daily in understanding, and her books teach her more and more.

Books with rhyming words are essential for language development. Continue reading Dr. Seuss, and try Mercer Mayer's inexpensive books about the "Little Critter," because they reflect your toddler's concerns. You can pick up reasonably priced books at the supermarket that cost no more than a candy bar, and have far fewer calories.

Signs

Familiar signs and symbols begin to mean something to your toddler. She may learn, for example, that a red octagon with white letters means "STOP." Point out to her your name on the mailbox or gate, the logo of your gas station, and the sign for her favorite restaurant chain. The idea isn't to teach reading, but to have her recognize that symbols have meanings.

Tactile Words

To develop your child's vocabulary, provide tactile experiences simultaneously with certain words, for example: rough, smooth, coarse, stringy, fuzzy, hairy, slimy, hard, soft, furry, sticky, spongy, crunchy, prickly, wiry, grainy, slick, soft, crinkly, gritty, sandy, velvety, satinny, bumpy, sharp, slippery, gooey.

Billy Is Blowing His Trumpet

(For you, when it's one of THOSE days.)

Billy is blowing his trumpet,
Bertie is banging a tin.
Betty is crying for Mommy,
And Bob has pricked Ben with a pin.
Baby is crying out loudly,
He's out on the lawn in his pram.
I am the only one silent,
And I've eaten all of the jam.

(Great Britain, Anonymous)

Typewriter/Computer

If you have an old typewriter, or can pick one up cheaply at a secondhand store or garage sale, let your child bash away at the keyboard. If you have a typewriter or a computer at home, let your toddler watch you use it and occasionally hold her in your lap and let her touch the letters and numbers.

Your toddler may well encounter her first computer at nursery school. Some computer programs are designed for children as young as one year old, and computer day camps abound for children starting at age four. Do let her know computers, and keyboards, are there, and that they are manageable.

If you have a home computer, look into some of the very good children's software programs on the market, and introduce your child to the functions. She may well outpace you in computer literacy.

Write a Story Together

Your toddler loves a story in which she is the central character. Write stories together about events in her life. A story has a beginning, a middle, and an end. Start a sentence and let her try to complete it. Say, for example, "[child's name] went to town, and she saw a ———." Write down her responses. Once you and she have written her story, illustrate it with drawings, photographs, or pictures from magazines. Your child can help select and glue in the pictures.

Make Up Stories About Your Toddler

Thinly disguise your toddler as the heroine in stories you make up. Give all of your stories happy endings with any conflicts resolved. Substitute a different name for the heroine, but let your child realize she is the STAR of the story. Feature familiar incidents, and perhaps help your shy or angry child to deal with difficult situations by resolving conflicts with happy endings. Acknowledge your child's frightening feelings and give her the distance required to be able to see solutions through her story.

Relate the Day's Events as a Story

"There once was a little girl named ———. One day she and her Daddy woke up, got dressed, and ———. They had a good time at the ———. They saw a ———, a ———, and a ———.

They had ——— for lunch. ——— had a nap. Later on, ——— went to ———.

She had a lovely day, didn't she? What will ——— do tomorrow?"

Use this opportunity to make plans for the next day with your toddler, so that she feels she has some say in her activities.

Concepts

Discuss letters, numbers, shapes, sizes, colors, and patterns as they occur in your child's daily life. She will absorb a great deal of information at this age. Some children even know how to count to ten and know the alphabet, even though they may not be talking yet. Discuss, for example, the circular shapes of the sun and moon, count objects up to ten, and point out and label all the colors in her environment. Talk about the red balloon, the white snow, the green grass, or the yellow flower. Make sure she is exposed to the concepts that structure our world and simplify our lives.

KITCHEN PLAY

Your older toddler can help in the kitchen in many ways. She can help you squeeze orange juice, shell peas, cut out cookies, and wash vegetables. She can also help you measure and sift dry ingredients, and she loves to help you stir. Take the time to teach her how to cook. Keep instructions clear, simple, and concrete. Repetition helps. Praise and encourage everything she does!!! Have your child participate whenever possible in your kitchen activities. The kitchen is an ideal place for creating wonderful smells and tastes. Talk about everything as she helps.

Pancakes

1 ½ cups sifted flour
   (all-purpose or a combination of whole grain
   flours)
Re-sift flour with:
      1 tsp salt
      3 Tbsp sugar or brown sugar
      2 tsps baking powder

Beat together:
      1 or 2 eggs
      3 Tbsps salad oil or melted butter
      1-1 1/4 cups milk

   Stir wet ingredients quickly into dry ones. Ig-nore any lumps. Cook on a lightly greased griddle, turning once. Serve immediately with jam or syrup.

Animal Pancakes

Y ou need pancake batter and a frying pan. Heat the frying pan and add a few drops of oil. As you drop the batter into the pan, move the spoon to make shapes. For instance, make a snake or a worm pancake by dropping the batter in a wiggly line. Make a mouse with an oval body, small drops for the head, ears, and feet, and a thin line for a tail. One big spoonful of batter sur-rounded by six droplets can make a turtle. Try making a bird, an elephant and a giraffe. These pancakes may encourage a picky eater, especially if she helps you make them.

Butterfly Sandwiches

B y cutting sandwiches diagonally and revers-ing the halves, you form a butterfly. You can make either one large butterfly or two small but-terflies from one sandwich. You can make open-faced butterfly sandwiches spread with cream cheese or spreading cheese. Decorate with banana slices, raisins, pickles, and/or pieces of soft fruit. Use pepper strips or vegetable sticks as antennae. Your toddler will be delighted to help decorate these sandwiches.

INDOOR GAMES

H ave your child accompany you in your household tasks. Have a mock pillow fight when you make the beds. She can help you sort the laundry and match the socks. Give her some responsibilities, like feeding the dog or cat, and help empty wastebaskets into the garbage bag. Helping with chores develops her sense of respon-sibility, as well as her sense of being part of the family. At the same time, she is learning matching and sorting skills that will last a lifetime. What to you is work is play to her, so let her help. It can be fun for both of you. Say favorite rhymes and sing favorite songs as you work together.

Junk Mail

Y our older toddler can play with the un-solicited mail that fills your mailbox. The best kind has pretty stickers and seals that are bet-ter than the ones bought in stores. Our favorites come from book clubs, record clubs, and a huge assortment of charities.

   HINT: The Post Office has 1¢ stamps that are cheaper and prettier than most of the stickers you buy as art materials. They look real for her "let-ters," too.

Sandbox

Place cornmeal, puffed wheat, puffed rice or puffed millet in a box or suitcase. Hide some small plastic toys under the cereal and ask her to find the toy. She is also ready to use her sandbox for a fishing expedition. Place a magnet on a string and hide some metal washers and nuts in the cereal. Have her "fish" for the metal pieces using her magnetic fishing line.

Plastic Animals

Buy small, inexpensive plastic animals, bugs, creepie-crawlies, turtles, flowers, dragons, and dinosaurs from the gift shops at museums, science centers, zoos, or dime stores. Bury them in her sandbox, or plop them in her bath. Don't forget some for busy bags (p. 145)!

Growing Plants

Teach your toddler to grow her own plants from seeds or cuttings. Soak orange, apple, grapefruit, lemon, or lime seeds in water for a day or two. Fill a planter with potting soil and place three or four seeds in each one about ½" deep. Water and place in a sunny spot. Soon you'll see green shoots!

You can also grow avocado pits, carrot tops, sweet potato vines, and potato eyes from your kitchen compost. Check your cooking supplies for popcorn seeds or dried beans that might grow, too.

Forcing Bulbs

As winter deepens throughout January, nothing is as cheerful as spring flowers. Daffodils, paperwhites, narcissi, amaryllises, crocuses, and hyacinths can all be made to bloom indoors during the winter. Place the bulbs in a shallow pot and cover with vermiculite, peat moss, or gravel. Follow the instructions that come with the bulbs. Place in a sunny window. Water and watch! Your toddler will love to help with the planting and watering.

QUIET TIMES

Set up an area into which your child can retreat for a while when she needs a break from too much action. Call this area her "cave" or "den" or "office," or her "special space." Furnish this special place with some colorful cushions, a child-sized desk or table and chair, and a few of her favorite books. She may retreat on her own, but at other times you may decide to separate her from an unpleasant situation, telling her to come back when she feels ready to participate.

Talk About Her Emotions

Ask your child how she is feeling, and discuss how you're feeling too. Talk about the facial expressions of emotions and how others are feeling. Share your own emotions with her. Say, "I'm happy," "sad," "frightened," "angry," "grumpy," "tired," or "bored." Let her know that we all have emotions and we can all deal with them.

Show her the facial expressions associated with various feelings. Cut pictures out of magazines that show the faces of people experiencing a variety of emotions.

If You're Happy and You Know It

(Do the actions as you sing.)

If you're happy and you know it, clap your hands!
        (Clap, clap)
If you're happy and you know it, clap your hands!
        (Clap, clap)
*If you're happy and you know it and you really
    want to show it,*
If you're happy and you know it, clap your hands!
        (Clap, clap)

Mad—stomp your feet...
Surprised—raise your eyebrows...
Sad—wipe your eye...
Agree—nod your head...
Tired—stretch and yawn...
Confused—turn around...
Happy—shout "Hooray!"...

Cramped—wiggle your fingers...
Unhappy—cry "boo hoo"...

(Traditional, Great Britain, North America)

Quiet Songs and Rhymes

Continue to recite quiet rhymes and to sing quiet songs during the transition to a nap or bedtime. Reading can be lots of fun during a very quiet time.

Bye'm Bye

Bye'm bye, bye'm bye, stars shining.
Number, number one, number two, number three,
Number four, number five, oh my!
Bye'm bye, bye'm bye, oh my! Bye'm bye.

(Traditional, Southern United States)

Sur Le Pont d'Avignon

Sur le pont d'Avignon,
L'on y danse, l'on y danse;
Sur le pont d'Avignon,
L'on y danse tout en rond.

(Traditional, France)

All For Baby

Here's a ball for baby,
> (Hands make a big round ball shape.)

Big and soft and round
Here's the baby's hammer
> (Pretend to hammer.)

See how she can pound.

Here's the baby's music
Clapping, clapping so
> (Clap hands softly.)

Here are baby's soldiers
Standing in a row.
> (Fingers up in a row.)

Here's the baby's trumpet
Toot, too, toot, too, too
> (Pretend to play trumpet.)

Here's the way that baby
Plays at "peek-a-boo"
> (Hide face and play peek-a-boo.)

Here's the big umbrella
Keeps the baby dry
> (Put up imaginary umbrella.)

Here's the baby's cradle
Rock-a-baby bye.
> (Rock imaginary baby, or use doll.)

(Emilie Poulson, United States, 1890)

OUTDOORS

Outdoor Boundaries

A country child has more freedom to explore her environment and to establish her own boundaries than a city child. These psychological boundaries indicate how far away from you she feels safe. Let a city child establish some boundaries in a large park or on visits to friends living in the country. Of course use common sense to keep tiny children from straying beyond your visual range.

Ideal Outdoor Play Space

Your child needs a safe and stimulating place to play outdoors. Perhaps there is a yard, park, or schoolyard that you and she can visit on your daily walk. Her ideal play area should include: a place to run, a place to climb safely, a place to slide, a place to play with sand and water, a place for riding and pedal toys, a place to swing, a place to roughhouse on the grass, and a place where grownups can sit comfortably and supervise the activities.

Balance Beam Walking

Once your toddler can walk steadily, hold her hand and have her walk on a curbstone (when there is no traffic), or on a low wall as though she were on a balance beam. Let her walk around the edge of her sandbox, if it's sturdy enough.

Show her how to balance with arms outstretched as she walks in a straight line. As her coordination improves, show her how to walk sideways along the beam, crossing her legs. As she approaches her third birthday, add hopping, jumping, and perhaps somersaults to her balance-beam walking. Tell her to keep her head up as she walks along.

Interesting Places

Make short expeditions to interesting places where your toddler can learn about her place in the world. Visit a beekeeper, an apple orchard, a sugarbush in the spring, a vegetable farm.

A trip to the fire station or police station will help her understand how police officers and fire fighters are able to help her if she gets lost or in trouble.

A trip to an airport, bus terminal, or railway station will provide her with a greater understanding of what her toys represent. A visit to a construction site, to watch the big machinery, is entertaining for children of all ages. One dad we know takes his daughter to sewage and water pumping stations, generators, and garbage dumps. They have a ball!

Gardening

Show your child how food and flowers grow. Garden plots are available in most cities, and sometimes farmers rent out space to "city folk" if you don't have your own garden, yard, or balcony space. Let your child have her own trowel and some seeds to plant (cress, radishes, lettuce, spinach, and chard grow quickly and are easy to tend). Even planting seeds in a flower pot can sometimes produce an edible crop. The most important part of the process for a toddler is digging in the dirt, and then seeing the product of her digging.

Plant your child's favorite vegetables or those that yield especially pretty and tasty crops. The most interesting vegetables for children to plant are radishes, zucchini, pumpkins, lettuce, tomatoes, carrots, peas, and beans. As you garden together, you can recite rhymes about farming, gardening, and agriculture.

Oats, Peas, Beans, and Barley Grow

(A circle game. One child—the farmer—stands in center. The others circle around the farmer, holding hands.)

Oats, peas, beans, and barley grow,
Oats, peas, beans, and barley grow.
You and I and everyone know
How oats, peas, beans, and barley grow.

First the farmer sows his seeds.
        (The farmer performs the actions.)
Then he stands and takes his ease,
Stamps his foot, and claps his hand,
And turns around to view his land.

Waiting for a partner,
        (The farmer selects another person
Waiting for a partner,
        to come into the center of the circle.)
So open the ring and let one in
So oats, peas, beans, and barley grow.
        (The person selected becomes the next
        farmer and the game continues.)

(Traditional, Great Britain, and North America)

Intery, Mintery

(This rhyme is frequently used to "count out" who is "it" in a game. All hands are extended into the middle of a circle while one person taps them with a fist as the rhyme is recited.)

Intery, mintery, cutery corn,
Apple seed and apple thorn.
Wire, briar, limber lock,
How many geese to make a flock?
One flew east and one flew west.
One flew over the cuckoo's nest.

(Traditional, United States)

C H A P T E R   E I G H T

What Are You Doing? Making a Mess!

Twenty-four to Thirty Months

The "twos" are a challenge! Your toddler realizes he is a separate person and he wants to express his own personality. Cooperation and sharing can be difficult, yet cooperation and even sharing sometimes occur spontaneously between two children when you least expect it. It is easier at this age to have two children the same age play together, since they keep each other entertained and require less adult participation. If your child is not in daycare, enroll him in a play group or nursery school and participate yourself. Several mornings a week is enjoyable for him.

Action songs and games continue to be important to him, and emerge in all parts of his life. Sing and dance with him whenever possible.

Your two-year-old's speech begins to echo adult speech patterns. He is learning about opposites: yes/no, under/over, up/down, fast/slow, in/out and yes/no. Make sure your play includes these concepts, as well as numbers, letters, shapes, and colors, in a matter-of-fact way. Don't try to "teach" him these concepts; just incorporate them into his daily life.

Your child enjoys manipulating objects, taking them apart, and putting them together again. He learns through constant construction and destruction, building towers out of blocks, for the joy of knocking them down again. He tests everything constantly: the limits you set, his own physical skills, his manual dexterity, and his own abilities.

He wants to do everything himself. Let him, as long as it is safe.

MOVEMENT

He wants to walk everywhere without your help. He loves rough-and-tumble games and climbing on gym equipment. He may have some difficulty running, jumping, climbing, walking, and turning corners, so accidents and frustrations are frequent. He can now open doors and unscrew jars. He still drops things often, because his fingers just haven't completely developed yet. Play lots of action and finger play games with him, and encourage him to focus on his movements so his coordination will improve.

Simon Says

Have your child mimic your actions as you jump up and down, take steps, make faces, and say funny things. When he is accustomed to mimicking your actions, tell him to imitate you when "Simon says," and to stay still when "Simon" doesn't say to do a certain action.

Jelly in the Bowl

Jelly in the bowl,
(March to the beat.)
Jelly in the bowl.
Wibble wobble, wibble wobble,
(Say in a funny voice and wiggle all over.)
Jelly in the bowl.
(March again.)

(Traditional, unknown)

Use regular, fast, and slow tempos, and high- and low-pitched voices. You can also mouth the words. Vary the actions according to tempo and pitch.

Teddy Bear, Teddy Bear

Teddy bear, teddy bear,
> (Sitting on floor, clap hands twice.)

Turn around.
> (Spin around on bottom.)

Teddy bear, teddy bear,
> (Clap hands twice.)

Touch the ground.
> (Tap the floor.)

Teddy bear, teddy bear,
> (Clap hands twice.)

Shine your shoes.
> (Wipe shoes with hands.)

Teddy bear, teddy bear,
> (Clap hands twice.)

That will do!
> (Cross arms emphatically.)

(Traditional, Great Britain, North America)

The Wheels on the Bus

The wheels on the bus go 'round and 'round,
> (Sitting on floor, make circles with hands, to show wheels turning.)

'Round and 'round, 'round and 'round.
The wheels on the bus go 'round and 'round,
All through the town-o.

The people on the bus go up and down...
> (Bounce up and down.)

The wipers on the bus go swish, swish, swish...
> (Move feet back and forth for wipers.)

The money on the bus goes clink, clank, clunk...
> (Drop coins in imaginary box.)

The babies on the bus go "Wah, wah, wah!"...
> (Rub eyes.)

The mommies on the bus go "Sh-sh-sh!"...
> (Place forefinger over mouth.)

The horn on the bus goes beep, beep, beep...
> (Honk imaginary horn.)

The driver on the bus says, "Move on back!"...
> (Point backwards while turning wheel.)

The daddy on the bus says, "be quiet———"

(Traditional, Great Britain, United States)

One Elephant Went Out to Play

(Children walk around the room, swinging arms to represent elephant trunks. One child selects a second, who selects a third, etc., until all the children are in an elephant parade.)

One elephant went out to play
Upon a spider's web one day;
He had such enormous fun
He sent for another elephant to come.

Two elephants went out to play
Upon a spider's web one day;
They had such enormous fun
They sent for another elephant to come.

(Traditional, Great Britain, North America)

Un éléphant se balançait
Sur une toile d'araignée.
Il trouva ça si amusant
Qu'il appela un autre éléphant.

Deux éléphants se balançaient
Sur une toile d'araignée.
Ils trouverent ça si amusant
Qu'ils appelerent un autre éléphant.

(Traditional, France)

"One Elephant, Deux éléphants" is one of Sharon, Lois & Bram's signature songs. The song originated in France.

A Ram Sam Sam*

A ram sam sam,
>   (Pound fists.)

A ram sam sam,
Guli, guli, guli, guli, guli,
>   (Pull fingers of both hands apart horizontally.)

Ram sam sam.

(Repeat.)

A rafi, a rafi
>   (Throw hands up in air.)

Guli, guli, guli, guli, guli,
Ram sam sam.

(Repeat)

(Traditional, Morocco)

*"Ram sam sam" is pronounced "Rum sum sum."
"A Ram Sam Sam" can be heard on *Songs and Games for Toddlers*, Bob McGrath and Katherine Smithrim, Kids' Records.

Pease Porridge Hot

(A chant for two people)
Pease porridge hot,
>   (Clap on stressed words: thighs, hands, partner's hands.)

Pease porridge cold,
>   (Thighs, hands, partner's hands.)

Pease porridge in the pot
>   (Thighs, hands, partner's right hand, own hands, partner's left hand.)

Nine days old.
>   (Thighs, hands, partner's hands.)

Some like it hot,
>   (Repeat actions.)

Some like it cold,
Some like it in the pot
Nine days old.

(Traditional, Great Britain, North America)

Little Rabbit Foo Foo

(A sitting-down circle game)

One child is selected to be Rabbit Foo Foo, one to be the Good Fairy, and the rest are field mice. This popular game provides opportunities to deal with fears in a safe way. In the second verse, the Good Fairy can indicate as many chances as there are children, so every child has a chance to be Rabbit Foo Foo.

Little Rabbit Foo Foo
>   (Rabbit Foo Foo hops around.)

Hopping through the forest,
>   (Pretends to scoop up a mouse.)

Scooping up the field mice,
>   (Claps hands, and taps another child

Bop them on the head.
>   lightly on the head.)

Down came the Good Fairy
>   (Child flits like fairy.)

And she said:
>   (Shakes head, wags finger.)

"Little Rabbit Foo Foo,
>   (Good Fairy hops around like Rabbit Foo Foo.)

I don't want to see you
>   (Shakes head, wags finger.)

Scooping up the field mice,
>   (She scoops up field mice

Bopping them on the head.
>   and claps hands.)

So I'll give you ——— more chances.
>   (Holds up number of fingers.)

And if YOU misbehave,
>   (Everyone wags fingers,

I'm going to turn you into a GOON!"
>   wiggles fingers in ears, and sticks out tongue.)

Next morning:

Little Rabbit Foo Foo
Hopping through the forest,
Scooping up the field mice,
Bop them on the head.

The Good Fairy comes and offers one less chance.
This continues until all the chances are used up. In
the Good Fairy's last appearance, she says:

"Little Rabbit Foo Foo,
I really warned you,
And you didn't stop.
Now you are a GOON! Poof!"

And the moral of the story is:
"Hare today, Goon tomorrow!"

(in unison)

(Traditional, North America)

As I Was Walking Down the Street

(One child walks, selects another child who joins
hands, and they dance to the rig-a-jig-jig. Con-
tinue, with the chosen friend selecting another
friend until everyone is dancing.)

As I was walking down the street
Down the street, down the street
A little friend I chanced to meet
Hi-ho, hi-ho, hi-ho.

A rig-a-jig-jig and away we go
Away we go, away we go
A rig-a-jig-jig and away we go
Hi-ho, hi-ho, hi-ho.

...A pretty bird I chanced to meet
...A great big dinosaur
...A huge long snake
...A kangaroo
...A big grey elephant

(Let the child pretend to be the animal sung...a
bird waves arms and cheeps...a snake crawls on
the ground on his tummy and hisses...a kangaroo
hops...whatever his imagination, and yours,
suggests.)

(Traditional, North America)

Triangle Stretches

S it on the floor with your child, facing each other in the straddle position, or as close as you can get to him and hold hands. Lean forward and have your child lean back, then alternate. Sing "Row, Row, Row Your Boat" (p. 58), or say some rocking rhymes like the one below as you lean back and forth.

See-saw, Margery Daw

(Hold hands and rock back and forth.)

See-saw, Margery Daw,
Jacky shall have a new master;
Jacky shall have but a penny a day
Because he can work no faster.

(Traditional, England)

Swivel Hips

Lie on the floor with your child. Flex one leg so your knee is above your chest. Put both hands on the knee and rotate your knee and leg out to the side and then back to center. Switch legs. Count, "1, 2, 3, switch, 4, 5, 6, switch." You may want to try this exercise as you sing "I Am Slowly Going Crazy."

I Am Slowly Going Crazy

I am slowly going crazy.
1, 2, 3, 4, 5, 6, switch.
Crazy going slowly am I.
6, 5, 4, 3, 2, 1, switch.
I am slowly going crazy . . . .

(Traditional, United States)

The traditional actions for "I Am Slowly Going Crazy" are cupping one elbow in the palm of the opposite hand and swinging the arm up and down as the counting proceeds. On "switch," the opposite elbow and palm are used. Sharon, Lois & Bram sing this song on their *Singing and Swinging* album, Elephant Records.

Tag

One child is "it," who then runs after another. When he touches the second child, the second child becomes "it," and the game continues. A rule can be no tag backs—the child who was "it" can't be made "it" again immediately. You may want to establish a "safe" place where children can't be tagged.

Musical Chairs

You need enough seats for all but one of the players, arranged next to each other, alternating front/back in a straight line. Players walk in one direction around the seats as music is played or is tapped on a percussion instrument. When the music stops, the players hurry to sit down. One player will be left standing. He sits down on one seat as the game continues. The other players resume walking when the music starts. Each successive time, another eliminated player takes a seat, so those remaining have to walk faster and search harder to get a place when the music stops. Make sure the players keep moving and don't wait for the music to stop.

Running, Jumping

Encourage your child to run and jump. Perhaps you can set up a slalom course in which he can control his running. An obstacle course in which he can crawl, climb, run, jump, and slither is useful in improving his coordination. Throwing balls and having him retrieve them is fun, and playing "catch" with a ball helps his hands do what his eyes tell him to do. Encourage as much physical activity as you can.

My Children Come to Me

(A group game)

This game requires two adults or older children, playing the roles of hawk and hen or rooster, and lots of space.

Draw two lines on the ground, about 60 feet apart. Behind one line is the hawk's nest; behind the other is the chicken coop. The children (chicks) run about in the central area, as the hawk tries to capture them and bring them to the nest. The hen or rooster tries to protect the chicks and to rescue any that have been caught.

Hen or Rooster: My children, come to me!
Chicks: We can't.
Hen or Rooster: Why not?
Chicks: Because the hawk is near.

To vary the game, some children can be baby hawks and capture other children. The chickens can run into the coop for safety at any time.

(Traditional, Tanzania)

WATER PLAY

B ath time may be complicated by the "I want to do it myself" phenomenon. This means that faces and ears don't get wet, while hands and feet are scrubbed amazingly well. To have your child wash his face and behind his ears, play "Simon Says." Use all your bathtub games, and sing more songs to the ducks.

Six Little Ducks

Six little ducks that I once knew,
> (Hold up six fingers; point to oneself.)

Fat ones, skinny ones they were too.
> (Spread arms out; bring hands in.)

But the one little duck with a feather on his back,
> (Wag hand behind back.)

He led the others with a quack, quack, quack.
> (Shake finger; open and shut palms
> horizontally.)

Chorus:
Quack, quack, quack—quack, quack, quack.
He led the others with his quack, quack, quack.

Down to the river they would go,
Wibble-wobble, wibble-wobble, to and fro.
But the one little duck with a feather on his back,
He led the others with a quack, quack, quack.

Home from the water they would come,
Wibble-wobble, wibble-wobble, ho hum hum.
But the one little duck with a feather on his back,
He led the others with a quack, quack, quack.

(Traditional, North America)

Five Green and Speckled Frogs

Five green and speckled frogs
Sat on a speckled log
Eating some most delicious bugs—
Yuummmmmmm, yuuummm!
One jumped into the pool
> (You may substitute your child's name.)

Where it was nice and cool.
Then there were four green speckled frogs.
Ribbit, ribbit!
...four, three, two, one.

(Traditional, North America)

When you're with a group of toddlers at the pool or beach, this song might help get the children into the water without chaos. As you sing each child's name, have him get in. This song also teaches backwards counting and how to wait for a turn. Start with as many frogs as there are children.

Un, Deux, Trois

Un, deux, trois, quatre, cinq, six, sept
> (Show number of fingers.)

Violettes, violettes.
Un, deux, trois, quatre, cinq, six, sept
A bicyclette, à bicyclette.
> (Pedal legs as if on a bicycle.)

(Traditional, French Canada)

I'm Bringing Home My Baby Bumblebee

(Tune: "Turkey in the Straw")

I'm bringing home my baby bumblebee.
> (Swing cupped hands.)

Won't my mommy be so proud of me!
I'm bringing home my baby bumblebee.
Oh-ohhhhh! He STUNG me!
> (Open hands on "Oh-hhhhh!")

I'm squishing up my baby bumblebee.
> (Clap hands together to squish.)

Won't my mommy be so proud of me!
I'm squishing up my baby bumblebee.
Oh-ohhhhh! He's all OVER me!

I'm wiping off my baby bumblebee...
                    (Wipe hands.)
Oh-ohhhhh! It's all over the FLOOR!
I'm vacuuming up my baby bumblebee.
Whirr-whirr-whirr-whirr...
              (Make vacuum cleaner sounds to tune of
              song.)
Oh, it's all GONE now!

(Traditional, North America)

CHANGING GAMES

B uy simple pull-on clothes that your child can manage by himself. Teach him how to put on a front-opening garment, such as a sweater, shirt, or coat. Lay the garment on the floor, front side up. Have your child reach into the sleeves while facing the top of the garment, and flip it over his head and down onto his body. Choose Velcro fastenings whenever possible, especially on sneakers. Continue to play lots of games that include finger movements.

Dressing Up

A s your child enjoys make-believe games more and more, uniforms for "let's pretend" become important to him. Dress-up clothes, handbags, small suitcases, kitchen utensils, lengths of cloth, dolls, stuffed animals, eyeglass frames, toy stethoscopes, hats of all kinds, and boxes all become necessary for his play.

Let's Pretend

Y our child needs to play pretend games that reflect the "real" world. Some enjoyable "let's pretend" games are: being Mommy, Daddy, a police officer, a firefighter, a nurse, a doctor, a dentist, surgeon, older child, animals, a storekeeper, going on a trip, shopping, a pilot, a truck driver, or attending a tea party. Think of your child's favorite occupations, people, or animals and perform the roles.

Make-Believe Shopping

S ave empty tea and cereal boxes, clean plastic containers, and juice cans with reclosable lids. Set up a "play store," perhaps in a kitchen cupboard, or give your child a toy shopping cart to fill up with "groceries." Give him a purse or wallet, containing some make-believe paper money and coins. Have him make up his own grocery list, and give him a shopping bag for his groceries. Take him with you when you do your own grocery shopping, too. Give him "grown-up" clothes to wear shopping, or a store manager's or cashier's "jacket," if you are pretending to be the customer.

Here Is the Sea

Here is the sea

> (Move both hands in wavy pattern.)

The wavy sea
Here is my boat

> (One hand into boat shape, palm up.)

And here is me.

> (Index finger of other hand between
> middle and ring finger of "boat.")

All of the fishes

> (Point index fingers and lower.)

Down below
Wiggle their tails

> (Wave fingers of both hands.)

And AWAY they go!

> (Move hands and arms behind back,
> quickly.)

(Traditional, unknown)

"Here Is the Sea" is consistently one of the favorites in Katharine's *Child•Music Classes.* You can hear it on the record *Songs and Games for Toddlers,* Kids' Records, and see it on the Golden Book Video of the same name.

MUSIC

Sing and dance with your child whenever you have a chance. Have him use his instruments and continue to play his record albums. Get him some toddler albums that feature lots of dancing and imaginative songs.

Your child is gaining more and more control over his singing voice. He is learning to feel the beat and dance spontaneously to his music. He loves rhymes, and he is learning some of his old favorites. He will sing and hum while playing, and he joins in when familiar songs are being sung.

My Grandfather Clock Goes

(Play sticks)

My grandfather clock goes
TICK TOCK TICK TOCK
My kitchen clock goes
Tick-Tock, Tick-Tock, Tick-Tock, Tick-Tock
My little wrist watch goes
tic-tic-tic-tic-tic-tic-tic-tic-tic-tic-tic-STOP

(Traditional, North America, adapted)

The Grand Old Duke of York

(Play sticks)

Oh, the grand old Duke of York,
He had ten thousand men.
He led them up to the top of the hill

> (Click sticks above head

And he led them down again.

> and back down again.)

And when they were up they were up.

> (Click sticks upwards.)

And when they were down they were down.

> (Click sticks downwards.)

And when they were only half way up,

> (Click at waist height.)

They were neither up nor down.

> (Click sticks up and down quickly.)

(Traditional, England)

Going to Kentucky

(Use shakers while singing.)

I was going to Kentucky,
I was going to the fair,
To see a señorita
With flowers in her hair.

Oh, shake it, baby, shake it,
Shake it if you can.
Shake it like a milkshake
And pour it in the can.

> (Tip shaker as though pouring.)

Oh, shake it to the bottom,
(Lower shaker.)
And shake it to the top,
(Raise shaker.)
And shake it round and round and round
(Shake shaker round and round.)
Until it's time to stop. HEY!

(Traditional, United States)

Nobody can better Kim and Jerry Brodey's version on the *Simple Magic* album, Kids' Records, or the *Hats On/Hats Off* video (Golden Book Video).

Bell Horses

(Shake bells to the beat.)

Bell horses, bell horses,
What's the time of day?
One o'clock, two o'clock,
Time to go away.
(Hide bells behind back.)

Little bell, little bell,
(Keep bells behind back.)
Where are you?
Here I am, here I am,
(Bring bells out quickly and shake vigorously.)
How do you do?

(Traditional, Great Britain, North America, adapted)

"Rags"

This is a favorite nursery school song that helps your child imitate actions. It also provides fun with language, role-playing, and pretending. The song encourages your child to improve rhythm and coordination.

I have a dog and his name is Rags.
He eats so much that his tummy sags.
His ears flip-flop,
And his tail wig-wags.
And when he walks he goes zig-zag.

Chorus:

He goes flip-flop, wig-wag, zig-zag.
He goes flip-flop, wig-wag, zig-zag.
He goes flip-flop, wig-wag, zig-zag.
I love Rags, and he loves me.
I love Rags, and he loves me.

My dog Rags he loves to play.
He rolls around in the mud all day.
I whistle, but he won't obey.
He always runs the other way.

Actions:

Tummy sags: Outline imaginary big tummy with your hands.

Flip: Place hands on either side of head (dog's ears), fingers pointing up, palms forward. Drop one hand forward, bending it at the wrist.

Flop: Same as flip, using the other hand.

Wig: Wiggle hips to the right.

Wag: Wiggle hips to the left.

Zig: With arms at sides, bent upwards, at the elbow, point to the left with right index finger and hold.

Zag: Same as zig, but point to the right with left index finger. The wrists cross over in front of you.

Rolls around: Rotate closed hands in front of you.

Runs the other way: Wiggle fingers (dog's feet), while moving first one hand and then the other in opposite directions.

I love Rags: Fling arms open to encompass the world.

And he loves me: Hug yourself.

(Traditional, United States)

Let's Tap Our Legs Together

Let's tap our legs together,
Let's tap our legs together,
Let's tap our legs together,
Because it's fun to do.

Let's clap our hands...
Let's stamp our feet...
Let's hammer the floor...
Let's touch our nose...
Let's wiggle our ears...
Let's all stand up...
Let's all sit down...

(Traditional, North American, adapted)

I Want to Do It Myself

(Sing or chant)

I want to do it myself,
Do it myself, do it myself.
I want to do it myself
And I MEAN it!!!

(Traditional, unknown)

A slightly different version of "I Want to do It Myself" was done by Katharine Smithrim and Bob McGrath on *Songs and Games for Toddlers*, Kids' Records.

ART

Creative play using art materials improves your child's control of his hands, fingers, arms, and shoulders. It also provides him with a sense of pride in his accomplishments of making marks on paper. His accomplishments are many, and he wants more.

Introduce Paints

Introduce your toddler to tempera paints or water colors. Provide a table and chair or an easel, and use masking tape to secure the paper. Use large, soft watercolor brushes. Limit his colors to two or three at the beginning, and supply a separate brush for each color. A green garbage bag, with holes cut for the head and arms, makes a perfect disposable paint smock.

Blowing Paint

Put a bit of thin, watery paint on a piece of paper and have your child blow it around with a straw. Add a second or third color if you wish. Talk about what happens when the colors combine, and experiment with different papers.

Toothpick Painting

L et your toddler dip toothpicks into paint and use the toothpick as a paintbrush. After the painting dries, let him glue the toothpicks he used onto his painting. Use leaves, pinecones, dried milkweed pods, feathers or other treasures he finds on his walks as a paintbrush.

Spatter Painting

C ollect some leaves, flowers, ferns, paper shapes, paper clips, elastics, string, or yarn. Place your objects on a piece of paper and have your child spatter paint over them. A toothbrush dipped in paint and rubbed over a piece of screening or a hand-held sieve makes fine droplets of paint, while a regular brush dipped in paint and splattered over the paper makes large droplets. Remove the objects from the paper, and talk to your child about the negative images that appear. Glue your paint-covered objects onto cardboard to make a collage.

Crayon Rubbings

P eel the paper off several crayons or use artist conté or charcoal. Then place a piece of paper over an interesting texture—a leaf, string, pavement, carpet, printed plaques, a piece of wood, tree bark, carved stones, or sidewalks. Rub the sides of the crayons over the paper. Perhaps you can go on a "rubbings" walk to collect an assortment of interesting textures. When you come home, cut up some of the textures to glue onto a collage.

Resist Drawings

T his type of painting relies on the principle that wax repels water. Have your child scribble with his crayons on a piece of soft construction, rice, pastel, watercolor, or other matte paper. Afterwards, have him paint the entire picture with a translucent watercolor paint, dye, or diluted ink wash. Use a thick-hair watercolor brush or

Chinese pen. The wax areas "resist" the ink and the painting glows. To save this type of picture apply a thin coat of varnish over the whole design before having it matted and framed.

Blotch Paintings

W et a sheet of soft paper, such as rice paper, watercolor paper, or construction paper. Have your child dribble drops of color onto the wet surface and watch the blotches spread. Secure the picture to a solid surface with masking tape so it will stay flat while drying.

Save Crayon Ends

D on't throw away those bits and pieces of crayons. Put them in the bottom of a muffin tin, heat them and then cool them to form crayon "cookies" that are quite manageable for small hands. Crayon bits can also be added to melted paraffin to make candles, or used in melted waxed paper masterpieces.

Butterfly Inkblots

D ab two or three blobs of wet paint onto a piece of paper. A tiny bit of black is a good color to use as a highlight—add just a bit to the other colors. Fold the paper and let your child smear the paint around with either his fist or his fingers. Unfold.

String Painting

D ip various types and lengths of string and yarn into paint and then drag them across a piece of paper. Compare the effect created when you drag the string across wet paper. Dab paint on another piece of paper, fold and pull a piece of string through the paint.

Three-Dimensional String Painting

Mix paint half-and-half with liquid starch. Wet some string in the paint/starch solution and drop it onto some paper. Let the painting dry. The starch will make the string stick to the paper.

Sandpaper

Fine sandpaper is a wonderful art paper. Use chalk, crayon, or water pastels on fine sandpaper for especially bright effects. Paste bits of paper onto the sandpaper to create contrasts in texture as well as color.

WORD PLAY

Words, Shapes, A, B, C, and 1, 2, 3

Your child is learning to distinguish and imitate sounds. He can compare and describe the sounds he hears. He begins to understand how words influence us, and how they can provide information about happiness, danger, sadness and mirth.

Present counting, shapes, and the alphabet as a natural part of your child's life. Supply simple, colorful ABC and counting books. Let him realize that words are made from letters, and that letters and numbers are essential in our daily lives. Point out the shapes in his world; for instance, a full moon is shaped like a circle, and a spruce tree is shaped like a triangle. Keep reciting poetry and rhymes to him, and if poetry and rhymes feature numbers or letters, so much the better.

The Counting Lesson

Here is the beehive.
> (Hold right fist upright with thumb tucked inside.)

Where are the bees?
Hidden away where nobody sees.
Soon they come creeping out of the hive.
> (Take thumb out of the fist on "one.")

One! Two! Three! Four! Five!
> (Then the other fingers.)

Buzzzzz-zzz-zz-zz-zz!
> (Flutter fingers away behind back.)

Once I saw an ant-hill
> (Hold left fist horizontal with thumb tucked inside.)

With no ants about;
So I said, "Dear little ants,
Won't you please come out?"
Then as if the little ants
Heard my call—
One! Two! Three! Four! Five!
> (Take thumb out on " one," then the other fingers.)

Came out. And that was all!

(Emilie Poulsson, United States, 1893)

One, Two, Three

One, two, three,
> (Hold up three fingers, one at a time.)

Mother* caught a flea,
> (Catch an imaginary flea.)

Put it in the teapot
> (Pretend to pop flea into teapot.)

And made a cup of tea.
> (Pour imaginary water.)

Oooops!
> (Act surprised.)

*Substitute "Daddy," "Auntie," "Nanny"...

(Traditional, England)

I Have Ten Little Fingers

I have ten little fingers,
          (Extend ten fingers.)
They all belong to me.
          (Point to self.)
I can make them do things,
          (Wiggle them.)
Would you like to see?

I can open them up wide,
          (Spread them apart.)
I can shut them up tight,
          (Make fists.)
I can put them together, and
          (Touch palms together.)
Put them out of sight.
          (Put them behind back.)

I can jump them high,
          (Raise hands above head.)
I can jump them down low,
          (Lower them to floor.)
I can fold them quietly,
          (Fold them.)
And sit just so.
          (Sit still.)

(Traditional, England)

The Ants Go Marching

(Tune: "When Johnny Comes Marching Home Again")

(This is one of those songs children adore, but can drive grownups around the bend after the eightieth repetition.)

The ants go marching one by one, hurrah, hurrah!
The ants go marching one by one, hurrah, hurrah!
The ants go marching one by one,
The little one stopped to suck his thumb,
And they all went marching down
To the earth to get out of the rain.
Boom, boom, boom.

The ants go marching two by two...The little one stopped to tie his shoe.
The ants go marching three by three...The little one stopped to climb a tree.
The ants go marching four by four...The little one stopped to knock at the door.
The ants go marching five by five...The little one stopped to do the jive.
The ants go marching six by six...The little one stopped to pick up sticks.
The ants go marching seven by seven...The little one stopped to go to heaven.
The ants go marching eight by eight...The little one stopped to close the gate.
The ants go marching nine by nine...The little one stopped to walk on a line.
The ants go marching ten by ten...The little one stopped to say, "THE END!"

(Traditional, United States)

As you begin each verse hold up the corresponding number of fingers. For the marching action, you and your child can use your fingers, or march around. If you can stand it, you might want to introduce "100 Bottles of Pop on the Wall," which of course descends to your tolerance level.

Make a Felt Board

Cover a heavy piece of cardboard, two feet by three feet, with felt. Cut different shapes, sizes, letters, and numbers from felt of contrasting colors to adhere to the board. Use the felt board to talk about concepts to your child in the same way that a teacher would use a chalk board. Let him handle and arrange the pieces himself. Tell the names of the shapes, colors, numbers, and letters. Line up, for instance, four squares of different sizes and colors. Have him organize the squares according to color, the big red square, the small yellow square. Line up a square, a triangle, an oval, a circle and a rectangle and ask him to bring you each shape you ask for.

Decorate the felt pieces by gluing on beads, macaroni, buttons, bits of felt in contrasting colors, or any other art materials.

HINT: During this stage, your child may sometimes become totally immersed in one activity. We observed one 29-month-old child at our nursery school for about an eight-week period, when she wanted to do art work. She would alternate between the creative table, where she had adult help and supervision, and the easel, where she worked alone. During this eight-week period her average time, per day, spent in these activities was 90 minutes.

If this type of prolonged interest in one activity occurs, go with it, but make sure it doesn't interfere with other essential activities, such as outdoor play, running around, and cuddling.

KITCHEN PLAY

Talk to your child about kitchen "magic": how the batter you pour into the pan turns into a cake; how a solid ice cube melts; how yeast, baking powder, or egg white make food rise as it is baked. Turn on the oven light so he can watch what's happening.

Taste and Smell

Have your child smell or taste a variety of foods and ask him to group them: sweet, salty, bitter, sour, spicy, or tangy. This helps him to not only understand the many flavors of food, but also to sort and classify. Give him blindfold tastes of his favorite foods (mild curry, ice cream, fried chicken, pickles, or cookies) and ask him to describe how the different foods taste.

White Substances

Show your child that not all things that look the same taste the same. Have him taste a variety of plain, white substances that you have in your kitchen, for instance, flour, baking powder, baking soda, alum, cream of tartar, arrowroot, cornstarch, sugar, and salt.

Magic Cookies

Your child will be thrilled to help roll out cookie dough and cut shapes with his own cookie cutters. These cookies can be poked, pushed, prodded, rolled, dropped, sliced, put through a cookie press, or thumbprinted with jam in the center. Add any flavorings or decorations you like.

2 cups sifted flour
1/4 tsp salt
1 egg or 3 egg yolks
⅔ cup soft butter
⅔ cup sugar
1 tsp vanilla   (or other flavoring)

If you have a blender or food processor, blend everything together at once with the steel blade and chill for ½ hour. Otherwise, blend together the butter, sugar, and egg. Add the sifted flour and salt, and mix well. Add the flavoring and chill for ½ hour.

Have your child help you measure and mix all the ingredients. He can also push the "on" and "off" buttons on a blender or food processor.

When you and your child have shaped the cookies, bake them in a 400°F oven for 10 to 12 minutes, depending on the size and thickness of the cookies.

Healthy (and Yummy) Cookies
⅓ cup vegetable oil
¼ cup brown sugar, firmly packed
¼ cup molasses
1 egg beaten
1 cup applesauce or grated apple*
Mix together well. Sift together and add:
1 cup sifted flour (whole wheat, unbleached, or
*   a combination of both)*
¼ cup skim milk powder
1 tsp baking powder
½ tsp allspice, plus ½ tsp cinnamon (if desired)

*or mashed banana, cooked orange squash or pumpkin, shredded zucchini, grated carrots, cooked sweet potato, or a combination of these.

Preheat oven to 400°F. Add dry ingredients to wet ingredients and stir well. Add ¾ cup of raisins or other dried fruit, and 1 ¼ cup quick rolled oats, wheat flakes, or bran cereal. Drop the cookies onto a lightly oiled cookie sheet and bake for about 10 minutes. Remove from pan and allow to cool on a rack before storing.

Your child can help you measure, sift, add, and mix the ingredients. Show him how to use a teaspoon to drop dough onto the baking sheet.

INDOOR GAMES

Your child's imagination starts to soar. Ask him to be a cat, a dog, a worm, a tiger, or a frog and show him how to hop, crawl, wiggle, walk or squirm on all fours. Ask him to be a streetcar, an ambulance, a spaceship, and a car. Continue to provide the basics of his most creative play—sand, water, blocks, and art materials.

Talk to Him—About Everything!

Talk to your child about how he lives and about how other people live. Talk to him about his own house. Then talk about houses where other people live. If you live in the city, talk about the country and what it is like to live there. If you live in the country, talk about the city. Talk about apartments, trailers, houses, and farms.

Talk about this person who "me" is. Tell about where he came from, his family history. Talk about what Daddy and Mommy do at work, and if possible, arrange a visit there. Talk to him about how people live in different countries and about how they are different in some ways from him and similar to him in other ways. Understanding his world through play is your child's work right now.

Puzzles

The more puzzles your child puts together, the more problems he is able to solve. Start with simple puzzles and progress to more complex ones as he matures. Puzzles are endlessly fascinating for him.

Make your own puzzles by gluing a picture to cardboard and cutting the pieces to fit together simply.

What's That Sound?

Talk about all the sounds you hear in your daily life. Make sounds for your child, and use your television and tape recorder as well. Ask your child to identify sounds with his eyes closed.

Match sounds with pictures, for instance, of a fire engine, or musical instruments, or animals.

Make pairs of musical shakers filled with grains, nuts, metal objects, and bells. Have your child match the same sounds.

QUIET TIMES

Teach your child some relaxation exercises. Lie on the floor with him, breathe deeply together, to unwind.

Shake Yourself Out

Lie down quietly in subdued lighting, and "shake yourselves out." Say, "Now we shake our right arm, our left arm, our fingers, our legs, our head and neck, our whole selves, and we breathe: in 1, 2, 3, out 1, 2, 3, in 1, 2, 3, out 1, 2, 3."

Breathe Animal Sounds

After you have shaken yourselves out, shut your eyes. Take a deep breath and breathe out all your air like a snake (ss-sss-sssss-sss-ss-s!) a bee (buzz-zzz-zz-zz-zz!), or an owl (whoo-oo-oooo-ooo!), or...?

Set the Table Together

When you aren't using your most precious dishes, have your child help you set the table. Count out the number of people who will be eating, then count out the same number of knives, forks, and spoons, and show him how to put them on the table properly. Count out the plates, and put them around. Add the napkins and glassware. Tell him that everyone at the table gets one of everything. Have him count the chairs as well, to make sure there are enough.

Put Away the Silverware

Your child can learn sorting and counting skills by helping you put away the clean knives, forks, and spoons. Place your silverware box or plastic utensil holder on the floor so he can put the pieces where they belong. As you take the utensils out of the drainer or the dishwasher, hand him each piece and ask "Where do the forks go?" "How many spoons are there?..."

Count Everything

Count cars parked along the street, your front steps, the number of petals on flowers, the number of peas on your child's plate. By counting, you show him that numbers are more than funny-looking, squiggly lines on a page.

What Fits in What?

Your child is learning about size relationships. Different kinds of nesting toys interest him. Let him experiment to find what goes inside what. Little toys go into some bigger toys, which fit into larger boxes. What does HE fit into?

Colored Lights

Colored lights fascinate your child. He will "oooh!" and "ahhh!" at Christmas lights, he will notice flares on the side of the road when breakdowns occur, and spot emergency vehicles before you do. He loves having candle-lit dinners. Put some cellophane in different colors over a flashlight and let him see the effects of translucent color.

Sing Lullabies and Say Soft Poetry

Even though he is getting quite grown up; he still loves to be cuddled. Have him hold his favorite doll or stuffed animal while you sing lullabies and recite gentle poems together. Rock together, and have him rock his baby as you both wind down.

There Was a Crooked Man

There was a crooked man
And he walked a crooked mile
He found a crooked sixpence
Against a crooked stile;
He bought a crooked cat,
Which caught a crooked mouse
And they all lived together
In a crooked little house.

(Traditional, England)

Little Boy Blue

Little Boy Blue, come blow your horn,
The sheep's in the meadow, the cow's in the corn.
Where is the boy that looks after the sheep?
He's under the haycock, fast asleep.
Will you wake him? No, not I!
For if I do, he's sure to cry.

(Traditional, England)

OUTDOORS

Finding His Way Around

It is important to introduce some sense of direction and purpose to your child's outdoor explorations. Talk about paths, trails, roads, streets, and how to find his way home. As your child approaches age three, he will be able to memorize his address and telephone number. Make sure you include his area code.

Paths and Trails

When you are at a sandy beach, or after a snowstorm, take a walk with your child and leave a trail of footprints in the sand or snow so you can find your way back again. If you are at the ocean, or the wind is blowing, you can point out the necessity of establishing permanent trails or landmarks, because footprints can be blown or washed away. To reinforce this, you can remind your child about how Hansel and Gretel could find their way home after leaving behind them a trail of stones, but got lost when they left a trail of breadcrumbs, eaten by the birds.

Mapping

On your daily walks, show your child landmarks and together draw a simple map of his neighborhood. Include his personal landmarks on his map: his friend's house, where his babysitter lives, the playground, the popsicle store, the fire station — anything that is of special importance to him. Highlight a route on the map from his house to a special place, such as the park. Take the map with you on your walks, and point out the landmarks as you pass them. Show him how to use the map to find his way home again.

When you plan a trip by car, show him the route on the road map, and point out prominent landmarks for him to watch for. Be sure to talk about them throughout your trip.

Follow a Trail

Find a footpath or trail marked out with blazes on trees, or arrows, or painted footprints on a sidewalk. Many cities have parks and zoos full of paths; choose one and follow the route. Have your child try to pick out identifying marks to look for along the way. Show him how he can get back to his starting point by turning around and using the marks to guide him back along the trail, so he won't get lost.

Treasure Hunt

Tie ribbons or crêpe-paper streamers around the park to make your own trail, or hang up arrows leading to a hidden treasure, perhaps a "busy bag" or a couple of small toys hidden in a tree, or covered by leaves (if you don't feel like digging). You can also draw a map that leads to the treasure.

One of the highlights of a trip to the West Indies with a two-and-a-half-year-old was a treasure hunt along a beach. With all the yachts around, a beautiful, warm beach, and a hand-drawn map to find pirate treasure near the brilliant turquoise sea, we felt like we had just stepped off the Spanish Main. The "treasure" of a couple of plastic cars dug up with a shovel and sand pail didn't dim the feeling that perhaps next time we would find pieces of eight.

Electronic Banking

Electronic bank accounts are a lifesaver, especially on those days when the lineups for tellers are long and slow, and your baby is cranky and bored.

What a wonderful way for your child to start to learn about numbers and money! Use your electronic card when there aren't any lineups at the banking machine. Show your two-year-old which buttons to press to make deposits, cash withdrawals and transfers, and to pay bills. Make it clear to him that he only does it when other people aren't waiting to use the machine. Press the security code yourself or your card may self destruct. The machines have cancel and correction buttons if your transactions become a bit confused. Your child will love putting deposit envelopes in the slot. By age three Jenny was able to put her allowance and monetary gifts into her account with minimal supervision.

Food Excursion

Visit a market, or a "food court" at a local shopping center—any place where a wide variety of foods are available. When the restaurants aren't too busy, show your child, and perhaps sample, some different foods from different cultures. Talk about and taste the different foods: sweet-and-sour won tons, tacos, fish and chips, satay, falafel, pizza—the world's the limit in your tasting experiences.

The Car Wash

Some toddlers love to ride through the car wash, and find the huge brushes and giant sprays exciting, other children are terrified. So sound out your child beforehand. Talk about what happens before the ride begins. You will soon know if he wants to be with you on this venture or not. Hold his hand or give him a cuddle if he needs it, and talk about how the car is getting its bath.

Seasons

Get outside and enjoy seasonal activities with your child. Dress comfortably, and play lots of active games.

Hopscotch

Look for a Hopscotch (Potsy) grid in your local schoolyard, or draw one on the sidewalk with chalk. Teach your child, after about age two, how to throw his marker onto consecutive numbers, and try to hop on one foot. (He will lose his balance most of the time.) Hopscotch is a good game for counting, coordination, balance, and improving physical agility.

Hoops

Hoops are marvelous toys for any child. Victorian children played with wooden hoops and sticks, rolling them through well-manicured parks and formal gardens. Today we have lightweight, inexpensive, colorful plastic hoops. About your child's second birthday, buy some hoops of various sizes. Let him use his own imagination and inspiration at first, and then introduce some games.

Jump Through the Hoop

Pretend to be a circus trainer and have your roaring lion, or a dog, or an elephant that gets stuck, jump through the hoop. Have him use "all fours" as well as stand upright. Take your turn being the animal, perhaps a frog or a kangaroo, and let your child be the animal trainer and hold the hoop for you. Make lots of animal sounds.

The Farmer in the Dell

(Have a group of children circle around, with one in the middle as the "farmer." The farmer selects another to join him, who selects another, and so on. The "cheese" becomes the next farmer.)

The farmer in the dell,
The farmer in the dell,
Heigh-ho, the derry-o,
The farmer in the dell.

The farmer takes a wife (or husband)...
The wife takes a child...
The child takes a nurse...
The nurse takes the dog...
The dog takes the cat...
The cat takes the rat...
The rat takes the cheese...
The cheese stands alone...

(Traditional, United States)

Make a Waterslide

In the summertime, secure a large plastic sheet, or cut-open green garbage bags, on a smooth, grassy incline. We use tent pegs to make sure the plastic is taut. Set up a sprinkler so the water splashes onto the plastic. Let your toddler slide down the water slide and play under the sprinkler.

Snow Angels

Lie down on your backs in fresh, powdery snow and make snow angels. Swing your arms up and down and your legs back and forth. This works on dry sand at the beach, too.

Sliding

If there is a long, gentle, sliding hill nearby, bundle yourselves up and go sliding or tobogganing. Stay out of the way of the more adventurous older children, and enjoy the best that winter has to offer.

Freezing Shapes

Freeze water in various shapes for outdoor winter construction. Use old cake pans, jelly molds, plastic containers, and tin cans. Cardboard milk cartons are perfect for making building blocks. If you wish, color the water first with non-toxic water colors. Pop the ice blocks out of their containers as they freeze, and make more. Place the shapes in the shade so they will last longer.

Ice Structures

Make a large quantity of ice blocks in various non-toxic water colors. Stick the blocks together with water as the "mortar," and build a wall with your child's help. Encourage your toddler to bring you the "red" or "green" or "blue" block to help build the wall. Your structure can be built up over several days, as long as it is out of direct sunlight, and freezing temperatures last.

Use non-toxic colors for your blocks. Water color paints work wonderfully. You can talk about temperature. For instance, the lighter color blocks will freeze faster and last longer than darker color blocks because the dark colors absorb more light.

Autumn Leaves

On an autumn walk, point out to your child how the leaves are changing color and dropping from the trees. Let him pick up some leaves to bring home. (They can be pressed between two pieces of waxed paper with a warm iron; be sure to use newspaper to protect your ironing board and iron.) Tell your child that falling leaves mean winter is coming, but that new leaves will grow again in the spring.

A Caterpillar Crawled

A caterpillar crawled
(Creep your fingers up child's arm.)
To the top of the tree.
"I think I'll take a nap," says he.
(Place one hand over opposite fist.)
So under a leaf he began to creep
To spin his cocoon.
And he fell asleep.

All winter long he slept in his bed
'Til spring came along one day and said.
"Wake up, wake up, little sleepyhead,
(Shake fist with other hand.)
Wake up, it's time to get out of bed."
So he opened his eyes that sunshiny day.
(Spread fingers, hook thumbs.)
Lo! He was a butterfly, and flew away.
(Flap hands as wings and fly away.)

(Traditional, North America)

Seed Pods

Show your child the magic of seed pods—milkweed in the fall, dandelions from early spring on. Show him how to blow the dandelion clocks or milkweed fluff so that the seeds fly away. Tell him that next year the seeds will sprout to make new plants.

CHAPTER NINE

Who's That?
What's That?
When's That?
Why?

Thirty to Thirty-six Months

Your child is organizing the world according to her sense of order. She is organized and she expects the world to be, also. She like rituals, and she can be inflexible when routines vary. "Past," "present," and "future" and "one", "two," and "many" are distinct concepts to her. She has the ability to care for herself reasonably well. With your guidance she is learning to dress herself, and she can undress herself completely.

She is interested in the differences between male and female. A girl wants to be like her mother and a boy like his father. She knows the names of most of the parts of her body, and she is eager to show them to you.

She is learning to concentrate, and may spend long periods involved in one special activity. Don't interrupt her when she gets involved: concentration is a priceless talent.

She loves to move, especially running, jumping, and climbing. By her third birthday she may be able to coordinate both the pedals and steering to ride a tricycle safely.

She is developing a vivid imagination, so provide lots of opportunities for dressing up and acting. She uses her toys more and more in her role-playing. She has a fine sense of the dramatic. Taking turns and sharing with her friends become important parts of her play rituals, and tea parties are lots of fun for everyone.

Your child loves to sing, play instruments, listen to and say her favorite rhymes. She loves musical games, especially with other children. Playmates and friends are very important to her. Keep providing painting and art activities, and spend lots of time with her playing with "goop." Let her help you with your cooking and meal preparations.

MOVEMENT

Introduce more sense of direction and purpose to your child's movements. Take her swimming at your local recreation center, and enroll her in good gymnastics or dance classes, if they are available. Talk about paths, trails, and ways to find her way home when she is out in the world. Play lots of movement games. Give her a skipping rope to use outside. She won't be able to use it yet, but she loves to try.

Controlled Jumping—Legs Apart

Have your child jump up and down, landing first with her feet together, then with her feet apart, then with feet together and so on. As you count, "One, two, one, two," have her land feet together on "one" and feet apart on "two."

Controlled Jumping—One Leg in Front

As your child jumps up and down, have her switch feet in front of her body. First the left foot is forward (count "one") and the right foot is behind; then the right foot is forward (count "two") and the left foot is behind. Again, count "One, two, one, two..."

Balancing Leans

Stand facing your child and hold each other's hands. Slowly lean to one side, lifting the opposite leg slightly off the floor or ground. Point your toes. Return to a straight position and lower your leg. Then lean to the opposite side, again lifting the leg and pointing the toes. Repeat. This is fun to do to music.

Baby Ballet

Choreograph a "modern ballet" on a carpeted area. Put on your favorite music and move in and out, over and under furniture, roll on the carpet, run, bend, lie, stretch, jump, prance, march, ooze and slither.

As the music changes, your movements can become graceful, energetic, slow, or fast.

In and Out the Windows

(Verse 1: One or two children go to the center of a circle of children, who are holding hands up high. The selected children thread in and out of the circle through the other children's arms.
Verse 2: The children in the center pick partners by stopping in front of another child.
Verse 3: The chosen children follow their partners as they thread in and out of the circle.
Verse 4: All the children join hands and circle in one direction.)

Go in and out the windows,
Go in and out the windows,
Go in and out the windows,
As we have done before.

Now stand and face your partner,
Now stand and face your partner,
Now stand and face your partner,
As we have done before.

Now follow her to London,
Now follow her to London,
Now follow her to London,
As we have done before.

Go round and round the village,
Go round and round the village,
Go round and round the village,
As we have done before.

(Traditional, England)

Hoop In and Out the Windows

Lay several hoops close together on the grass, patio, or living room floor. Jump in and out of the hoops to music, or while singing "In and Out the Windows."

Engine, Engine

(Children sit in a line to form a train, and rock backwards and forwards to the beat.)

Engine, engine number nine,
Coming down [your town's] line,
If the train goes off the track
Do you want your money back?
Yes, no, maybe so.

(Then do a fast verse as the train gathers speed, and a slow verse as the train comes into the station. When the song ends, toot the whistle, tooooot-too.)

(Traditional, Great Britain, North America)

Blind Man's Buff/Guess Who?

One child, blindfolded, stands in the middle of a group of players, who move around. When the "blind man" yells "stop!" the group must stand still in one place. The children may stoop down or move one foot to keep away from the "blind man." The "blind man" may take up to three steps to catch and identify a player by touch. If the blind man guesses who the captured person is, that person becomes the next "blind man."

Bean Bags

Bean bags are lots of fun. They can be tossed in games of "catch," balanced on feet, heads, or hands, and used in relay races. They can be used to play "Leapfrog," when other children aren't around. They can be tossed into simple "basketball" nets, or used as markers in "Hopscotch." Make or purchase about half a dozen beanbags and use them daily.

Leapfrog

"Leapfrog" can be played with any number of children, even one, as long as she has a line of objects to jump over. It's most fun with four, five, or more children. Have the children form a line of bodies tucked into a crouching position. The last person in line vaults over the tucked backs of each child in front of her, then scrunches down quickly at the head of the line. The child at the end of the line becomes the next jumper. As the children become more competent at this game, the next jumper starts to jump as soon as she is jumped over, making the line move quickly. If you like, you may next sing "A Busy Buzzing Bumblebee" (p.122).

In a Cabin

In a cabin in a wood,
        (Outline imaginary cabin.)
A little man by the window stood,
        (Circle fingers for eyeglasses.)
Saw a rabbit hopping by
        (Bounce hands in front of you.)
Frightened as could be.
        (Simulate fright.)
"Help me! Help me! Help me!" he said,
        (Throw hands up in the air.)
"Or the hunter will bump my head!"
        (Tap head.)
"Come little rabbit, come with me;
        (Motion "come.")
Happy we will be."
        (Pat hand.)

(Traditional, United States)

Lucy Locket

(A drop-the-handkerchief circle game. One child goes around the outside of the circle and drops the "pocketbook" behind another child. The second child picks it up and becomes "it." The first child sits in the second child's place.)

Lucy Locket lost her pocket,
Kitty Fisher found it.
Not a penny was there in it,
Only a ribbon round it.

(Once the children get used to taking turns, the second child can "race" the first child back to the empty space. The last one back is "it" for the next turn.)

(Traditional, England)

Zoom, Zoom, Zoom

Zoom, zoom, zoom,
(Standing, rub hands upwards
I'm going to the moon.
against each other to symbolize rocket
launch.)
If you want to take a trip,
Climb aboard my rocket ship.
(Climb imaginary ladder.)
Zoom, zoom, zoom,
(Repeat hand-rubbing.)
I'm going to the moon.
10, 9, 8, 7, 6,
(Crouch down gradually until "one.")
5, 4, 3, 2, 1—
Blast off!
(On BLAST OFF jump up high and clap loudly.)

(Traditional, Germany, adapted)

Skip to My Lou

(This song is good for establishing skipping movements.)

Chorus:
Skip, skip, skip to my Lou,
Skip, skip, skip to my Lou,
Skip, skip, skip to my Lou,
Skip to my Lou, my darling.

Lost my partner, what will I do?
Lost my partner, what will I do?
Lost my partner, what will I do?
Skip to my Lou, my darling.

Can't get a red bird, a blue bird will do...
Flies in the buttermilk, shoo, fly, shoo...

(Traditional, United States)

A Busy Buzzing Bumble Bee

(Tune: "Battle Hymn of the Republic," "John Brown's Body")

A busy buzzing bumble bee went busily buzzing by
A busy buzzing bumble bee went busily buzzing by
A busy buzzing bumble bee went busily buzzing by
As they all went marching home.

They were only playing leap frog
They were only playing leap frog
They were only playing leap frog
As a busy buzzing bumble bee went busily buzzing by.
Buzzzzzzzzzz-zzzz OUCH!!!!

(Traditional, North America)

The Monster Hunt

Every so often, a Daddy we know comes home from work after dark. He says, "I think I heard a monster upstairs (or in the cellar, in the attic or anyplace else dark and spooky); let's go look." He and his daughter each get a flashlight and climb up the stairs on their tummies, crawling under beds, and searching behind bureaus with their flashlights. Great searchings are made, with a few bumps and rumbles coming from the monster. Usually, only a tiny monster, not worth bothering, is found. But you never know....BOO!

The Tiger Hunt

The Tiger Hunt is a game that gives your child a chance to have fun with her language, as she uses her body to represent actions, and the order of events, while pretending and "making believe." You can vary the game according to her age and interests, for instance, swimming across the ocean, riding a horse, sailing a boat, or climbing a mountain. Add your own creative variations (for example, an alligator in the swamp, a jellyfish in the ocean, a soaring hawk coming to say "hello") to create a new game every time you play this. Ask your child to mimic all of your actions and to repeat everything you say:

(Tap beat of words.)

Going on a tiger hunt,
Gonna catch a big one.
> (Hold arms out wide.)

I'm not scared.
> (Point to self and shake head.)

Oh, look!
> (Shade eyes with hand, peering off in distance.)

There's some ooey, gushy mud.
> (Make squishy noises.)

Let's go through.
> (Curl fingers and move them up and down.)

Glump! Glump! Glump!
> (More squishy noises.)

There's some long, wavy grass.
> (Make wavy grass motions with hands.)

Let's go through.
> (Part grass with hands.)

There's a river—no bridge.
> (Act startled.)

Let's swim across.
> (Make swimming motions.)

There's a big tree.
> (Arms up for tree.)

Let's climb up and look.
> (Make climbing motions, fist over fist.)

Oh, look, a great big cave.
> (Circle hands over eyes to make binoculars.)

Let's climb down and look!
> (Motion downwards.)

We're in the cave.
> (Use soft, spooky voice.)

Everybody light a match.
> (Scratch imaginary match.)

Oh, look!
> (Act surprised.)

A big pair of yellow eyes—
> (Startle and gasp.)

The tiger!!! Run!!!
> (Retrace all actions very quickly back to the beginning. Finally, blow out the match and say:)

Phew!!!

(Traditional, Great Britain, North America)

Mike and Michelle Jackson do a wonderful version of "The Bear Hunt" on their *Playmates* album, Elephant Records, using the same rhythms as "The Tiger Hunt."

WATER PLAY

Let your child have many opportunities to play with water, both inside and outside. Remember to keep towels and a dry set of clothes handy in case of spills.

Washing the Mirrors or Windows

Add 3 or 4 Tbsps of distilled white vinegar to a spray bottle and fill it with water. Show your child how to spray her bottle at a mirror or window and shine it with a crumpled newspaper, a rag, or a paper towel, to make the glass shine. The object isn't really to clean house (although this may be a by-product), but to teach her how to manipulate the spray bottle. Don't expect a perfect job; just have fun spraying and polishing.

Wash the Floor Together

Give your child her own small mop or sponge so she can help when you are washing the floor. You can't hold her back! She wants to get water everywhere, and it's fun mopping it up.

Does It Sink or Float?

At bath time ask her if different objects will sink in the bath, or if they will float. Test her boat, ducks, sponge, soap, facecloth, pieces of paper, crumpled aluminum foil, full and empty containers. Ask her if she can think of any reasons why some objects float and why others don't.

CHANGING GAMES

Open Them, Shut Them

Open them, shut them,
>   (Open hands wide, then make a fist.)
Open them, shut them,
>   (Repeat.)
Give a little clap.
>   (Clap hands.)
Open them, shut them,
Open them, shut them,
Put them in your lap.
>   (Place hands in lap, folded.)
Creep them, creep them,
Creep them, creep them,
>   (Slowly walk fingers up body to chin.)
Right up to your chin.
Open your little mouth
>   (Open mouth.)
But do not put them in.
>   (Shake head to indicate "no.")

Open them, shut them,
Open them, shut them,
To your shoulders fly.
>   (Flutter hands like bird to shoulders.)
Let them flutter to the sky,
>   (Flutter hands up.)
Falling, falling, falling,
Almost to the ground.
>   (Flutter hands down.)
Quickly pick them up again
>   (Hold hands up.)
And turn them round and round,
>   (Revolve them.)
Faster, faster, faster, faster,
>   (Revolve them quickly.)
Slower, slower, slower, slower,
>   (Revolve them slowly.)
Clap, clap, clap.
>   (Clap them.)

(Traditional, North America)

Raindrops, Raindrops!

Raindrops, raindrops!
Falling all around.
>   (Move fingers to imitate falling rain.)
Pitter-patter on the rooftops,
>   (Tap fingers softly on head.)
Pitter-patter on the ground.
>   (Tap fingers softly on feet or floor.)
Here is my umbrella.
>   (Pretend to open umbrella.)
It will keep me dry
>   (Place umbrella over head.)
When I go walking in the rain
I hold it up so high.
>   (Hold umbrella high in air.)

(Traditional, North America)

MUSIC

Some of her favorite songs now will be her favorites for a long time to come. She still loves some of her "baby" songs, so don't eliminate any. Start adding songs that place greater demands on her memory, and are more musically complex. Now is the time for songs that have lots of verses, show different moods and are more interesting listening. Your child will begin to participate in the production of her own music, and will initiate family singing with the slightest encouragement.

During long family car rides, take along a list of favorite songs for everyone to sing, and her most loved tapes. The miles just zip by.

Sing more complex action songs, finger plays, counting songs, alphabet songs, color songs, animal songs, and songs dealing with abstract concepts such as up/down and in/out. She may be able to master the musical concepts of slow/fast, loud/soft, and musical pause. She may dramatize her songs in her own creative play.

Make lots of music together. The more action in her songs, the more fun it is for everyone.

She'll Be Comin' Round the Mountain

She'll be comin' round the mountain,
when she comes—"Toot toot"
>   (Pull an imaginary train whistle.)
She'll be comin' round the mountain,
when she comes—"Toot toot"
She'll be comin' round the mountain,
She'll be comin' round the mountain,
She'll be comin' round the mountain,
when she comes—"Toot toot"

She'll be drivin' six white horses,
when she comes—"Whoa back!"
>   (Pull back reins.)
She'll be drivin' six white horses,
when she comes—"Whoa back!"
She'll be drivin' six white horses
She'll be drivin' six white horses
She'll be drivin' six white horses,
when she comes—"Whoa back, toot toot"
>   (Do the actions.)

...And we'll all go out to meet her,
when she comes—"Hi Babe"
>   (Wave hand in greeting.)
...We'll kill the old red rooster,
when she comes—"Chop, chop"
>   (Chopping motions.)
...We'll all have chicken and dumplin's,
when she comes—"Yum yum"
>   (Rub tummy.)
...She'll be wearin' red pajamas,
when she comes—"Scratch, scratch"
>   (Scratch.)
...She'll have to sleep with Grandma,
when she comes—"Move over"
>   (Make pushing motions.)
...We'll have a great big party,
when she comes—"Yahoo!"
>   (Swing arm over head as for a lasso.)

(For the last line of each verse, perform the actions for that verse and all preceding ones. The last verse will include "Yahoo, move over, scratch scratch, yum yum, chop, chop, hi babe, whoa back, toot toot!")

(Traditional, United States)

Skinnamarinky Dinky Dink

Skinnamarinky dinky dink,

(Hold right elbow in left hand, wave fingers.)

Skinnamarinky doo,

(Hold left elbow in right hand, wave fingers.)

I love you.

(Point to eye, heart, and to other person.)

Skinnamarinky dinky dink,
Skinnamarinky doo,
I love you.

I love you in the morning

(Raise arms over head in circle.)

And in the afternoon.

(Lower circled arms to waist.)

I love you in the evening

(Lower circled arms to knee level.)

Underneath the moon.

(Swing them up to one side to make a crescent moon.)

Skinnamarinky dinky dink,
Skinnamarinky doo.
I love you, you, boo-boo-be-do.
Oh, yeah...(whispered)

(Traditional, North America)

"One Elephant, deux éléphants" and "Skin-namarinky Dinky Dink" are Sharon, Lois & Bram's signature songs on records, videos, and *The Elephant Show.*

Little Arabella Miller

(Tune: "Twinkle, Twinkle Little Star")

Little Arabella Miller

(Or use your child's name.)

Had a fuzzy caterpillar
First it crawled upon her mother
Then upon her baby brother
They said Arabella Miller
PUT AWAY THAT CATERPILLAR!

(Said quickly and loudly.)

Little Arabella Miller
Had a great big green SNAKE (sss-ss-s-s)
First it crawled upon her mother
Then upon her baby brother
They said Arabella Miller
PUT AWAY THAT GREEN SNAKE!!!!

... Orange dragon
... Brontosaurus dinosaur

(Make up lots of scary, interesting pets.)

(For the last verse repeat the first verse, singing softly and sweetly, with the final line "Little Arabella Miller, how we love your caterpillar.")

(Traditional, North America)

Walk When the Drum Says Walk

Have your child move around to the beat of a drum as you are playing it. Start with walking and tap the beat of the entire song. Add gallop and running. When she can anticipate when the drum will stop, interrupt the song and change the beat of the song randomly. This teaches her how to listen and move to the beat.

Walk, walk, walk
            (Walk around to the drum beat.)
When the drum says walk.
When the drum says stop, we stop.

Gallop, gallop, gallop
            (Gallop to a galloping beat.)
When the drum says gallop
When the drum says stop, we stop.

Running, running, running
            (Run around on tiptoes quickly.)
When the drum says running
When the drum says stop, we stop.

(Katharine Smithrim)

"Walk When the Drum Says Walk" can be heard on *Songs and Games for Toddlers,* by Bob McGrath and Katharine Smithrim, Kids' Records.

ART

Scissors and Cutting

Get your child a pair of blunt-ended, plastic or rubber-covered sharp children's scissors. Supervise any cutting that she does, and show her how to place the scissors in her hands to use them. Have her cut scraps of paper to make them smaller, styrofoam pieces, cards, ribbon, straws, and pictures from magazines. Make a collage with her, gluing her bits together.

Translucent Paintings

This activity is a bit messy and requires adult participation. You need sheets of double-coated waxed paper, crayons or oil pastel shavings (use a pencil sharpener or a grater), a hot iron, and newspapers.

Have your child color on one sheet of waxed paper and add bits of crayon shavings. You cover her waxed paper with another sheet of waxed paper, and gently place the painting on an ironing board covered with newspaper. Place another piece of newspaper over the painting and iron everything with a hot iron. She can then cut the painting, using her scissors, into shapes (perhaps raindrops) to decorate her window. This process makes wonderful "stained glass" and Christmas ornaments.

Variation: Instead of using wax shavings as the "paint," have your child cut pieces of pretty tissue paper into interesting pieces to put between sheets of waxed paper. Iron as above.

Stamp Printing

Make some "stamps" out of vegetables— potatoes, carrots, onions, turnip, cabbage. Show your child how to dip the vegetable into tempera paint and press it onto a piece of paper. Carve a design or texture into the stamp, and do more stamping. You can also make stamps using cut-up sponges or cookie cutters.

Paper Batik

Have your child completely color a piece of soft matte paper (such as rice or construction paper) with wax crayons. (No empty space should show through.) Have her crumple her picture carefully into a tight ball, paying particular attention to the edges of the paper. Gently unfold the picture and notice how the surface has cracked. Brush a dark or contrasting ink or water paint over the entire painting to create a mosaic effect.

Allow the picture to dry, then place it on a sheet of newspaper, and cover it with a piece of thin drawing paper. Iron over the drawing paper with a hot iron, using a "patting" rather than a "sliding" motion. This will smooth out the cracks in the original paper, and also transfer the original image to the drawing paper. Voilà. The same picture for both grandmothers, if this matters in your family.

Marble Painting

Show your child how to drop marbles into various colors of paint and roll them across a piece of paper.

WORD PLAY

Continue to use lots of jokes, riddles, counting games, alphabet games, and tongue twisters.

A Twister of Twists

A twister of twists once twisted a twist,
The twist that he twisted as a three-twisted twist;
If in twisting the twist, one twist should untwist,
The untwisted twist would untwist the twist.

(Traditional, England)

One Old Oxford Ox

One old Oxford ox opening oysters.
Two toads totally tired trying to trot to Tisbury.
Three thick thumping tigers taking toast for tea.
Four finicky fishermen fishing for funny fish.
Five frippery Frenchmen foolishly fishing for
*   frogs.*
Six sportsmen shooting snipe.
Seven Severn salmon swallowing shrimp.
Eight eminent Englishmen eagerly examining
*   Europe.*
Nine nimble noblemen nibbling nectarines.
Ten tinkering tinkers tinkering ten tin tinder-boxes.
Eleven elephants elegantly equipped.
Twelve typographical topographers typically
*   translating types.*

(Traditional, England)

As I Was Going to St. Ives

As I was going to St. Ives,
I met a man with seven wives.
Each wife had seven sacks,
Each sack had seven cats,
Each cat had seven kits:
Kits, cats, sacks, and wives,
How many were going to St. Ives?

Answer: One was going to St. Ives. 7 wives + 49 sacks + 343 cats + 2401 kits + 1 man were coming from St. Ives, for a total of 2,801.

(Then you can discuss if the sacks should be counted...)

(Traditional, England)

KITCHEN PLAY

Start a Recipe File

Make or buy your child her own recipe box or pretty index card file. Copy out her favorite recipes, using simple words, pictures and symbols. Draw symbols for ½ cup, or a picture of the green mixing bowl, if that is what she uses in the recipe. Write out recipes that you make together. As well as include some simple "no-cook" recipes that she can make with a minimum of supervision.

Fruit or Vegetable Kebabs

Cut your child's favorite fruits or vegetables, for example, bananas, pears, oranges, or cucumber, celery and green pepper. Have her thread the fruit or vegetables onto a wooden skewer or toothpick. Feast on her favorite foods.

Fruit Slices Supreme

Spread a whole meal or graham cracker with her favorite sandwich spread and top with a slice of fruit and some raisins. Serve with a glass of milk for a super snack.

Banana Porcupines

Cut a ripe banana into ¾-inch slices. Have your child roll the slices in a bowl of her favorite crunchy cereal, to make "porcupines." Have her add some raisins for eyes.

Celery Boats

Cut celery into pieces 2 to 3 inches long. Help your child fill the inside of the celery with cream cheese, or any other soft spreading cheese that she likes. If she wants to make different shapes, stick two pieces of celery together along the filling, and you cut crosswise.

Bread Dough Figures

Thaw some frozen bread dough and allow it to rise, or make your own dough to the punched-down stage. Give your child workable amounts of the dough to shape: a figure, a person, an animal, a snowman, or whatever she likes. Allow the shape to rise, then brush with melted butter, and bake.

Thumbprint Cookies

(Have her help measure, cream, sift, beat the egg, dissolve the soda and water, and stir. Her fingers are just the right size to make good thumbprints for the jam. Help her with rolling the balls.)

1 cup butter or margarine
1 ½ cups light brown sugar
1 egg
1 tsp baking soda, dissolved in ¼ cup hot water
3 cups sifted flour
¼ tsp salt
1 tsp vanilla
½ cup granulated sugar

Cream butter and light brown sugar well. Add beaten egg, dissolved soda solution, sifted flour, salt, and vanilla. Roll about 1 tsp of dough at a time in the granulated sugar to make a ball, and place on an ungreased cookie sheet. Have her make her thumbprint in the center of each cookie, and add a small dab of jam to the center of each thumbprint. Apricot jam is best. Bake the cookies about 12 minutes in a 325°F oven.

INDOOR GAMES

Family History

Dig out old family photograph albums and talk about your child's own family history. Tell her how her parents met, anecdotes about how Grandma and Grandpa lived, what life was like when you were growing up and how it is different from her history. Write down and read aloud some of your family's special stories. Have older members of your family tell her what their life was like when they were little. If you have a tape recorder, tape some of these "interviews." Take out your child's baby diary and photo albums and tell her about her own history.

Jokes and Riddles

Along with a vivid imagination, your child is developing a sense of humor. She loves riddles and jokes, even if she usually misses the punch line. She likes to ask riddles, but sometimes gets lost half way through the joke. Many classic nursery rhymes (such as "Humpty Dumpty") were originally riddles. Encourage her developing sense of fun with words.

Knock, Knock

Knock, knock.
Who's there?
Boo.
Boo who?
Don't cry, ——, that's all right.

Knock, knock.
Who's there?
Lettuce.
Lettuce who?
Lettuce in and find out!

Knock, knock.
Who's there?
Cows go.
Cows go who?
No, cows go moo.

Knock, knock
Who's there?
Banana.
Banana who?
Knock, knock.
Who's there.
Banana.
Banana who?
Knock, knock.
Who's there?
Orange.
Orange who?
Orange you glad I didn't say "banana"?

As Light as a Feather

As light as a feather,
As round as a ball,
Yet all the king's men
Cannot carry it at all.
(Ask your child "What is it?" Answer: A bubble.)

(Traditional, England)

A Shoemaker Makes Shoes Without Leather

A shoemaker makes shoes without leather,
With all the four elements together,
Fire, water, earth, air,
And every customer takes two pair.
(Ask your child "Who makes these shoes?"
Answer: A blacksmith or farrier)

(Traditional, United States)

QUIET TIMES

Touching and Identifying

Completely remove the top from a large juice can. Cut an old grown-up-sized sock off at the ankle, saving the upper part. Stretch the ribbed part over the top of the can. The top of the sock then becomes a "tunnel" for your child's hand to reach through. Inside the can place six or eight different objects, for example, a whole walnut, or chestnut, a small furry toy, a small piece of cloth, a large coin, a large button, a marble, a small spoon, a matchbox car, a thimble, or a shell. Have her reach inside the opening and ask her to select one of the objects, and ask if she can guess what it is. Take turns reaching inside the can and guessing what each object is, one at a time. Vary the game by describing one of the objects you touch, and asking your child to guess what it is. Then reverse roles. Change the toys in the can frequently. This game helps build her descriptive language.

Imagination Time

Ask your child to describe what it would be like if she were ten years old, a giant, a tiger, a dragon, a Mommy, a Daddy, a bird, a snake. What would she like to be?

Imagine Being a Balloon

Lie on the floor together, eyes shut, and pretend you are balloons. Blow yourselves up big, and lift up onto your feet. Float over to the wall and—whoops!—you hit a nail sticking out. Pop! Slowly blow the air out, slither to the floor, and rest for a moment. Then puff up with air again and slowly leak all the air out. Blow yourself up again and let the air out even more slowly. Finally, fill up with air again and go pop! Now rest together for a minute with your eyes shut.

Sing a Song of Sixpence

Sing a song of sixpence,
A pocket full of rye.
Four and twenty blackbirds
Baked in a pie.

When the pie was opened
The birds began to sing,
"Was that not a dainty dish
To set before the King?"

The King was in his counting house
Counting out his money.
The Queen was in the parlour
Eating bread and honey.

The maid was in the garden
Hanging out the clothes.
Along came a blackbird
And snapped off her nose.

As it fell upon the ground
'Twas spied by Jenny Wren
Who took a stick of sealing wax
And stuck it on again.

As they saw the nose stuck on
The maids cried out "Hooray!"
Till someone said, "But it is stuck
The topsey-turvey way!"

They took her to the King,
Who just replied, "What stuff!
'Tis better far put on that way,
So nice for taking snuff!"

They bought a pound of Lundfoot*
And threw it in her face.
She sneezed, "Achoo!" which twisted it
Into its proper place.

*A brand of snuff

(Traditional, England)

Good Night, Sleep Tight

Good night, sleep tight,
Don't let the bedbugs bite.
But if they do, take your shoe
And beat them till they're black and blue.

(Traditional, United States)

OUTDOORS

The Naturalist

Your child is seeing all the wonders of nature, so make sure she experiences the great outdoors. Talk together about what you are seeing. She is a natural explorer and scientist. She can spend ten minutes investigating one acorn, leaf, or stone she has found. Be patient; she's slow now, but soon you won't be able to keep up with her. Take the time to slow down and look at her leaf. Take time to discover the world as she sees it. Use a magnifying glass or binoculars, a microscope, or a telescope, if possible, to show her the details of her wonderful discoveries. Give her a small knapsack or a pail to carry home her treasures. Glue some of them into a book describing her expeditions. Use others in her art work. Make a nature shelf for special finds. Recite poetry and rhymes and sing songs about the animals, plants and bugs she sees on her walks.

Blindfold Trails

Stretch a rope across a variety of interesting surfaces, blindfold your child, and have her hold the rope as you lead her along the path. Make the trail across grass, pavement, gravel, and sand. Have her talk about what she is experiencing.

Sail Boats Away

Make paper or leaf boats with your toddler, and let them sail away down a stream, or onto a lake. Talk about where the water flows. Introduce and try reading the wonderful book, *Paddle to the Sea,* by Holling C. Holling, published by Houghton Mifflin. If you simplify the story and show her the Caldecott Medal-winning illustrations, she will understand her boat might reach a destination far away.

Mud Pie

Hand-mix sand, clean dirt, and water in a large bowl or pail. Keep the mixture really thick. Pour part of it into a cake pan or pie plate. Sprinkle with grass. Add another layer of mud. Sprinkle with flower petals. Bake in the sun until ready to serve.

Round and Round

You and your child stand inside a hoop, arms spread out wide as you hold the hoop and lean back. Lean from side to side, moving and turning slowly. Then spin suddenly in one direction, like a top. Stop before you get dizzy.

Frogs on a Lily Pad

This is fun for school, at a party, or when you have visiting children and adults. Spread several hoops on the grass and tell the children that the hoops are lily pads and that they are "safe" when they are on a lily pad. There is a huge mean hawk (a selected adult) who just LOVES to eat little frogs. The hawk makes a scary sound and swoops after the frogs. When they hear the sound the children must hop to the lily pad for safety. (Each lily pad can hold many frogs.) The children play outside the hoops and the hawk comes. The adult should pretend to be a wicked, evil hawk, spreading wings, and glowering at the children. By the time the hawk gets to the frogs, they will be on their lily pads. Sometimes a child may WANT to be caught. When one is caught, pick her up from behind, arms around her waist. Swing her around a few times and carry her off. When a child is caught, she becomes a baby hawk and helps capture other frogs. Or, captured frogs can be freed when the hawk is away.

Hoop Dancing

Lay several hoops in a line, touching each other. First walk, then hop, run, gallop, skip, walk crookedly, dance, and boogie through the hoops. This is great for coordination and can be done as you run, skip or dance to the music.

Weather

Your child will want to play outdoors in most weather conditions. Dress up accordingly, go outside and enjoy!!!

Watch the Sky

Watch the sky for impending changes in the weather and talk about them. Sunny, cloudy, stormy, rainy, hailing, foggy and snowy have different cloud formations. Watch the clouds, and talk about how they look and how they change. Mention that the wind moves the clouds along in the sky, and that the wind also indicates changes in the weather. Make a trip to the weather office at a local airport and ask the meteorologist to show you around. Ask if your child can have an old weather map for her wall, too.

Watch a Thunderstorm

Have an expedition to a place where you and your child can watch a thunderstorm together, safely. Watch from a porch at a lake cottage, or farm, or warm and dry in a high-rise building. Talk about the thunder, lightning, and rain that come from this special type of storm. You may want to tell your child a story about giants bowling, Rip Van Winkle, Thor throwing lightning bolts, or talk about blacksmiths using anvils.

If you prefer, keep the talk scientific. When she has good experiences and understands to take precautions, she will never need to fear thunder and lightning. Point out the special anvil-shaped cloud formations that make thunderstorms, and point out that thunder showers come in individual clouds.

Boom, Bang, Boom, Bang!

Boom, bang, boom, bang!
Rumpety, lumpety, bump!
Zoom, zam, zoom, zam!
Clippety, clappety, clump!
Rustles and bustles
And swishes and zings!
What wonderful noises
A thunderstorm brings!

(Traditional, North America)

The Rain Walk

Jenny and I love to get all dressed up in rain slickers, boots, hats and umbrellas and go for a walk in the rain. We sing rain songs and say some nursery rhymes about rainy weather. We talk about how important rain is, how it brings water to drink, waters the garden, makes flowers bloom, makes the grass green, makes the trees grow, and cleans up everything. We talk about how rain fills Aunt Marilyn's cistern, and how it brings water to the brooks, rivers, lakes and oceans. We love our rainy days.

It's Raining, It's Pouring

It's raining, it's pouring,
The old man is snoring,
He went to bed and he bumped his head
And he couldn't get up in the morning.

(Traditional, Great Britain, North America)

Rain, Rain, Go Away

(melodic chant)

Rain, rain, go away
Come again another day.
Little [child's name] wants to play.
Rain, rain, go away.

(Traditional, Great Britain, North America)

Dr. Foster Went to Gloucester

Dr. Foster went to Gloucester
In a shower of rain.
He stepped in a puddle
Right up to his middle
And never went there again.

(Traditional, Great Britain)

Slip on Your Raincoat

Slip on your raincoat,
Pull on your galoshes;
Wading in puddles
Makes splishes and sploshes.

(Traditional, North America)

One Misty, Moisty Morning

One misty, moisty morning,
When cloudy was the weather,
There I met an old man
Clothed all in leather;
Clothed all in leather,
With a cap under his chin,
How do you do, and how do you do,
And how do you do again?

(British Broadside Ballad c. 1680)

Rain on the Green Grass

Rain on the green grass
And rain on the sea.
Rain on the housetops
But not on me!

(Traditional, England)

Enjoy a Sunrise

If your child wakes up before dawn, go outside to watch the sun come up. Talk about the changes as the sky gets lighter and lighter. Talk about the changes in the wind, the smells, the amount of moisture in the air, what the weather is like. Say "Good morning" to Mr. Sun. When the sun is bright enough, your child can dance with her shadow.

Oh, Mr. Sun

Oh, Mr. Sun, Sun, Mr. Golden Sun,
Please shine down on me.
Oh Mr. Sun, Sun, Mr. Golden Sun,
Hiding behind a tree.
These little children are asking you
To please come out so we can play with you.
Oh Mr. Sun, Sun, Mr. Golden Sun,
Please shine down on, please shine down on,
Please shine down on me.

Oh Mr. Moon, Moon, Mr. Silvery Moon...
To please come out so we can dream with you...

(Traditional, Southern United States)

The Night Sky

On a warm summer evening, take a blanket outside, lie down, and look at the heavens. Look for the moon, and watch the stars come out. Look for the first star, constellations, planets, and satellites. If possible, use opera glasses, binoculars, a telephoto lens or a telescope, to see greater detail in the night sky.

When you stargaze, don't forget to wish on the first star you see. Talk about the monthly changes in the moon as it goes from full to new, and back again. Talk about the astronauts who have been to the moon. Find a book about stars and share it with your child. A visit to a planetarium or an observatory will show her more about the universe. The stars and moon have a magical quality for a child.

Star Light, Star Bright

Star light, star bright,
First star I see tonight,
I wish I may, I wish I might
Have this wish I wish tonight.

(Traditional, unknown)

C H A P T E R   T E N

Records, Television, Books, and Public Entertainment

RECORDS

Music is an essential part of your baby's life. It is never too early to give your child a chance to become familiar with good children's music. The records or tapes he hears at four months contain seeds of his favorite songs at 18 months, when he'll begin to sing some of the words.

Records give more value per dollar than almost any of your child's toys. When in doubt about a child's gift, give a record.

The basic requirements of a good children's record are: a sing-along quality, a good tune, and lively, interesting lyrics that are easy to learn and slip easily off the tongue. Good toe-tapping music doesn't hurt. A collection of old favorites, containing "Old McDonald," "This Old Man," and some familiar nursery rhymes, is a perfect first purchase. Also collect the songs of popular children's entertainers, such as Raffi; Sharon, Lois, & Bram; Bob McGrath; and Fred Penner.

In addition to children's songs, there is great value in presenting him with the great music of the world. Don't let your Mozart gather dust in the corner, play it for your baby as background music. Remember, Mozart wasn't much older than your toddler when he composed his first pieces. Help develop your child's ear for music; play him the best, often, on a good sound system.

Play all types of music for him. See if he likes rock 'n' roll, Greek dances, Irish jigs, Italian Arias, reggae, calypso, and African, Maori or South American music. Try to put him to sleep with soft, structured classical music. Have fun with your own records and give your child's record collection variety and depth. Though the sing-along songs are the mainstays, he has the right to make selections from the world's treasury of music.

Use your public library to test records for your baby. They have records for the very young. If he falls in love with the songs, then buy the record. Using the library for testing can save you many dollars. There are some clinkers on the market, along with some real finds. You can't afford to waste your money on the bad when good music is so essential to your baby's happiness.

Your baby will soon want to put on his music "by myself." He needs his own tape recorder or record player.

There are many simple, sturdy, inexpensive record players and tape decks available. Remember that the player you choose should be made for small hands. Small-format, 33⅓ records are just the right size for little hands, too. Disneyland Records makes many small-format records, including *A,B,C, Counting Fun, Mother Goose Rhymes, Manners, The Best of Disney from Film Favorites,* and *The Little Engine That Could.* Some Mercer Mayer books, such as *Just for You* and *Just Grandma & Me,* are recorded in the Golden Book and Cassette, Disneyland Storyteller Series. Most of these small-format records and tapes are packaged along with a book.

Remember that the first children's records you buy will be damaged by frequent use. Expect to replace favorite records every six months or so, until small hands learn to use the record player properly. Keep an extra needle in stock as well. Let your child put records and tapes on, and have some say in what he wants to hear. Don't deprive him of a sense of mastery and accomplishment for the sake of a few scratched records.

Tape recorders are a blessing because they allow you to assemble tapes of your child's favorite music as he grows. He can learn to operate simple cassette recorders and select his own tapes between 24 and 30 months. You will just have to remind him not to touch or pull the tape itself. Don't forget to play children's music on the tape deck of your car when you are taking trips.

Another technical marvel is the compact disc player; the records are virtually indestructible because they play by laser transfer. Even very small hands can manipulate compact discs and not destroy them. Even if they're stepped on accidentally, the discs will not be damaged.

Get to know the songs your child is hearing wherever babies gather. Get him the record album or tape that has these songs so he can enjoy them on his own and so you can both learn the words by heart. Sing together.

Your toddler entertains himself by singing his favorite songs. He also feels more comfortable with other children when he knows the same songs they do. Music and songs are basic ingredients of the shared cultural experience of childhood.

Following are my recommendations for children's records. Try them and see if you agree that they're wonderful. These selections are based on the joy Jenny and I have shared together and with other children.

RECOMMENDED RECORDS

For Under Ones

The Baby Record, Bob McGrath and Katharine Smithrim; Kids' Records (Includes instructions for games that parents can play with babies.)

Bunyips, Bunnies & Brumbies, Mike and Michelle Jackson; Elephant Records (The Australian version of "Old McDonald" is exceptional. Especially good, rollicking dance music for babies.)

Singable Songs for the Very Young and *More Singable Songs for the Very Young*, Raffi; Troubadour Records (Words included for lots of favorite songs.)

There's a Hippo in My Tub, Anne Murray; A & M Records (Country-and-western-flavored music for children. Many traditional songs.)

Peter, Paul & Mommy, Peter, Paul and Mary; Warner Brothers' Records (Folk-flavored children's music. Many lullabies and fun to grow on.)

For Under-Threes

Songs and Games for Toddlers, Bob McGrath and Katharine Smithrim; Kids' Records (Instructions provided; much loved, especially when imaginative play emerges.)

If You're Happy and You Know It Sing Along With Bob, Vols. 1 & 2, Bob McGrath of "Sesame Street"; Kids' Records (Provides words to many favorite songs.)

The Wonderful World of Nursery Rhymes, Vera Lynn and Kenneth McKellar; London Records. (A good selection of rhymes with a professional musical performance.)

One Elephant, deux éléphants, Sharon, Lois & Bram; Elephant Records (Lots of fun!)

Mainly Mother Goose, Sharon, Lois & Bram; Elephant Records (Primarily nursery rhymes; some familiar songs.)

The Cat Came Back, Fred Penner; Troubadour Records (Played over, and over, and over, and over.)

Everything Grows, Raffi; Troubadour Records. (The masterpiece by the master.)

Records to Grow Into

One Light, One Sun, Raffi; Troubadour Records
Baby Beluga, Raffi; Troubadour Records
Rise and Shine, Raffi; Troubadour Records
Corner Grocery Store, Raffi; Troubadour Records
Fiddle up a tune, Eric Nagler; Elephant Records
Come On In, Eric Nagler, Elephant Records
Smorgasbord, Sharon, Lois & Bram; Elephant Records
In the School Yard, Sharon, Lois & Bram; Elephant Records

Singing and Swinging, Sharon, Lois & Bram;
     Elephant Records
1, 2, 3, 4, Look Who's Coming Through the Door,
     Sharon, Lois & Bram; Elephant Records
Stay Tuned, Sharon, Lois & Bram; Elephant
     Records
Simple Magic, Kim and Jerry Brodey; Kids'
     Records (Really good to grow into.)
Family Pie, Kim and Jerry Brodey; Kids'
     Records
Playmates, Mike and Michelle Jackson, Elephant
     Records
Special Delivery, Fred Penner; Troubadour
     Records
The Cat Came Back Again, Fred Penner;
     Troubadour Records
Polka Dot Pony, Fred Penner; Troubadour
     Records
A Home For Me, Fred Penner; Troubadour
     Records
Merry-Go-Round, The Travellers; Elephant
     Records

DISTRIBUTORS OF CHILDREN'S RECORDS

S ome of these records may have to be ordered
by your local record store or through the distributor. A catalogue of children's records is available from:

Educational Record Center
472 East Paces Ferry Road
Atlanta, GA, USA 30305
1-800-438-1637
(404)233-5935

Elephant Records

Canada:

Elephant Records
24 Ryerson Avenue
4th Floor
Toronto, Ontario, Canada
M5T 2P3

United States:

A & M Records
1416 N. Labrea Avenue
Los Angeles, CA USA
90028

Kids' Records

Canada:

Kids' Records
68 Broadview, Suite 303
Toronto, Ontario, Canada
M4M 2E6

United States:

Silo Records
Box 429
South Main Street
Waterbury, VT, USA   05676

Lemonstone Records

Lemonstone Records
P.O. Box 607
Cote St-Luc, Quebec, Canada
H4V 2Z2

Troubadour Records

Canada:

Troubadour Records
6043 Yonge Street
Willowdale, Ontario, Canada
M2M 3W3

United States:

A & M Records
1416 N. Labrea Avenue
Hollywood, CA USA 90028

TELEVISION

It is estimated that, on average, pre-school children watch 25 hours a week of television. Watching TV is a passive activity, so never allow television viewing to interfere with your baby's active play. He needs his games with you, he needs his outdoor play, he needs his "go to bed" ritual of books, records, good cuddling, and singing.

Never use television as a babysitter, but for fun and information. Never restrain your child when he is watching television. Give him room to roam and toys to play with while the TV is on. He simply can't sit still in one place for very long.

Used in moderation, and selectively, television isn't all bad. There are times when everyone gets tired and needs some passive time. Sick children benefit from the time they spend quietly in front of the television.

You are your child's prime resource person, the great question answerer. Take time to sit with him and watch his shows, as often as you can. Just cuddle in front of the set and explain the concepts being discussed.

For example, when "Sesame Street" discusses in/out, up/down, behind/in front of, you and your child can make a game of it, going in and out of the room, standing up and sitting down and standing in front of or behind a chair.

Many parents have found that the key to television success with young children is to utilize public broadcasting (PBS), or the local educational station. Send for your local educational station's TV guide and circle possible shows.

The benefits of television include access to information on a host of subjects. There is no easier way to see a beluga whale in its natural habitat or footage on wild animals. "Wild, Wild World of Animals," "Nature," or "World of Survival" are excellent choices for your budding naturalist, especially before a trip to the zoo.

Save your own television viewing for times when your baby is asleep.

Selecting Television Shows

VCRs, satellite TV dishes, pay television, and expanded cable services have all facilitated increased depth in children's programming. We are no longer held captive by the networks and their advertising. Beware of violence in children's programming, even if it does come packaged with a moral. Remember, your child internalizes the violence he sees on television. He is not able to resolve the conflict in the way a nursery rhyme or story allows. Be careful that no program your child watches conflicts with your own parental approach and values.

Draw up a schedule of available children's programming. Include network, educational television, and local cable programming. Include the Disney Channel and Nickelodeon pay-TV stations if they are available in your area. List all the quality children's programs available to you, such as "Sesame Street," "Mr. Roger's Neighborhood," "The Elephant Show," "Polka Dot Door," "Edison Twins," "3-2-1 Contact," "Fred Penner's Place," "Fraggle Rock," "Today's Special," "Muppet Babies," "Jeremy," and "Passe-Partout."

View these shows with your child and find out which ones appeal to him. Respect your child's interests. If a program bores him, turn it OFF.

Boom Ball

One Daddy I know has converted his 20-month-old daughter into a fanatical Sunday afternoon football fan. Rather than passively watching the games, he and his daughter play "Boom Ball." At the completion of almost every play, they roughhouse and scream "Boom!" at the top of their lungs as they tackle each other to the floor. During beer ads they will have mock arguments, with the Daddy yelling "Less filling!" and his daughter countering with "Light!"

Kideo Video

A video cassette player is a boon for parents. Not only can you eliminate commercials for useless toys and snacks of dubious nutritional value, but you can also create your own library of favorite shows. Imagine being able to entertain a bed-ridden toddler with "Sesame Street" and "The Elephant Show" rather than soap operas! And what better way to capture priceless moments for grandparents living far away? Simply rent the camera, film the special (or not-so-special) event, and mail the tape. Your child will love to see himself on television, especially long ago as a "baby," now that he has reached the ripe old age of four. Warning: you might get all mushy, too.

Children's movies can be rented at reasonable prices from your local variety store. Every child loves to select and enjoy classic films, such as *The Wizard of Oz, Chitty-Chitty Bang-Bang, Mary Poppins,* and *Willie Wonka and the Chocolate Factory.*

Kid Vids

Although still in its infancy, the Kid Vid market is burgeoning. Of great merit, and widely available, is a series of videos available from Golden Book Video. They claim to offer "The Best in Children's Entertainment," and they do. While most children's videos are designed for older children, Golden Book has made some that appeal to under-threes. Of special note for ages two to four is Katharine Smithrim's *Songs & Games for Toddlers,* in which some of the songs and games in this book are performed. View this video with your toddler until he learns the words and actions. We also found that children up to six and seven loved doing this tape, as well.

The Golden Book Video "Storybooks Brought to Life" series features excellent videos, especially when used in conjunction with favorite books such as Mercer Mayer's *Just for You.* Golden Book has also taped several quality children's television shows, including The Polka Dot Door's "Dinosaurs" and Today's Special's "Storms," that under-threes find appealing. You might use these shows along with some of your other play activities, to enhance the ideas these shows present.

By the time your child turns three, Sharon, Lois & Bram's "At the Zoo", and "Live at Young People's Theatre"; Eric Nagler's "Making Music With Eric"; "Troupers", featuring Robert Munsch; and "Hats On/Hats Off" by Kim and Jerry Brodey will attract your child. These videos cost no more than an average toy, and provide good entertainment value, without commercials.

For older age groups, the children's video market expands tremendously, including all the Disney favorites. Also, Fairie Tale Theatre videos, from CBS-Fox Video, are fun to rent once your child is old enough to appreciate fairy tales, usually around age four. These best-loved fairy tales are re-enacted with exceptional casts of well-known actors and actresses. You will probably decide to buy one or two of your favorites.

BOOKS

It is never too early to get into the habit of reading to your child. If books are a daily event in your child's life, the basis of a desire to read all by himself is easily established. Build his reading habit by reading to him every day, preferably at the same time. Choose a comfortable spot where you won't be interrupted.

At first, you may feel slightly uncomfortable reading out loud, but within a few weeks you will fall in love with the experience of children's books and the playful attitude of children's writers towards language.

Begin with Mother Goose. You may remember many of the rhymes from your childhood. Proceed to Dr. Seuss, especially *ABC* and *Hop on Pop,* and enjoy his delightful rhymed words. Children love ABC books. Find books you and your child can enjoy. Borrow stacks of books from your library and discover the wide variety of titles available.

Use books for their beautiful illustrations as well as their stories. Encourage your child to recognize the details in the pictures. Point to items and give them their proper names. Enunciate your words so your child will learn to speak well. Ask questions such as "Where is the bear?" "Why is the bear crying?"

Use lines from books to enrich your conversations. Favorite lines and concepts from her favorite books are fun to toss about. When your child bumps his head and you both know he's okay, say "The sky is falling! The sky is falling!" if you've been reading *Chicken Little*. It helps bring laughter to a sad situation. It's hilarious to watch your toddler trying something new while singing, "I think I can, I think I can, the little blue engine said," from *The Little Engine That Could*.

Your child from birth to age three is learning his language. Books give your child words to speak as well as phrases to explain his feelings, thoughts and ideas. The more your child speaks, the more confidence he will have and the greater his fascination with the language we share as human beings.

Books are shared experiences. When you read with your child you share a common language and grow closer to each other. Books explain your child's culture and he learns the words he uses. Books introduce ideas. Books help your child use speech and learn about relationships with others. Books provide fun and material for his imaginative play. For instance, reading about the friendship between an owl and a moon that followed him home can create a game of trying to outwit the moon when he is outside after dark. (*The Owl at Home*, Arnold Lobel, I Can Read, Harper and Row.)

The habit of reading to your child allows for continual emotional and intellectual growth. Your child accumulates information daily. As his knowledge and skills grow, so does the pleasure you'll experience as his parent.

As you read to your child, you will discover many interesting aspects of his blossoming individuality, for instance, how intelligent he is, or what a superb memory he has. By two-and-a-half, many children are able to recognize the words in many books because they have memorized them. It becomes a game to try to figure out if your child is actually reading, or if he simply remembers the exact words you read to him a few days, weeks, or months ago. The memories of young children are extraordinary.

Store your child's books on low bookshelves to invite browsing. Your child's book corner may become his favorite spot. Don't forget to put alphabet and number friezes on his wall, and refer to them often.

Ideally, there are bookshelves in your child's room, filled to overflowing with children's classics waiting to be read. If not, begin his library as soon as possible. Select books from the "My First Golden Books" series when you are at the grocery store—they cost about the same as a bag of potato chips and have greater lasting value.

RECOMMENDED BOOKS

Under One Year

Heavy cardboard books to cut his teeth on, literally
Floating plastic tub books
Friezes of alphabet letters and numbers to hang in your child's room
Small, well-illustrated Mother Goose rhymes
pat the bunny, Dorothy Kunhardt, Golden Books
Hand, Hand, Fingers, Thumb, Al Perkins, Random House
Hop on Pop, Dr. Seuss, Random House
Colors, Shapes, Numbers, Sizes, ABC, etc., by Jan Pienkowski, Heinemann/Cape
I Can Count, etc., Dick Bruna, Methuen
B is for Bear, Dick Bruna, Methuen
Gobble, Growl, Grunt, Peter Spier, Zephyr Books, Doubleday
Good Night Moon, Margaret Wise Brown
Once: A Lullaby, b.p. nichol

One to Two

Dictionaries for babies (Get your baby to point to "apple" or "baby." Say, "What's this?") Books that match your child's toys, for instance, *Raggedy Ann and Andy, Paddington Bear, Barbapappa*, books about Sesame Street characters.

"Easy-to-Read" series (Dial Books)
The Five Senses Series: *Sight, Touch, Smell, Taste, Hearing*, Barron's NY
Richard Scarry's Busy Book and other books by this author
Just Me and My Dad, Me Too, and other Mercer Mayer titles in the "Golden Look Look Books" series
I Can Do It Myself, Sesame Street, Golden Press
Green Eggs and Ham, Dr. Seuss, Random House, New York
Jelly Belly and *Alligator Pie*, Dennis Lee, Macmillan, Toronto
Babar Loses His Crown, Babar Learns to Cook, and many other Babar books
Each Peach, Pear, Plum, Allan and Janet, Kestel
The Oxford Ox's Alphabet, Ferelith Eccles Williams, World's Work
One to Ten and Back Again, Anne Ferns, illus. Susanne Ferrier, Hamlyn
Dr. Seuss's ABC, Dr. Seuss, Beginner Books, Random House, New York
The Counting Book, Judy Hindley and Collin King, Usborne/Hayes First Book
The Alphabet Book, Heather Amery and Collin King, Usborne/Hayes First Book
Wake Up Farm, Alvin Tresselt, illus. Roger Duvosin, World's Work
Over in the Meadow, Ezra Jack Keats, Hamish Hamilton
Father Bear Comes Home, Elsa Holmelund Minarik, illus. Maurice Sendak; an I Can Read Book, Harper and Row (New York)
ABC of Things, Helen Oxenbury, Stoddart
A is for Angry, Sandra Boynton, Workman Publishing
Spot books, Eric Hill, the Putnam Young Readers Group

Two to Three

Your First Adventure Books, Bantam. Kids love choosing the stories' plots; the illustrations are wonderful and the story themes are great.
Natural history books on shells, reptiles, snakes, stars, rabbits, dinosaurs, snakes, birds, trees
How Animals Live, Anne Civardi and Cathy Kilpatin, Usborne/Hayes
Dinosaurs, Peter Zallinger, Random House Picturebook
Make Way for Ducklings, Robert McClosky, Picture Puffin

Nursery rhymes with detailed illustrations, e.g.,
Lavender's Blue, Kathleen Lines, illus. Harold Jones, Oxford University Press
Peter Rabbit, Jemima Puddle-Duck, Squirrel Nutkin, etc., by Beatrix Potter (a wonderful size for small hands and beautifully illustrated)
Earth, Sky, Moon, Sesame Street, Golden Press
One Fish, Two Fish, Red Fish, Blue Fish, Dr. Seuss, Beginner Books, Random House, New York
Good Night Owl!, Pat Hutchins, Bodley Head/Puffin
The Little Engine That Could, Retold by Watty Piper, illus. George and Doris Hauman, Platt & Munk, New York
Bears, Ruth Kauss, illus. Phyllis Rowland, Harper and Row
Mr. Gumpy, John Birmingham, Cape/Puffin
The Cat in the Hat, Dr. Seuss, Random House

The Caldecott Medal

The Caldecott Medal is awarded annually to the artist or illustrator of the most distinguished American picture book published the preceding year. While the text need not be the work of the artist, it must be worthy of the book. Ask your librarian for a complete list of Caldecott Medal winners, and look for the gold medal printed on the outside cover of books both at the library and at the bookstore.

Caldecott Medal winners include such classics

as *Make Way for Ducklings*, by Robert McCloskey; *The Snowy Day*, by Ezra Jack Keats; *Where the Wild Things Are*, by Maurice Sendak; *Noah's Ark*, by Peter Spier; and *Ox Cart Man*, by Barbara Cooney. EVERY Caldecott book is a winner. These are books to be treasured.

You may see other books with a gold medal printed on the cover — The Newberry Award. While the text is too advanced for preschoolers, they are books for your child to cherish when he is older.

PUBLIC ENTERTAINMENT

Only you know your lifestyle, your baby's personality, and what to expect in terms of attention span and coping ability for both you and your baby. Some babies can be taken to restaurants, movies, shows, and sporting events from the time they are born. Others cannot. Use your own judgment in each situation. Sit near an exit in case you need to make a speedy getaway.

Movies

Gabriel started going to movies in her pouch carrier within a week of her birth. The only problem occured when Bill, Thoma and Gaby weren't allowed into a theatre because Gaby was under 18. The movie had a Restricted rating. Jenny was an active baby who didn't have the patience to put up with a feature movie until she was about three.

Ice Shows/The Circus

Generally, the first half of a show is fine for under-threes. After intermission, however, boredom may set in. If you can roam around a large stadium or arena without disturbing others, an ice show or circus can be lots of fun. If you feel anxious, or if your child is bored, it's best to leave.

Concerts/Ballet/Opera/Theatre

Hire a babysitter unless you're attending an open-air event. For events in a park, bring a blanket, sit on the grass, and play between acts or sets. Don't forget to pack a few small toys and bring along a picnic or some favorite snacks and a thermos of juice.

Children's Concerts

Depending on the performers, the pace of the show, and the average age of the audience, children's concerts can be fun. Sharon, Lois & Bram; Raffi; and Fred Penner concerts are wonderful. If your child can clap his hands, jump up and down, and sing along, it's guaranteed he'll have a good time. Outdoor concerts are best.

Major Sporting Events

Jenny attended her first major league baseball game for her first birthday. She thought it was the best party EVER. She cheered and booed at all the right moments, and jumped up and down with excitement. She became a baseball addict, and by three recognized her favorite players by first name on television.

She also went to the horse races with her grandparents at ten months. She was the best handicapper of the day, picking her horses at random from the Daily Racing Form. She spent an entire afternoon squealing every time the horses ran past her.

If you like sports, take your baby along. He'll let you know the first time out whether he enjoys it. Again, take snacks, juice, and small toys along.

Fairs/Exhibitions/Theme Parks

Many theme park rides are designed for older children, so check first to make sure there are rides suitable for your child if he is under three. Some rides are ideal for little ones, but others are simply too much. Respect your child's decisions to try out rides—he may go "ooooh" and "ahhh" at everything or he may be frightened.

Take a picture on the merry-go-round or swan
boats for Grandma's album. (Never force the is-
sue, allow his choices.)

Flower Shows/Boating Shows/ Sportsmen's Shows/Home Shows

Take along his stroller, his blanket, a special
cuddle animal, and his special food, and
browse to your heart's content. Show him everything you find interesting and let him get his
"hands on" everything possible.

Zoos

Zoos are marvelous for the whole family, if you
remember to wear comfortable shoes and
clothing, and take along enough food and diapers
for the day. Bring your own stroller from home.
With infants and toddlers, a slow pace is essential.
Don't be in a hurry to see every animal in one day.
Plan to take in a few exhibits and observe each
animal in great detail. It is better to really SEE one
animal than to exhaust yourself rushing from exhibit to exhibit. Modern zoos are so spacious that
after a few miles, you might get cranky. Your baby
can sleep in his stroller, but you can't. A trip to the
zoo must be fun for all, YOU included. Once the
fun is gone, go home. Plan to stop by the gift shop
on the way out, if possible—they usually stock
beautiful plush toys and excellent children's books
about animals.

The Aquarium

The aquarium is a great place to visit on a rainy
day. Infants and toddlers are fascinated by the
multi-colored fish swimming in their tanks. Like
the zoo, an aquarium requires in-depth viewing, so
relax, enjoy a slow pace, and give yourselves
plenty of time. If your aquarium has a dolphin
show, don't miss it!

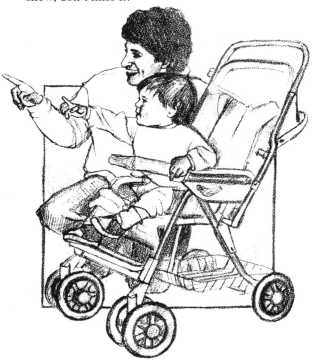

CHAPTER ELEVEN

Toys, Toys, Toys

Toys are a major ingredient of childhood. As a rule of thumb, select toys that can be used in a variety of ways. The more limited a toy's use, the faster your child will become bored with it. The toys that give the most satisfaction are traditional ones—balls, stuffed animals, cuddly dolls, and blocks—toys enjoyed by children of all cultures for centuries.

Expensive is not necessarily best when it comes to toy selection. Some expensive toys are fragile, or have limited play value, so that your child will soon outgrow them. Toy designers keep adult buyers in mind when marketing toys, which means your child may sometimes find the packaging of more interest than the contents.

The Safety Factor

Monitor toys for safety as your child plays with them, and get rid of or replace toys if they become unsafe. Consider the following when checking the safety of toys for under-threes:

- Can the toy, or parts of the toy, be swallowed or inhaled?
- Will the toy break easily?
- Does the toy have sharp edges?
- Will the toy wear out quickly?
- Does the toy contain batteries?
- Is the toy made of glass or brittle plastic?
- Are all parts of the toy non-toxic?
- Could pieces of the toy pinch tiny fingers?
- Could hair get caught in the toy?
- Could a long cord or string on the toy wrap around a child's neck?
- Will it hurt her if she eats it?

Homemade Toys

Many toys can be made from simple household items. Old socks can be stuffed and sewn to make dolls, with pretty embroidered faces. Plastic food containers can make a set of nesting toys. Pots and pans can be banged. Pieces of wood can be sanded to make stacking blocks. Macaroni and other hollow, dried pasta can be colored and strung for beads.

The Toy Library

Toy libraries exist in many areas. The public library, nursery school or a community resource organization may know if one is in your community. Find and use one close to you. These libraries are perfect for testing toys, especially expensive ones. If your child's interest in the toy lasts as long as the loan period, the toy is probably a worthwhile investment. If not, you haven't wasted any money.

Toy libraries are especially wonderful for puzzles—once a child has solved a puzzle, she is eager to try many new ones. Toy libraries provide a much larger range of puzzles than you will find in most department stores.

If a toy library is unavailable to you, perhaps you and friends or relatives can set up your own toy library or a toy exchange for outgrown toys.

HINT: Most well-loved toys can be disinfected and brightened with sodium hypochlorite (Javex or Chlorox bleach) dissolved in hot water, then washed with detergent and hot water and rinsed thoroughly. The "gentle" cycle of an automatic washer will clean small plastic toys, especially those covered with bits of teething biscuit.

The Busy Bag

A "busy bag" containing toys and treats can entertain your child while she is waiting in a doctor's office, for the bus, streetcar, subway—all those places where her usual toys are unavailable.

A busy bag for a baby could include a small photo album displaying pictures of babies, a bright book, a special toy animal, and a bottle of water. A busy bag for an older child could include a box of crayons or markers and a small pad of paper, small cars, a box of raisins, a favorite book, or a set of flash cards.

Make several busy bags and alternate them on trips. Always keep one stashed in your diaper bag.

Alternate Her Toys

A major problem with toys is that familiarity breeds contempt. Your child will see the same toys day after day and become bored with them. Alternate the toys that are in daily use. Have a hidden shelf high up in your closet for toys on vacation. Keep one or two toys as a special treat or when a new toy is just what is needed to cheer up a bored, cranky baby.

Don't forget the very inexpensive busy books, magic slates, small metal cars, small plastic dolls, new balls, and a new package of crayons and coloring book as a way of introducing new magic.

Toy Organization

Whatever your housekeeping style, you will soon realize it is almost impossible to keep toys under control without organizers. Your best organizers are bookshelves, plastic bins, plastic baskets, and your own self-discipline. All of the pieces to one toy belong together, and it is essential that you form the habit of spending five minutes in the morning and five minutes at night putting together pieces of toys that belong together. Open shelves make the job easier. Save small plastic tubs, bins, and metal cookie tins for dominos, marbles, magnetic letters, interlocking building pieces. Keep blocks in a simple drawstring bag.

Once you've disciplined yourself regarding toy storage, it is easier to help your child learn to put her toys away. Your child can only make effective use of her toys if she has all the parts. A puzzle with half the pieces missing is frustrating as well as a boring waste of time. Avoid using toy boxes and playpens as storage areas, because they inspire disorder. You can never find all the pieces when it's time to play.

A Room Without Toys

If you find yourself overwhelmed by toys, you can perhaps establish one room in the house where toys aren't permitted, except on temporary "visits." In a suburban "open-concept" house this might be difficult, but it can make life less cluttered if there is a place where the toys haven't taken over.

Toys Away Game

Your baby needs to be with you when tidying up. From the time she is about nine months old, she will be able to help you. Even if she drops just one block into a basket, as a game, it is a "win." By turning a chore into a game, it becomes fun, and the realization evolves that toys live in special places when they aren't in use. Simple chants such as "Toys Away" and "Tidy Up" make a game of getting toys picked up.

Tidy Up

(Use this chant once to indicate that toys need to be cleared.)

Tidy up,
Tidy up,
Everybody tidy up
Right now.

(Traditional, North America)

Toys Away

Toys away, toys away,
(Chant two or three times.)
Time to put your ——— away.
(Name the toy.)

(Traditional, North America)

TOYS FOR DIFFERENT AGES

Toys that our children liked at certain ages are the basis for the following recommendations. The popularity of some toys will span several age groups. Often your child will return to old favorites at a much later stage, especially when role-playing and imaginative play begin. As with everything, your child is a unique individual and there are many toys that she may not like that our children enjoyed, and she may enjoy toys not listed that our children didn't like.

Birth to Three Months

You will probably be inundated with toys as baby gifts. Put most of them away for a while. The only toys your infant needs are some bright faces to look at, some small fuzzy animals to grasp, a special stuffed toy to sleep with, and one or two small rattles. She also needs a mobile (see p. 19) over her crib or in her window, and perhaps a music box.

Three to Six Months

Toys start arousing your baby's curiosity. She will try to wriggle towards a toy she wants. Place a toy just outside her reach, and watch her go! She will wiggle and squirm to get to the toy, and the beginnings of locomotion occur. She will be quite frustrated when she ends up going backwards, but it won't be long before creeping and crawling will get her to that toy she wants. She is beginning to control her hand movements, so she can grasp small toys, perhaps ones suspended above her.

Provide a soft doll or cuddly animal who sleeps with her. Her friend will soothe her and she may be able to calm herself without your presence occasionally.

Your baby may enjoy a crib activity center. Soft cloth balls and blocks, squeaky plastic squeeze toys, wind chimes, chiming balls, and small textured toys are also favorites. When she is in her stroller, or infant chair, suspend some soft toys for her to grab and strike.

She loves to look at flowers, both real and plastic; hang some plastic ones where she can reach them.

Make her a discovery box. By the time she can sit up, she is able to open a small cardboard box. Place three or four small plastic toys inside for her to find and play with. She likes teething rings, a rattle that has several moving pieces on a ring, and toy keys.

While you are changing her, give her a clean diaper to play with or a small toy to hold to keep her from wiggling.

Six to Nine Months

A baby now finds balls of all sizes and colors appealing. Get her an assortment of balls ranging from a ping-pong ball to a beach ball. She will also enjoy large, blow-up cylinders that are bottom-heavy and can be knocked over, such as inflatable clowns that rock and chime. Give her toys with parts she can manipulate, for instance, a string to pull or a knob to push to make something happen. Color and noise are guaranteed to fascinate. She starts to love her special stuffed animal or doll. She needs toys that are rugged and can be banged together, toys that float, and toys that pour sand or water. She also needs a set of nesting or stacking toys.

Introduce your baby to the telephone, preferably a real one so she can listen to Daddy or Grandma on occasion. Buy her a toy phone.

Nine to Twelve Months

A nine- to twelve-month-old will find stackable soft blocks intriguing. She also likes pull toys that can be dragged around after her as she crawls, and soft balls. In fact, she loves balls of all sizes.

She has learned that some toys fit inside other toys, so provide some blocks that fit inside a box or a cylinder, or a very simple shape sorter. Stacking rings, animal toys, books, toy cars, small plastic toys of all kinds, and balls in a bowl are all fun at this age.

Twelve to Fifteen Months

Your baby will want to bring home objects she has discovered when you are out exploring together. Pine cones, acorns, chestnuts, seeds, leaves, sticks, seed pods, pebbles, seashells, nuts, feathers, dried weeds, grasses, rocks, and sand all attract her attention. Some of these can be placed inside containers to make rattles. Some can be pasted into books to touch or glued to paper to make art pieces. Be sure to save some of her priceless possessions.

Simple jack-in-the boxes, pull toys, stacking rings, snap-lock beads, indoor slides, small houses with people to go inside, a toy phone, a small riding toy propelled by feet, not pedals—all suit her newly developed mobility and coordination skills. The most essential toys for twelve- to fifteen-month-olds are blocks, stacking rings, and stacking and nesting blocks.

Fifteen to Eighteen Months

Your toddler loves push or pull toys, especially if they make NOISE. She will love a "popcorn popper," a lawnmower, or a whirling insect push toy. Pull toys on wheels like ducks, horses or trains are also lots of fun for her. Larger toys on wheels, such as a doll carriage, or a shopping cart, or a walking frame, also become popular as her walking improves.

It is now time to introduce lots of shape sorters and containers with lids for smaller toys to rattle around inside. Provide an assortment of blocks, spools, and large beads for her to put into her containers. She loves to play with some of the pieces of larger toys, even though she may not be playing with the big toy yet. Cuddly toy animals are a big part of her life, especially her special friend.

HINT: You may notice that your toddler has fallen in love with a blanket or a toy that is getting quite "ratty." Never throw out a well-loved snuggle item. Let her eventually reject the toy on her own terms, maybe years from now. This is a personal relationship that you don't want to destroy. After all, who ever said that love is rational?

Eighteen to Twenty-four Months

Provide your toddler with puzzles, balls, paints, finger paints, and stickers. She needs to experience both "goop" and real dough playing with Mom or Dad. She loves large stuffed animals. Sandboxes and water buckets are essential. More complex blocks that fit together, such as alphabet blocks that make words, or DUPLO blocks, are fun for her. Give her some "mail" to play with and a "suitcase" (perhaps an old purse or lunchbox). Surprise her by hiding a small box of raisins or a book in her suitcase. She likes toy animals. Get her a foam or plastic baseball bat and ball, or a plastic hockey stick and rubber ball. Insist on her following the real hockey rules, and tell her to keep the stick on the ice or pavement.

Twenty-four to Thirty Months

Your older toddler loves shape sorters, puzzles, her special teddy or panda bear, big wooden beads and shoelaces to string them on, and a large dumptruck for her sandbox. She loves playdough, art materials, stickers, and sticky papers. Show her how to use magnets to display her artwork on the refrigerator. A barn and farm animals will appeal to her. She also loves riding toys that she can push with her feet. A magnet and iron or steel washers will win lots of attention. Try using the magnet in her sandbox.

Thirty to Thirty-six Months

With the development of imagination, your child wants toys that will support her imaginative play, for example, hand puppets and finger puppets. A good puppet theatre is a small table turned over on its side. Dishes for tea parties, hats of all kinds, old clothes and jewelry, masks, and makeup are important props in her role-playing. She loves playing with "goop" and her art materials.

She likes musical toys and you might want to give your child a musical block or a toy glock-enspiel. She can now master "ride'em" toys, so a tricycle is a good gift for her third birthday, provided she has the coordination required to steer and pedal at the same time and a safe place to ride.

A pajama bag makes a comforting toy for her bed, and she loves to store her pajamas there in the morning. Water play, growing plants, and sand-play all fascinate her. She likes to match colors and shapes, and enjoys magnetic letters, numbers, flash cards, and peg boards.

She loves dressing up. Provide her with makeup, scarves, hats, jewelry, and old clothes so she can "pretend" and "make believe."

CHAPTER   TWELVE

Birthdays, Unbirthdays, Holidays, and Other Excuses for a Party

We all need some gilt on our gingerbread. Your baby needs carefree, fanciful times as much as you do. Everyone has fun when the daily routine is disrupted by a holiday.

Create your own family holidays by celebrating every special occasion. If you are feeling glum and out of sorts, it's time for a party. Celebrate victories and accomplishments, major and minor. Daddy got a new job! Grandma won at the racetrack! Mommy swam twelve lengths of the pool without stopping! Baby got a new tooth! The Garbageman came today and carted off the garbage! The first robin arrived at the birdfeeder! Baby found an acorn on his walk! The first snowfall since spring! A party can be as simple as lighting candles and dimming the lights at dinnertime to make a more festive meal.

Besides family parties, organize parties for children your child's age, and share the party-giving with other mothers. For example, Thoma has the Hanukkah party, Elaine has the Christmas party, Helene has the Twelfth Night party, and Judy has the Groundhog Day party. By sharing the party giving, everyone can enjoy themselves and no one needs to do all the work.

Where to start celebrating? Start with ALL family birthdays. Add traditional holidays and make up your own holidays. Have a holiday whenever you or your child needs one.

Baby's Own Birthday

Your baby's birthday is most important day of the year for him. He is the center of attention, and it is his holiday, alone. No sharing, no waiting while other people open presents, they are all his. Invite your child's friends and limit the number of young guests to three or four. Have a cake, candles, noisemakers, music, and dancing. Make it a special occasion. Drape streamers around the house and blow up balloons.

Have a sing-song, featuring many of his favorite songs, such as "Wheels on The Bus" (p.101), "Alouette!" (p. 62), "Bumpin' Up and Down" (p. 85) and "Old McDonald" (p. 49). Organize a rhythm band, using pots and pans, plastic ice cream containers, and bells. Play your baby's favorite instrumental songs.

Play lots of circle and action games like Hokey Pokey (p.87), Looby Loo (p. 87), B-I-N-G-O (p. 87), Ring Around A Rosy (p. 71), Simon Says (p. 100), Frogs on a Lily Pad (p. 132), What Time Is It, Mr. Wolf (p. 161), and Musical Chairs (p. 104).

Serve simple refreshments, such as popsicles, ice cream, cake, and toddler finger foods. Make sure you have favors—little presents—for all your small guests to take home in their loot bags.

Play lots of children's records. Sing and dance along. Costumes or face makeup might be part of the fun. Remember, though, to be sensitive to the children who do not like to dress up or have their faces made up.

The Birthday Cake

Your child needs his own very special birthday cake with lots of decorations, including candles. Add one candle for every year, and a big one "to grow on." Have him make a wish before blowing out the candles. If you have him practice blowing out the lights in his bedroom before going to bed, or blowing out a flashlight (as you control the switch), he will have plenty of "puff" before his first birthday.

Special Birthday Cake

This birthday cake has been made for at least five generations of birthdays in our family. It has no fat. Follow the instructions exactly, for a perfect cake every time. (This cake is not suitable for the first birthday, as it contains egg whites.)

2 eggs, yolk and white separated
⅔ cup cold water
1 ¼ cups sugar
1 ½ cups unbleached cake flour, sifted
½ tsp baking powder
½ tsp salt
½ tsp cream of tartar
1 tsp vanilla or almond extract

In a large bowl, pour the egg yolks and the cold water. Beat until the volume looks enough to make 4 cups, with a hand or electric beater. Add 1 cup of sugar and beat for seven minutes. Sift together the flour, baking powder, and salt and add to the egg yolk mixture, beating until well mixed. In a chilled bowl, beat together the egg whites and the cream of tartar. Slowly add ¼ cup sugar, beating until the egg whites hold peaks. Add the flavoring.

Fold the egg white mixture into the egg yolk mixture and bake in a greased tube pan or 8-inch x 8-inch square pan in a 350°F oven for 45 minutes, or until done.

I usually ice the cake with a lightly sweetened whipped cream, and decorate with fresh fruit, such as strawberries, kiwi, grapes, orange segments, raspberries, or whatever is in season. Candles look especially festive when placed in strawberries.

Butter Icing (Alternative)

Cream ¼ cup butter until soft. Gradually stir in ¾ cup sifted confectioner's sugar. Add ½ tsp vanilla and a dash of salt. Add another ¾ cup confectioner's sugar alternately with 2 ¼ Tbsp cream or hot milk, beating until smooth after each addition. Add a drop or two of food coloring, if desired.

Unbirthdays

In our family, Daddy and Grandma have birthdays right after Christmas, when everyone is partied out. We've formed the habit of having "unbirthdays," birthday celebrations at times other than actual birthdays—perhaps three, six, or nine months after the day itself. We celebrate on the same day of the month, however. An "unbirthday" is a day when a person who has a "mis-timed" birthday can have a truly personal celebration.

At the unbirthday party, everyone carries on as though it were a regular birthday party, with a few exceptions. Silly hats, costumes, and makeup are mandatory. Silly games are played, such as "Musical Floor" (nobody gets out because everybody has a place to sit down), and "Pin the Tail on the Gorilla." If your child is learning jokes, tell some of his really silly favorites. If presents are given, they should be delightfully silly.

Note: We celebrate unbirthday parties for adults, although we invite as many small children to an unbirthday as we would to a child's birthday party. An unbirthday party should NEVER replace your child's own birthday party, even if his birthday happens to fall on Christmas Day. On his actual birthday, make sure he has his own separate birthday presents, and a birthday cake of his own.

We add a bit to unbirthdays and get away with more silliness, without hurting anyone's feelings. For instance, for Daddy's unbirthday Mommy was distracted during the construction of the cake. The supervision was slightly bananas and Jenny (34 months) followed most of the recipe. The cake didn't come out quite right because the dry stuff didn't get sifted together, the stirring didn't get done quite thoroughly, and, well, it was a bit lopsided. It was still a very special cake with a very special candle that Jenny had made at a crafts class. So what if the candle was purple and uneven? Daddy still puffed it out! We added a few sparklers to the cake (it was almost a firecracker day) to add to the festivity. The icing was lumpy and a little bit runny, but still tasted wonderful.

Unbirthday Songs

At our unbirthday parties we sing lots of silly songs, like "Aikendrum" including Willy Wood (p. 90), "Old McDonald" (p. 49) with the silliest animals we can think of, and "The Ants Go Marching" (p. 112). We also sing some old university rugby club songs with freshly laundered lyrics.

A CALENDAR OF HOLIDAYS

All traditional holidays are causes for celebration. The celebrations we enjoy with our children establish family traditions that last for years, and sometimes for generations.

Children are included at our parties. We believe housewarmings, cookouts, and traditional grown-up celebrations such as New Year's are a time for families to include children. With an assortment of finger foods of varying degrees of sophistication, appropriate libations, a huge stack of tapes of dance music for both children and adults, and one room full of toys, both kids and grownups have a grand time. Let's not exclude our children from our party lives.

New Year's Eve

New Year's Eve is special in our family. New Year's Eve is when we get together with friends to welcome the new year. We gather together early in the evening, and roast weiners in the fireplace for the children (and some adults who are hungry), along with toasted marshmallows. If weather permits, we go skating, or go for a walk outdoors. Later in the evening the adults and the children who are still awake sit down to a formal dinner. Usually the host family provides the main course, and guests bring appetizers, salad, soup, dessert, or rolls, according to a previously designed "master plan." We have a "midnight countdown" and sing "Auld Lang Syne." After midnight it's time for dessert, coffee, and best wishes for the coming year. Often the party continues into brunch at someone else's place.

New Year's Day

Every country has its "renewal holiday." New Year's Day is a time of hope and magic. It is a time to make a fresh start. Celebrate the New Year's Days of all cultures. The Chinese New Years occurs in mid-winter, and Rosh Hashanah in early fall.

Groundhog Day/Candlemas Day (February 2nd)

Candlemas Day, or Groundhog Day, is the halfway point of winter. It is the day the sun is halfway between the winter solstice and the vernal equinox. It is day, traditionally, to predict the end of winter. In North America, if the groundhog sees his shadow, he returns to his hole because winter is going to last another six weeks. If he doesn't see his shadow, winter is over.

Take a ride in the country, or take a long walk to look for the groundhog. Talk about the changing seasons. Look at the trees for signs of buds. One way to experience the coming of spring is to force bloom some forsythia sprigs indoors. After it blooms try to start a new forsythia bush by leaving woody forsythia branches in water until roots appear after blossoming. Plant your new bush outside when spring officially arrives.

Candlemas Party

Candlemas Day or Groundhog Day is the day to have a party for school friends if your child has a birthday in the summer. Have a cake and candles, and a theme of "spring is coming," but don't call it a birthday party. Play lots of your favorite games and sing songs.

St. Valentine's Day (February 14)

St. Valentine is the patron saint of lovers. Make Valentine's day your special "I Love You" day. Hearts, flowers, cuddles, and chocolates are a wonderful part of this day.

Start your preparations right after Groundhog Day. Make valentines from red and pink paper. Cut paper "snowflakes" from tissue paper and paste on colored hearts. Make "I Love You" messages for all your family members, the elderly in your neighborhood, and your babysitter. Make "secret admirer" valentines for neighbors who have become your child's special friends. Decorate your valentines with stickers, paper doilies, and ribbons. Send valentines to friends and relatives who live far away.

Flowers

One daddy I know brings his little girl flowers on Valentine's Day. Her eyes light up, and she goes "Oh-hh-hh-h-h." Those flowers from her dad are the most special event of her day.

Valentine's Party

Have a party and serve cupcakes with candy hearts on top, or a cake baked in a heart-shaped pan. Decorate your house with red and white crêpe paper streamers and blow up red and white balloons.

Sing love songs such as "Can You Make Me a Cambric Shirt" (p. 41) and "Skinnamarink" (p. 126).

Make a big red heart to put up on the wall, and play a game of "Pin the Arrows on the Heart" instead of "Pin the Tail on the Donkey." Serve a big dish of red, spicy, heart-shaped candies. Make some rolled cookies and cut them in heart shapes. Decorate them with silver dragées and heart-shaped candies. Read some love poetry, and recite some traditional Valentine's Day rhymes.

The Rose Is Red, the Violet's Blue

The rose is red, the violet's blue,
The honey's sweet, and so are you.
Thou art my love and I am thine;
I drew thee to my Valentine.
The lot was cast and then I drew,
And fortune said it should be you.

(Traditional, Great Britain)

I Love You Because...

Play "I Love You Because" games. "I love you because you have big feet," "I love you because your eyes are blue (green, brown)," "I love you because you are a special person," "I love you because you are pudgy and bald," "I love you because you are a rotten little kid," and — "I love you because you're you!"

Purim (late February, early March)

During the Jewish holiday of Purim, the story of Esther is read from the Torah. In the story is a villain named Hamen who is hissed and booed every time his name is mentioned. Children are given rattles, noisemakers and whistles to scare Hamen away.

A special type of "trick or treat" occurs during Purim, when children dressed in costume go from door to door saying, "Today is Purim, tomorrow it's o'er. Give me a penny and show me the door."

The children are given pennies, fruit, candy and special "Hamentaschen" treats. Hamentaschen are sweet pastries made from a sweet bread, biscuit, or cookie dough that is stuffed with either a poppy-seed or prune filling. A record featuring songs and stories of Purim and Hanukkah, *Latkes and Hamentaschen* by Fran Avni, is available from Lemonstone Records.

Shrovetide

S hrovetide is the four-day period before the beginning of the Christian Lent. On Ash Wednesday, a traditional period of fasting begins, lasting until Easter, approximately six weeks away. Before this fast there is much festivity, such as Mardi Gras in New Orleans, and Carnival in Brazil and Trinidad. Bright costumes, music, and dancing highlight Carnival time, which ends at midnight on Shrove Tuesday.

Shrovetide includes the Sunday before Ash Wednesday, Collop* Monday, Shrove Tuesday, and Ash Wednesday. Historically, during Lent, a fast lasted until sundown. No meat or rich foods were allowed, and all milk, eggs, and fat had to be consumed before the fasting period began.

*Collops are thin slices of meat

Celebrate Mardi Gras

H ave a Mardi Gras or Carnival party with bright costumes, makeup, and dancing. Supply noisemakers, streamers, balloons, and, if you can stand the mess, confetti. Alternate reggae and calypso records with your favorite children's music. Serve simple snacks, including fresh tropical fruit, especially oranges and bananas.

Mardi Gras Picnic

M ardi Gras is the perfect time for an indoor picnic. Shut the blinds, turn on all the lights, and spread beach towels and blankets on the floor. Put on tropical shirts, shorts, sunhats, or bathing suits.

Make some crêpe paper palm leaves and bright flowers for the walls and ceilings. Play tropical music and eat grapefruit, bananas, oranges,

mangoes, papayas or pineapples. If you have a fireplace, have a weiner roast. Spread out an old shower curtain or split open a green garbage bag and set out a bucket of water and your indoor sandbox. Put on your sunglasses and pretend you're in Trinidad.

An indoor picnic can be a lifesaver anytime during the winter.

Thread the Needle

(A group game)

"Thread the Needle" is an ancient game played during Shrovetide, on May Day, and during harvest festivals. Children hold hands and form a long line, with alternate children facing in opposite directions. The first two children face each other, arms raised to form an arch—the eye of the needle. The last child in the line becomes the leader and the whole line follows him through the eye of the needle, still holding hands. The last pair then becomes the eye of the needle. Sing songs and chant rhymes as the needle is threaded.

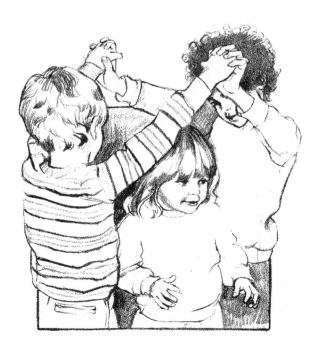

Pancake Day

On Shrove Tuesday, pancakes are traditionally served to rid the house of milk, butter, and eggs, as these rich foods are not allowed during Lent. Pancake races through the village were traditional on Pancake Day, and were followed by lots of "Thread the Needle" games. Needless to say, huge platters of pancakes and syrup are served.

Basic Pancake Race

Make stacks of pancakes (p. 96). Establish a starting line and a finish line. Have the children line up, holding pancakes on spatulas. Say, "One, two, three, go!" and see who crosses the finish line first, without dropping any pancakes.

Pancake Relay Race

Establish two teams of runners, and divide them equally between the start and finish lines. On "Go!" two contestants race to the finish line, and pass pancakes from spatula to spatula; the next two runners race back to the start line; the next two runners race to the finish line and so on. If a pancake drops to the ground, it can be picked up. Below are some "start-the-race" rhymes.

One to Make Ready

One to make ready,
Two to prepare,
Good luck to the rider,
And away goes the mare!

(Traditional, Great Britain)

One for the Money

One for the money,
Two for the show,
Three to make ready,
And four to go!

(Traditional, Great Britain, United States)

April Fool's Day (April 1)

This day's objective is to make a joke at someone else's expense so that that person becomes the "April Fool." Fooling finishes by noon, or the person trying to play a joke becomes the fool. April Fool's Day is the only day of the year when your worst jokes are appreciated. And just in case you need some groaners:

Why do bees hum?
Because they don't know the words.

What do you get if you cross a rooster with a poodle?
A cockerpoodledo.

What do you get if you cross a cow with a duck?
Cream quackers.

What do you get if you pour boiling water down a rabbit hole?
Hot, cross bunnies.

Good Friday

Another wonderful centuries-old tradition is the eating of hot cross buns from Good Friday until Easter. Small buns with crosses have been made since Egyptian times (such buns were even found in the ruins of Pompeii). In England, hot cross buns became popular during the 1300s, as pilgrims travelled to distant churches for Easter services. They are still a wonderful picnic food. In recent years, hot cross buns have become available during the entire Lenten season.

Hot Cross Buns! Hot Cross Buns!

(Have your child play his bells as you sing this song.)

Hot cross buns! Hot cross buns!
One a penny, two a penny,
Hot cross buns!
If your daughters do not like them
Give them to your sons;
But if you haven't any
Of these pretty little elves,
You cannot do better
Than eat them yourselves.

(Traditional, London street chant)

Easter (March or April)

Easter is the Christian festival celebrating the resurrection, the coming of spring, and the rebirth of the land. Participants dress up in their new spring finery and sometimes take part in parades. Take your toddler to an Easter parade, or have an informal parade in your neighborhood. Children in decorated wagons and tricycles, or pushing doll carriages, can troop around singing their favorite Easter songs.

One symbol of Easter is the egg, signifying rebirth. The Easter Bunny brings children pretty baskets filled with candy eggs and chocolate rabbits. Children sometimes search for candy Easter eggs that have been hidden around the house. If weather permits, you can have an outdoor Easter egg hunt, using hard-boiled eggs. After the eggs are found, it is fun to have relay races, passing an egg in a spoon to other team members, or an egg-rolling contest, pushing the egg along the ground with your nose.

It is fun to get a group of children together to decorate eggs. Melt a crayon or two, and paint a design on the egg using a fine-pointed brush, perhaps an old eyeliner brush. Then lower the egg into a non-toxic Easter egg dye (egg decoration kits are available). The wax in the crayon acts as a resist, and makes attractive contrasts.

Traditionally, Easter dinner is usually either roast lamb or baked ham and is served with spring's first fresh vegetables. Easter is also a day to get together with friends or relatives for brunch. Prepare some hard-boiled Easter eggs. Open-faced egg salad sandwiches topped with smoked salmon bits, served with a watercress salad, is a perfect way to celebrate the arrival of spring.

After your lunch or dinner, go for a walk to find the flowers. The first crocuses, daffodils, and tulips may be starting, and you will feel that winter is over.

Great Easter books for under threes include *It's Not Easy Being a Bunny*, by Marilyn Saddler, illustrated by Roger Bollen, Random House; *Tales of Peter Rabbit*, by Beatrix Potter; and *The Golden Egg Book* by Margaret Wise Brown.

Passover

Passover is an eight-day Jewish holiday, a time of homecoming, prayer, song, and feasting. Only unleavened bread is eaten during this festival, in remembrance of the unleavened dough used during the Jews' flight from Egypt. All other foods eaten must be specially Kosher for Passover, and many food rituals are enjoyed by the whole family. Children are a special part of this festival, as the purpose of the Seder ceremony is to pass on Jewish history to the children.

The Ceremonial Cleaning (The night before Passover)

All leavened bread and cracker crumbs must be removed before Passover begins. Parents scatter a few cracker crumbs in the corners of the kitchen when the children aren't looking. After synagogue, the whole family searches for any remaining crumbs. The children brush up the crumbs with a goose feather. Then the mother burns the crumbs with a candle as the rest of the family watches.

Ritual Dishes

Special serving dishes are used at Passover, as well as the finest table linen, fruits, and flowers. Every person has a goblet, and a special goblet for the prophet Elijah is provided. A special plate receives the traditional Passover foods of Seder—three perfect matzos; a roasted lamb bone; a roasted egg; bitter herbs; horseradish; a combination of chopped apple, nuts, and wine; sweet herbs of watercress, parsley, and endive; salt water; the special goblets, and the book of the Seder, one for each person.

Afrikomen

The traditional dessert served at the Seder supper is the Afrikomen, a piece of the ritual matzo. One child searches for the last hidden piece of the matzo; when this dessert is eaten, the supper ends.

Sham-al-Nessin (March 21)

A Moslem holiday corresponding to the Christian Easter and Jewish Passover is the Egyptian Sham-al-Nessin. This holiday celebrates the first day of spring. The entire family goes out together to search for the loveliest spot where they can be together to enjoy the fragrances of spring.

In the morning the parents and children engage in serious discussions of both family issues and the wonders of nature. Everyone eats a huge lunch. After lunch the parents and children enjoy singing, storytelling, games, and kite-flying.

May Day (May 1)

In northern climates, the arrival of spring has been celebrated for centuries on May Day, also called Beltane, or Walpurgis Day. May Day is a time for gathering flowers, and going to the woods. Construct a maypole using a broomstick and some brightly colored ribbons or crêpe paper. Show three or four children how to weave in and out as they dance around the maypole. It is also a traditional time of matchmaking and matrimony.

Take your child to a park, or go for a walk in the woods. You might pick some common wild flowers to make nosegays for your neighbors. Place nosegays on doorsteps, trying not to be caught in the act. May First is a perfect day to get children out and skip, hop and jump around to burn off winter. Get together with other parents and make May Day an event. Plan a picnic with lots of action games, such as tag, "B-I-N-G-O" (p. 87) "Ring Around the Rosy," (p. 71) and "Thread the Needle" (p. 154) is also played on May Day, accompanied by some special May Day songs.

Here We Come Gathering Knots of May

(Drop the hankie. One child walks around the outside of a circle of players and drops a hankie behind another child. Both run around the circle to take the empty place. The last one back is "it" for the next game.)

Here we come gathering knots of May,
Knots of May, knots of May.
Here we come gathering knots of May,
At six o'clock in the morning.

(Traditional, England)

Good Morning, Mistress and Master

If your child gives "May baskets," here is a traditional chant:

Good morning, Mistress and Master,
I wish you a happy day;
Please to smell my garland
'Cause it is the First of May.

A branch of May I have brought you,
And at your door I stand;
It is but a sprout, but it's well budded out
The work of our Lord's hand.

(Traditional, England)

Firecracker Days

The Fourth of July, Victoria Day, Canada Day, and Bastille Day (July 14) are all celebrated with outdoor fireworks displays and can be combined with an evening picnic or band concert performance. Summer evenings can be cool, so take along sweaters, a blanket or two, and a thermos of hot liquid. Don't forget your baby's favorite toys and blanket.

If fireworks are legal in your area, get a package of sparklers for your baby to enjoy so he can go ooohhh and ahhhh. For several years on Victoria Day, we have had a small neighborhood fireworks display in the largest backyard. Each family contributes a modest sum in advance or brings some favorite fireworks. Children are not allowed to go near the "blast zone," and one parent is selected to light all the fireworks, set in a big sandbox. Everyone enjoys.

Some babies love fireworks, others are apprehensive, and some will let you know immediately that they want no part of this at all. Provide lots of reassurance, if necessary.

Summer Vacations and Holidays

If you slow down your usual pace when your baby is travelling with you, the dividends are tremendous! Include special children's places such as zoos, parks, playgrounds, and beaches.

When travelling, take extra breaks and stretch your legs frequently. We have made some major changes in our travel routine since Jenny's birth. From our front door to Grampa and Grandma's front door is 600 miles. When we travelled by expressway in one day we got there tired, cranky and good for nothing the next day. We now take two days, use the back roads, stop to explore our interests and arrive invigorated, rested, and eager to talk about our travelling experiences and adventures. We also don't lose a day to "travel grumps." We know we can get onto the expressway if we get bored with our explorations.

Travelling With Baby by Car

Take along an assortment of busy bags and some favorite cassette tapes, if you have a portable tape recorder or a tape deck in your car. As the miles pass, sing songs and play "I Spy" (p. 84), looking for certain colored cars, or interesting landmarks.

One of the advantages of your baby's car seat is that he is able to see, so talk about everything you and he can see. Even on a boring expressway, you can count red cars or tractor trailers.

Stop frequently to stretch your legs and have a snack. Take along a bag of healthy cookies, muffins, foil-wrapped cheese, and fresh fruit, in case you can't face another fast-food outlet. Include a thermos of cold juice.

Make sure your child's special cuddly animals and blankets are along, especially for reassurance in strange hotel rooms.

Try to stop early enough in the evening to explore a bit as a family. Room service is "manna from heaven" for travelling families, although sometimes children, toddlers, and babies can be angelic in even the classiest hotel dining rooms. We have found that travelling is special family time when we take the time to enjoy it.

Harvest Festivals

Nearly all countries celebrate the harvest with a huge meal of thanksgiving. Usually a roast turkey with stuffing, cranberry sauce, potatoes, and vegetables is served, and everyone eats like a glutton. Another meal to commemorate a good harvest is a "boiled dinner": corned beef, cabbage, carrots, onions, peppers, potatoes, beets, and cabbage simmered in a pot. The remains of the boiled dinner are turned into "red flannel hash."

September Blow Soft

September blow soft
Till the fruit's in the loft.

(Traditional, United States)

Old Roger

(You need a large group of all-sized people to play this rollicking game.)

Old Roger is dead and laid in his grave,
> (Old Roger —a parent or older child— lies down on the floor.)

Laid in his grave, laid in his grave;
Old Roger is dead and laid in his grave,
Heigh-ho*, laid in his grave.

They planted an apple tree over his head,
> (The smallest child stands at Old Roger's head as the apple tree.)

Over his head, over his head;
They planted an apple tree over his head,
Heigh-ho, over his head.

The apples grew ripe and ready to fall,
> (The rest of the group — except the old woman — surrounds the apple tree, to become apples.)

Ready to fall, ready to fall.
The apples grew ripe and ready to fall,
Heigh-ho, ready to fall.

There came an old woman a-picking them all,
> (The tallest person — the old woman — picks the apples, one by one.)

A-picking them all, a-picking them all.
There came an old woman a-picking them all,
Heigh-ho, a-picking them all.
> (Repeat verse until all apples are picked.)

Old Roger jumps up and gives her a knock,
> (Old Roger jumps up quickly.)

Gives her a knock, gives her a knock;
> (Taps the old woman.)

Old Roger jumps up and gives her a knock,
> (Chases her around the circle.)

Heigh-ho, gives her a knock.

Which makes the old woman go hipperty hop,
> (Old woman goes hopping off.)

Hipperty hop, hipperty hop;
Which makes the old woman go hipperty hop,
> (Old Roger goes after her, takes her by the hands, and they dance around in a circle.)

Heigh-ho, Hipperty hop.

*In the traditional Appalachian version, "H'm ha!" is substituted for "Heigh-ho."

(Traditional, Great Britain, Appalachia)

"Old Roger" can be sung again, as "Wind the Clock" is played (see below). The old woman takes the apple tree's hand, and the clock is first wound up, and then unwound. The traditional instrument for playing "Old Roger" is a dulcimer.

Wind the Clock

Players join hands, arms outstretched, with the tallest person at the end of the line. Everyone begins to sing. The tallest player stands still as the player at the opposite end leads the line around and around the tallest player, until the entire line is wrapped around the player in the middle and nobody can move. The surrounded player can try to pull his or her way out, with everyone following, or the group can reverse direction and unwind itself. (The latter activity is better if very young children are playing.)

Sukkoth

Sukkoth is a Jewish thanksgiving festival celebrated in late September or early October. A thatched hut is built outside for the children to play in. The roof is made of leaves or branches through which the stars shine at night. The inside of the hut is decorated with hanging fruits and vegetables, paper chains, and drawings.

Lots of fruits and vegetables are served during the Sukkoth festival, and strudel is a favorite dessert.

Halloween   (October 31)

Your child's birthday is the only holiday that may be more important than Halloween. There is a magical quality about Halloween. Most children over two love dressing up, trick-or-treating, making Jack-O'-Lanterns out of pumpkins, and bobbing for apples. Encourage your child to get involved in the spirit of Halloween. There is something wonderful about scaring yourself silly and enjoying every second of it.

If trick-or-treating makes you apprehensive, have a party at home instead. Bobbing for apples, eating donuts from a string, dressing up in costume, and making up faces are all wonderful and safe ways to enjoy the holiday. If you do decide to go trick-or-treating, go to houses you know. Never overwhelm your child by trying to do too much trick-or-treating, and respect his wishes about costumes and makeup. Some children love to dress up in scarey costumes, but others find it frightening.

Bobbing for Apples

Float some apples in a plastic tub or a pail with water. Each child holds his hands behind his back while he tries to pick up an apple with his teeth. HINT: Shallow water is best for very young children, and have lots of towels handy to wipe up spills.

Donuts on Strings

Hang donuts on strings at an appropriate height. Each child tries to eat the donut while his hands are behind his back.

Read Scarey Stories

The Spookey Old Tree by Stan and Jan Berenstain, Random House, is perfect for Halloween, as is *A Woggle of Witches* by Adrienne Adams, Atheneum. Read *Hansel and Gretel* and recite Halloween rhymes.

I'm a Jack-O'-Lantern

I'm a Jack-O'-Lantern with a great big grin.
> (Smile.)

I'm a Jack-O'-Lantern with a candle in.
> (Hold index finger in front of mouth.)

Poof! goes the wind and
> (Blow quickly at finger.)

Out goes the light.
> (Shut eyes.)

Away fly the witches
> (Flap arms.)

On Halloween Night.

(Traditional, North America)

Late One Dark and Stormy Night

Late one dark and stormy night,
(Use spooky voice.)
Three little witches are stirring a pot.
(Stir imaginary pot.)
Two little ghosts to say, "How d'ye do?"
(Lower voice gradually.)
Went tip toe, tip toe, tip toe.
(Barely whisper.)
Booooo!
(Very loud "boo!")

(Traditional, North America)

On a Dark, Dark Night

(Use scary whisper until the word GHOST.)

On a dark, dark night,
In the dark, dark woods,
In a dark, dark house,
In a dark, dark room,
In a dark, dark cupboard,
In a dark, dark box,
There's a GHOST!

(Traditional, North America)

Hinx, Minx

Hinx, minx the old witch winks,
The fat begins to fry.
Nobody's home but Jumping Joan,
Father, mother and I.
Stick, stone, stone dead,
Blind men can't see;
Every knave will have a slave,
You or I must be he.

(Traditional, Great Britain)

Bat, Bat

Bat, bat, come under my hat
And I'll give you a slice of bacon!
And when I bake, I'll give you a cake
If I am not mistaken.

(Traditional, Great Britain)

Scary Games

Play some scary games with the children. At least one of the players should be a grown-up to keep the game going.

Craney Crow

(Hide 'n' Seek. The "chicks" hide as the rhyme is chanted, and the hours to 12 are counted. The witch then tries to find the chicks.)

Chickamy, chickamy, craney crow,
I went to the well to wash my toe.
When I got back, my chickens were gone.
What time is it, Old Witch?

(Traditional, Great Britain)

What Time Is It, Mr. Wolf?

One child plays the wolf. The rest line up in a "safe" zone some distance from the wolf. The group asks, in unison, "What time is it, Mr. Wolf?" The wolf says, for example, "Four o'clock" and everyone takes four steps forward. This continues until the players are close to the wolf. He then says, "Dinner time!" and gives chase, trying to catch as many children as possible before they reach the safe zone. The last child to reach the safe zone, or the first child caught, is the next Mr. Wolf. Play "What Time is it, Mr. Wolf?" frequently, not just at Halloween.

Jack-O'-Lantern

Decide in advance if you want to carve a happy, sad, or scary face on your pumpkin or the more traditional turnip. Make your Jack-O'-Lantern no sooner than the night before Halloween, so it won't start to spoil or collapse. Cut the lid off first, dig the stringy pulp and seeds out, and place the seeds aside to roast later. Your toddler might help separate the seeds from the pulp (soak in water first). Once all the pulp is removed, use a spoon to scrape all the fiber from the bottom and sides, until only solid pumpkin is left. Carve the features for the face, using a thin-bladed, very sharp knife. The finer the features, the more difficult the carving, and the smaller the knife blade required.

Save the chunks of cut-out pumpkin for a pumpkin pie or pumpkin soup. With some care, your entire Jack-O'-Lantern can be used later for cooking.

Cut a hole in the base of the pumpkin the size of a votive candle, so the candle will stand securely inside. Do not leave the Jack-O'-Lantern unattended when the candle is lit.

HINTS: A boning knife for chicken or fish is recommended, as it has a flexible blade. To steam a pumpkin, peel and cook it as for winter squash, 15-20 minutes, or until tender. Strain or process in a food processor after cooking.

Halloween Party

Decorate in orange and black, the traditional Halloween colors. Use flashlights rather than candles in Jack-O'-Lanterns. Dress up in costumes, make up faces, and serve plain donuts, apples, cider and cheese. Get into the spirit of Halloween several days before the big day, and let your child choose his costume.

Guy Fawkes Day (November 5)

Guy Fawkes Day is Great Britain's "Firecracker Day." Guy Fawkes was one of the conspirators in the Gunpowder Plot to over-throw the British Parliament in 1604. A "Guy" is now a dummy burned in a bonfire as part of the celebrations. Children beg for money to buy fireworks, saying, "A Penny for the Guy, Sir," and bonfires are lit. "Parkin" is a special cake served on Guy Fawkes Day. If the weather permits, you might organize the year's last outdoor cookout.

The Fifth of November

The Fifth of November, they bid you remember,
The bright little boys with the funny old Guy.
In his chair up and down, he'll be borne through
*   the town,*
Then burned in a bonfire, he'll be by-and-by.

And those who remember, the fifth of November
Some money will give to the boys with the Guy.
If all gave a penny, I wonder how many
Wheels, crackers, and squibs they'd be able to buy?

(Thomas Crane, Great Britain 1883)

Parkin

Mix in a bowl:

⅔ cup rolled oats
1 cup all-purpose flour
½ tsp. ginger
¼ tsp. cloves
½ tsp. cinnamon
½ tsp. baking soda
1 tsp. grated lemon rind
½ cup raisins

Melt together:

½ cup butter and
⅔ cup dark corn syrup or golden syrup (treacle)

Add:

⅔ cup milk to the butter mixture and add to the dry ingredients.

Pour the entire mixture into a greased 8 x 8 inch pan and bake at 350° until the cake pulls from the side of the pan, approximately 35 minutes. Cut into bars, and allow to cool.

Hanukkah

Hanukkah, the Jewish Feast of Lights, com-memorates the Macabees' recapture of the Temple in Jerusalem from the Romans. Every night for eight days, the eldest child in a family lights a candle in the Menorah (a special candle-stick) until all eight candles burn on the eighth day (A ninth candle is used to light the others.)

Children receive gifts of gelt (chocolate coins covered with gold foil) or real money, often hidden in the pockets of visiting relatives and friends. Dreidels, four-sided tops imprinted with the first four letters of the Hebrew alphabet, are spun to foretell the future. Some children gamble their Hanukkah gelt by wagering on the results of the Dreidel spin. A special food for the holiday is Latkes.

Spinning the Dreidel

Each player starts with ten pennies, pieces of gelt, beans, raisins, or poker chips.

1. Each player puts one piece in the center.
2. The Dreidel is spun. The letter facing up when the top stops indicates what to do next:

   נ NUN—Do nothing. The next player has a turn.

   ג GIMEL—Take all the pieces.

   ה HAY—Take half the pieces.

   ש SHIN—Pay two pieces.

3. The player with the most pieces at the end of the game is the winner. If at any time no pieces are left, start the game again.

The words on a dreidel form the sentence: "A great miracle happened here." This commemorates the miracle of the oil that burned for eight days when there was only enough for one after the purification of the Temple.

Latkes

(These potato pancakes are often served during Hanukkah.)

6 medium potatoes
1 small onion (optional)
1 tsp salt (or to taste)
1 egg, beaten
3 Tbsps flour, matzo meal, or bread crumbs
½ tsp baking powder

Wash, pare, and grate potatoes. Strain off the liquid. Grate the onion. Add the onion, salt, and egg to the potatoes. Beat well. Add remaining ingredients, mixed together, and beat well again. Drop by spoonfuls into hot fat in a frying pan. Brown the pancakes on both sides. Serve with applesauce, sour cream, or plain yogurt, and sprinkle with cinnamon.

Christmas

The Christmas season is an enchanting time for your child. Remember your own special Christmas memories, and put in the effort to make your baby's Christmas as magical as it was for you. Start your preparations early, and make or do something special every day during the Advent Season.

A sure way to destroy all the fun and joy of the season is to treat it as shopping in crowds for a couple of days combined with a hectic dinner and gifts on the holiday itself. Treat Christmas as the season from the beginning of Advent four Sundays before Christmas, until Epiphany on the sixth of January. Spread out the magic to make a long and happy festive season for everyone.

By all means, play down the commercial aspects of Christmas, but do delight in the wonders that abound during the holiday season. Take your child to a major department store to see the

Christmas window displays. Drive around residential neighborhoods to see the Christmas lights. Go ice skating and drink hot chocolate together. Prepare gift packages for needy children, and set aside non-perishable food gifts for distribution by charities. Perhaps visit a senior citizens' home with your toddler and let the generations enjoy each other at this special time of the year.

Stir Up Sunday

The Sunday before Advent, "Stir Up Sunday" is traditionally the day when fruit cake and plum pudding are made in time to mature before the holiday. Carrot puddings and suet puddings are also traditional desserts served on Christmas Day. The following recipe for steamed molasses pudding doesn't contain large amounts of saturated fats, and has been the family's traditional Christmas pudding for five generations.

Steamed Molasses Pudding

Beat 1 egg thoroughly. Add ¾ cup molasses, and 1 tsp baking soda, dissolved in ½ cup warm water.

Sift 1½ cups all-purpose flour, with ½ tsp salt and add the flour mixture to the liquid. Add 1 cup raisins and ¼ cup salad oil. Stir well. Fill a greased pudding mold or heatproof ceramic bowl no more than ¾ full. Add some good luck charms, if desired (see below). Put a rack in the bottom of a large pot, and pour in about an inch of hot water. Place the pudding on the rack, cover the pot tightly, and steam for 1¼ hours. Just simmer the water in the pot, and add more if necessary. Wrap the unmolded pudding in cheesecloth moistened with rum or brandy, and store in an airtight container. As the cloth dries out, add more brandy or rum. Serve with flaming brandy or rum-soaked sugar cubes around the pudding, along with egg sauce or hard sauce.
HINT: One plum pudding is NEVER enough. Make two and serve one on Boxing Day, December 26.

Good Luck Charms

Good luck charms, such as silver or gold coins, silver buttons, rings, and thimbles, are traditionally placed inside a plum pudding. Clean the charms well before you put them into the pudding, and tell the guests to watch for them.

Egg Sauce for Plum Pudding

Beat one egg white until stiff. Add ½ cup powdered sugar and ½ tsp vanilla, rum, or brandy to taste. Add one well-beaten egg yolk. Stir in ½ pint whipped cream, unsweetened. Serve immediately.

Little Jack Horner

Little Jack Horner
Sat in the corner,
Eating a Christmas Pie,
He put in his thumb,
And pulled out a plum,
And said, "What a good boy am I!"

(Traditional, England)

Flour of England, Fruit of Spain

Flour of England,
Fruit of Spain,
Met together in a shower of rain;
Put in a bag,
Tied round with a string;
If you'll tell me this riddle,
I'll give you a ring.

(Answer: Plum Pudding)

(Traditional, England)

Make an Advent Wreath

An Advent wreath is used as a centerpiece. It has a candle lit on each of the four Sundays before Christmas. Make an Advent wreath with your toddler, perhaps using materials he has collected on his walks such as nuts or pine cones. Or make one from baker's clay and macaroni. Make a doughnut-shape and add four candle holders.

Make Christmas Ornaments

Set aside some time throughout the Advent season to make special Christmas decorations with your child, and some ornaments for the tree. Store his ornaments separately. If you make sturdy ornaments, they will last until he has his own family.

Fill Your Home With Smells of Baking

Bake cookies, bars, and special treats with your baby. Put assortments of these treats into decorated boxes as gifts. Have him with you to help measure, sift, and stir. You may want to set up a cookie exchange with your friends to increase the bounty and cut the work.

The Advent Season

Make meals festive during the entire Christmas season. Light candles for the table. Use holiday dishes, either a special set you use only during Christmas, or paper plates printed with Christmas decorations. Spread a special holiday tablecloth. Light the candles in the advent wreath for Sunday dinner.

Advent Calendar

Patience, patience; the big day is approaching. On December 1 hang up an Advent calendar with small, numbered doors and windows, each one to be opened consecutively each day before Christmas. Some Advent calendars have small chocolates hidden behind the doors. Provide one calendar for each child.

Make an Advent Chain

Everyone gets impatient waiting for Christmas to come—it never comes FAST enough. On the first Sunday of Advent make a chain with your child. Use sticky paper, sticky ribbon, or bright paper and glue. Create one link about 8 inches long by ¾ inch wide, for every day until Christmas. Glue the first link together, overlapping the ends by about ¾ inch. Pass the next strip of paper through the first link, glue the ends together. Continue until you have the number of days until Christmas. Every day, have your child cut one link from the chain.

Make other chains of pretty paper or ribbons to decorate the Christmas tree, stairwells, hang from the ceiling, or...

Decorate, Decorate, Decorate

Decorate your house festively for the Christmas Season. Make a wreath for your front door. Use baker's clay (p. 94) and colored macaroni (p. 77) to make special ornaments for your Christmas tree, and hang some paper angels too. String stale popcorn and cranberries together to make a garland for the tree. When Christmas is over, hang the popcorn and cranberry decorations outside for the birds and the squirrels.

The Christmas Tree

To find an extra-special Christmas tree, take your toddler with you to a "cut-your-own" tree farm, and have a wonderful day in the country. If there is snow, take along his sleigh. If a trip to the country is too complicated, have him choose the tree he likes best from the corner lot.

Make Your Own Gifts

You and your toddler can make special home-made gifts that will please the most dis-criminating. Bake special holiday breads, make pomanders, or shape baker's clay dishes, or pin trays inscribed with "I LOVE YOU." Help him make some simple bird feeders, and combine these with specially painted bags of birdseed, or a bird book.

Pomanders

You will need a large quantity of cloves and a small orange, or a lemon. Using a nail or the point of a knitting needle, poke a hole in the orange and then put in a clove. Cover the orange with holes and cloves until the original fruit can-not be seen. Place the pomander in a paper bag in a dark, cool, place and allow the fruit to dry—two or three weeks. Remove and use to provide a spicy smell for linens or in a closet. Add a bright ribbon, if you want to hang the pomander. The smell will last for years.

Bird Feeders

Tie a string or piece of bright yarn to a large pine cone. Have your child spread the pine cone with peanut butter and roll it in birdseed.
HINT: Chickadees love sunflower seeds.

Shortbreads

Sift together 4 cups all-purpose flour, ³/₄ cup sugar and ¹/₄ tsp salt. Cut 1 lb. butter into pieces and add to the dry mixture, rubbing the butter in so that an even dough is formed (a food processor can be

used). Roll dough out on a floured pastry cloth or wooden board. Cut with cookie cutters. Sprinkle a little sugar over the cookies. Bake at 325°F for about 25-30 minutes, until the shortbreads are pale golden. Cool on a wire rack.

Christmas Dinner

Plan your Christmas dinner well in advance, and decide with your toddler what your meal will be. Decide on turkey, roast beef, or goose (or your favorite feast), and take him to a farmers' market or to the supermarket to shop for the ingredients.

Serve your Christmas dinner with ALL the fixings, making all your preparations well in advance.

Hang Stockings on Christmas Eve

Hang Christmas stockings for Santa Claus to fill on Christmas Eve. Leave cookies and milk out for Santa, and don't forget to leave a snack for the reindeer, too. HINT: Rudolph's favorite is a carrot. If you have a fireplace, hang the stockings on the mantlepiece. If you don't have a fireplace, Santa Claus also comes in through the front door, the back door, or a special window. Some of the best stocking gifts from Santa are activity books, crayons, and small toys to keep the children busy all morning. An orange and apple somewhere near the toe of the stocking are helpful in case you want to postpone breakfast.

Visit Santa Claus

Many children enjoy sitting on Santa's knee to tell him what gifts they want for Christmas. Others are scared silly. Pay a visit to Santa, but be tactful if your child is frightened.

Some communities have a special Santa Claus telephone number, so a timid child can talk to Santa without being afraid. Help your child write a letter and mail it to: Santa Claus, North Pole, Canada, H0H 0H0. Include a self-addressed, stamped envelope for a personal reply. If you live outside Canada send an International Reply Coupon, available at your post office.

Read "A Visit From Saint Nicholas," by Clement Moore, sometime during the Advent season, perhaps on St. Nicholas Day, on December 6th.

Christmas Music

Immerse yourselves in wonderful Christmas music. Take your child to a candlelight Christmas Eve carol service. Go to a carol sing-along at a shopping mall. Go carolling with some friends. Be on the lookout for Salvation Army bands. Watch *The Nutcracker* on television, and play the album. Enjoy *Raffi's Christmas Album*, (Troubadour Records), and play grown-up Christmas music often, too. Teach your child all the Christmas songs you know.

Vive le Vent

(Tune: "Jingle Bells")
(Ring bells rhythmically while singing.)

Vive le vent, vive le vent,
Vive le vent d'hiver!
Qui s'en va sifflant, sifflant
Dans les grands èpins verts, OH!
Vive le vent, vive le vent.
Vive le vent d'hiver.
Vive le vent, vive le vent,
Vive le vent d'hiver.

(Traditional, French Canada)

We Wish You a Merry Christmas

We wish you a Merry Christmas,
We wish you a Merry Christmas,
We wish you a Merry Christmas,
And a Happy New Year!

Good tidings to you, wherever you are;
Good tidings, Merry Christmas,
And a Happy New Year.

Je vous sou hai te un Joyeux Noel,
Je vous sou hai te un Joyeux Noel,
Je vous sou hai te un Joyeux Noel,
Et un heureuse Annee!

(Traditional, England, France)

Away in a Manger

Away in a manger, no crib for a bed,
The little Lord Jesus laid down his sweet head.
The stars in the heavens looked down where he lay,
The little Lord Jesus asleep on the hay.

The cattle are lowing, the Baby awakes,
But little Lord Jesus, no crying he makes.
I love thee, Lord Jesus; look down from the sky,
And stay by my cradle till morning is nigh.

Be near me, Lord Jesus, I ask thee to stay
Close by me for ever, and love me, I pray.
Bless all the dear children in thy tender care,
And fit us for heaven, to live with thee there.

(Traditional, unknown)

A Visit From Saint Nicholas

'Twas the night before Christmas, and all through
   the house,
Not a creature was stirring, not even a mouse.
The stockings were hung by the chimney with care,
In hopes that Saint Nicholas soon would be there.
The children were nestled all snug in their beds,
While visions of sugarplums danced in their heads;
And mamma in her kerchief, and I in my cap,
Had just settled down for a long winter's nap—
When out on the lawn there arose such a clatter
I sprang from my bed to see what was the matter.
Away to the window I flew like a flash,
Tore open the shutter, and threw up the sash.
The moon on the breast of the new-fallen snow
Gave luster of midday to objects below;
When what to my wondering eyes should appear
But a miniature sleigh and eight tiny reindeer,
With a little old driver, so lively and quick,
I knew in a moment it must be Saint Nick!
More rapid than eagles his coursers they came,
And he whistled and shouted and called them by
   name.
"Now, Dasher! now, Dancer! now, Prancer and
   Vixen!
On Comet! on, Cupid! on, Donner and Blitzen!—
To the top of the porch, to the top of the wall,
Now, dash away, dash away, dash away all!"
As dry leaves that before the wild hurricane fly,
When they meet with an obstacle mount to the sky,
So, up to the housetop the coursers they flew,
With a sleigh full of toys—and Saint Nicholas, too.
And then, in a twinkling, I heard on the roof
The prancing and pawing of each little hoof.
As I drew in my head and was turning around,
Down the chimney Saint Nicholas came with a
   bound:
He was dressed all in fur from his head to his foot,
And his clothes were all tarnished with ashes and
   soot:
A bundle of toys he had flung on his back,
And he looked like a peddlar just opening his
   pack.
His eyes, how they twinkled! his dimples, how
   merry!

His cheeks were like roses, his nose like a cherry;
His droll little mouth was drawn up like a bow,
And the beard on his chin was as white as the
   snow.
The stump of a pipe he held tight in his teeth,
And the smoke, it encircled his head like a wreath.
He had a broad face and a little round belly
That shook, when he laughed, like a bowl full of
   jelly.
He was chubby and plump—a right jolly old elf:
And I laughed when I saw him, in spite of myself;
A wink of his eye, and a twist of his head,
Soon gave me to know I had nothing to dread.
He spoke not a word, but went straight to his
   work,
And filled all the stockings: then turned with a
   jerk,
And laying his finger aside of his nose,
And giving a nod up the chimney he rose.
He sprang to his sleigh, to his team gave a whistle,
And away they all flew like the down of a thistle.
But I heard him exclaim, ere they drove out of
   sight,
"Happy Christmas to all, and to all a goodnight!"

(Clement Moore, December 23, 1823)

The Coventry Carol

Lullay, lullay, thou little tiny Child,
By, by, lully, lullay;
Lullay, lullay, thou little tiny Child
By, by, lully, lullay.

O sisters, too, how may we do,
For to preserve this day;
This poor Youngling for whom we sing,
By, by, lully, lullay.

(Traditional, England)

What Child Is This?

(Tune: "Greensleeves")

What Child is this, who laid to rest
On Mary's lap, is sleeping?
Whom angels greet with anthems sweet,
While shepherds watch are keeping?
This, this is Christ the King;

Whom shepherds guard and angels sing:
Haste, haste, to bring him laud,
The Babe, the Son of Mary!

So bring Him incense, gold and myrrh,
Come peasant, King to own Him.
The King of Kings, salvation brings,
Let loving hearts enthrone Him.

Raise, raise, the song on high,
The Virgin sings her lullaby:
Joy, joy for Christ is born,
The Babe, the Son of Mary!

(Traditional, England)

Deck the Halls With Boughs of Holly

Deck the hall with boughs of holly,
Fa la la la la, la la la la.
'Tis the season to be jolly,
Fa la la la la, la la la la.
Don we now our gay apparel,
Fa la la, la la la, la la la.
Troll the ancient Yule-tide carol,
Fa la la la la, la la la la.

See the blazing Yule before us,
Fa la la la la, la la la la.
Strike the harp and join the chorus,
Fa la la la la, la la la la.
Follow me in merry measure,
Fa la la, la la la, la la la.
While I tell of Yule-tide treasure,
Fa la la la la, la la la la.

Fast away the old year passes,
Fa la la la la, la la la la.
Hail the new, ye lads and lasses,
Fa la la la la, la la la la.
Sing we joyous all together,
Fa la la, la la la, la la la.
Heedless of the wind and weather,
Fa la la la la, la la la la.

(Traditional, England)

After Christmas

To give the new year an auspicious start, evil spirits must be warded off in the magical time between December 25 and Epiphany (January 6). The entire period is a time to be happy, to ensure good luck through the coming year, and to ensure that the year is well started. It is a time to go out wishing your neighbors good health and prosperity—this is the time to go "wassailing." To "wassail" is to go door-to-door, toasting the health and prosperity of your friends and neighbors while singing Christmas Carols and wassailing songs, such as "I Saw Three Ships," and "Here We Come A-Wassailing." Traditional wassailing drinks are hot brown ale, mulled wine, and hot cider. Bring along a thermos of hot chocolate for the children. They get cold, too. Don't forget to sing "Jingle Bells." The most magical night in the Christmas season is Twelfth Night on January 5th.

Good Cause Wassailing

If you gather together a group of wassailers with good voices, you can raise funds for that needed major piece of equipment for your nursery school or a favorite charity. Have the smallest children carry a bag or hat for money, and let your neighbors know in advance about the fundraising. Sing "Hold, Men, Hold," the traditional Mummers' begging song for the post-Christmas season, while passing the hat.

Hold, Men, Hold

Hold, men, hold,
We are very cold.
Inside and outside,
We are very cold.
If you don't give us silver,
Then give us gold
From the money in your pockets.
Hold, men, hold.

(Traditional English mummer's song)

Here We Come A-Wassailing

Here we come a-wassailing
Among the leaves so green.
Here we come a-singing,
So fair to be seen.

Chorus:

Love and joy come to you,
And to you your wassail too.
And God bless you, and send you
A happy New Year.
And God send you a happy New Year.

We are not daily beggars
Who beg from door to door.
But we are neighbors' children
Whom you have seen before.

Oh, we have got a little purse
Of pretty leather skin;
We want a little money
To line it well within.

Bring us out a table
And spread it with a cloth,
And give to us a bit of cheese
And of your Christmas loaf.

God bless the master of this house
And bless the mistress too,
And all the little children
Who round the table go.

(Traditional, Yorkshire, England)

Wassail Bowl

(hot mulled cider)

1 gallon apple cider
1 orange, cut in chunks
1 lime, cut in chunks
1 lemon, cut in chunks
4 cinnamon sticks (or 1 tsp ground cinnamon)
1 small piece of fresh ginger or (¼ tsp ground ginger)
1 tsp cloves, allspice, and/or star anise (if desired)

Heat all the ingredient together and serve in heatproof cups, or pour into a thermos to take wassailing. Adults may want to add either brandy, *rum, or vodka as flavoring, although a wassail bowl tastes wonderful without any additives.*

Twelfth Night Eve (January 4)

Twelfth Night marks the end of the Christmas season. In the Christian tradition, Twelfth Night represents the night the Holy Family fled into Egypt. On Twelfth Night Eve it is traditional to drink a toast to the family ox to wish him good health for the coming year.

We Drink to Thee

We drink to thee and thy white horn,
Pray God send master a good crop of corn,
Wheat, rye, barley, all sorts of grain:
If alive at the next time
I'll hail thee again.

(Traditional, England)

Twelfth Night (January 5)

On Twelfth Night, all the evil spirits that could bring bad luck to the new year have been banished to the nether regions. Twelfth Night is also called "Apple Tree Night." An apple tree is toasted and wished good health to ensure a bumper crop the next harvest. Have the whole family visit a tree by night. A happy memory for us is the crunch of snow on snowshoes, miles from anywhere, on a farm in rural Quebec. We went to toast an apple tree on an overcast winter night. It was a magical experience for two two-and-a-half-year-old girls. When the apple tree is toasted in Devon, England, a blunderbuss or shotgun is discharged into the oldest tree; each piece of lead supposedly ensures an apple in the season to come.

Have a bowl of hot soup when you come in from the cold! (See recipe below.)

Here's to Thee!

Here's to thee, old apple tree!
Stand fast root, bear well top.
Pray God send us a youling crop!
Whence thou may'st bud
And whence thou may'st blow
And whence thou may'st bear apples enow;
Hats full and caps full,
Bushels full and sacks full,
And our pockets full too.
Apples and pears, with right good corn,
Come in plenty to everyone;
Eat and drink good cake and hot ale,
Give earth to drink, and she'll not fail.

(Don't forget, give earth her due.)

(Traditional, England)

Great Grandmother's Red Soup

This soup tastes even better when re-heated on the second day.

2 3-lb. soup bones with meat and marrow
1 large onion, thinly sliced
1 small turnip, cubed
½ medium cabbage, thinly sliced
3-4 carrots, thinly sliced
4 good-sized potatoes, cubed
1 green pepper, chopped
2 stalks celery, chopped
2 medium cans tomatoes
2 cans tomato paste

Cover the soup bones with cold water and cook slowly for 3 hours. Chill overnight and remove fat on top. Return to stove, add vegetables, and simmer.

One hour before serving, add tomatoes and tomato paste. This soup is best when it is cooked long and slowly. It can't be overcooked.

Serve with hot biscuits (p. 80), or rolls and pickles.

Untrim-the-Tree Party

On Twelfth Night, Christmas is officially over. Organize an "Untrim-the-Tree Party." Invite friends in, make lots of snacks for the children. Serve hot mulled cider (p. 170), and sing "The Twelve Days of Christmas."

The Twelve Days of Christmas

On the first day of Christmas
My true love gave to me
A partridge in a pear tree.

On the second day of Christmas
My true love gave to me
Two turtle doves and a partridge in a pear tree.

On the third day of Christmas
My true love gave to me
Three French hens, two turtle doves
And a partridge in a pear tree.

Fourth day: four colly* birds...
                    (Count backwards, repeating items in
                     preceding verses.)
Fifth day: five golden rings...
Sixth day: six geese a-laying...
Seventh day: seven swans a-swimming...
Eighth day: eight maids a-milking...
Ninth day: nine pipers piping...
Tenth day: ten drummers drumming...
Eleventh day: eleven lords a-leaping...
Twelfth day: twelve ladies dancing...

*Colly birds are grimy, covered in coal dust.

(Traditional, England)

Twelfth Night Eggnog

1 egg, beaten
¾ cup milk
¼ cup cream
1 tsp honey or sugar

Beat ingredients together, and add flavoring to taste. Try a dollop of ice cream on top, and a sprinkling of nutmeg.

Non-Traditional Holidays

In case you need an excuse to have a party when there isn't an official holiday on the calendar, here are some occasions you can celebrate:
- changing seasons
- a perfect day
- an imperfect day
- Baby's first accomplishments—first friend, first tooth, first crawl, first word, first step, first day at nursery school...
- your own accomplishments (...I made it through the DAY!)
- a change of job
- a full moon
- a new moon
- the first day of the month
- Grandma and Grandpa's visit

The Elegant Meal

Once in a while, plan a festive meal where your good dishes are used, the lights are dimmed, and candles are on the table. Anything from grilled-cheese sandwiches and a tired salad to gourmet fare can be served elegantly to create a festive occasion.

At some point in his life, your child will outgrow Tupperware and Melmac. Provide opportunities where he can learn to eat from fine china and drink from crystal glassware.

HINT: Buy him a special "crystal" glass of his own, or use the last of a set; Jenny's favorite is a red "cranberry" glass obtained at a yard sale for almost nothing.

The Goof-off Day

Make days when you and your child are together, doing exactly what you want to do, without restrictions. My favorite holiday of all is what I call our "goof-off day." I never know in advance when the "goof-off day" is going to happen, or what is going to occur. Generally, the "goof-off day" happens on a clear, bright Friday when it is either wonderful bicycling or skiing weather. "Goof-off days" can mean a trip to the zoo. They can mean a picnic. They can mean simply unplugging the phone, drawing the blinds, lighting the fire, and reading a huge pile of books together.

On a typical "good-off day" Jenny and I are out of the house by 8:00 a.m. We take a snack with us — fruit, juice, cheese — and we pick up muffins at a take-out. Jenny rides behind me on my bicycle in a carrier, or trudges along beside me on cross-country skis.

"Goof-off day" is a day for no hassles, no housework, no telephone, and no deadlines. It is a day to explore new parts of the world together away from our neighborhood, or a day to explore our inner worlds. We find new playgrounds, out-of-the-way bicycle paths, and new restaurants. After lunch we head home for a nap (sometimes as much as a 10-mile bicycle ride away). After naptime, we paint or create together, doing far more complex activities than we normally take the time to do. It is a wonderful day for us. We phone out for pizza for dinner, and spend ALL our time together.

I generally try to have one goof-off day a month in the winter, and one goof-off day a week in the summer. But again, I never know in advance when one is going to arrive.

Index

MOVEMENT

Birth to Three Months

Three to Six Months

Six to Nine Months

Nine to Twelve Months

Twelve to Fifteen Months

Fifteen to Eighteen Months

± *Baby Music,* Katharine Smithrim
* *Baby Dance,* Thoma Ewen

± *Baby Music,* Katharine Smithrim
* *Baby Dance,* Thoma Ewen

± *Baby Music,* Katharine Smithrim
* *Baby Dance,* Thoma Ewen

MUSIC

± *Baby Music,* Katharine Smithrim
* *Baby Dance,* Thoma Ewen

± *Baby Music,* Katharine Smithrim
* *Baby Dance,* Thoma Ewen

± *Baby Music,* Katharine Smithrim
* *Baby Dance,* Thoma Ewen

KITCHEN PLAY

± *Baby Music,* Katharine Smithrim
* *Baby Dance,* Thoma Ewen

± *Baby Music,* Katharine Smithrim
* *Baby Dance,* Thoma Ewen

QUIET TIMES

± *Baby Music,* Katharine Smithrim
* *Baby Dance,* Thoma Ewen

OUTDOORS

± *Baby Music,* Katharine Smithrim
* *Baby Dance,* Thoma Ewen

Thirty to Thirty-Six Months

± *Baby Music,* Katharine Smithrim
* *Baby Dance,* Thoma Ewen